Carrots, Sticks, and Ethnic Conflict

Carrots, Sticks, and Ethnic Conflict

Rethinking Development Assistance

Milton J. Esman and Ronald J. Herring, Editors

Ann Arbor

THE UNIVERSITY OF MICHIGAN PRESS

First paperback edition 2003
Copyright © by the University of Michigan 2001
All rights reserved
Published in the United States of America by
The University of Michigan Press
Manufactured in the United States of America
⊚ Printed on acid-free paper

2006   2005   2004   2003   5   4   3   2

A CIP catalog record for this book is available from the British Library.

Library of Congress Cataloging-in-Publication Data

Carrots, sticks, and ethnic conflict : rethinking development
    assistance / Milton J. Esman and Ronald J. Herring, Editors.
        p.   cm.
    "This book originated in a conference held at Cornell University
as part of a series of inquiries—originally sponsored jointly by
the Peace Studies Program and the Institute for European Studies of
Cornell's Mario Einaudi Center for International Studies—on the
implications of ethnic conflict for international affairs. Two
earlier volumes focusing on international organizations and on
international law (Milton J. Esman and Shibley Telhami, eds.,
International Organization and Ethnic Conflict, and David Wippman,
ed., International Law and Ethnic Conflict) were published in this
series in 1995 and 1998, respectively, by Cornell University Press."
    Includes bibliographical references and index.
    ISBN 0-472-11177-9 (cloth : alk. paper)
    1. Economic assistance—Congresses. 2. Ethnic relations—
Congresses.
    I. Esman, Milton J. (Milton Jacob), 1918–   II. Herring, Ronald J.,
    1947–
    HC60 .C2957   2000
    338.91—dc21   00-010716

ISBN 0-472-08927-7 (pbk. : alk. paper)

Contents

Preface

This book originated in a conference held at Cornell University as part of a series of inquiries—originally sponsored jointly by the Peace Studies Program and the Institute for European Studies of Cornell's Mario Einaudi Center for International Studies—on the implications of ethnic conflict for international affairs. Two earlier volumes focusing on international organizations and on international law (Milton J. Esman and Shibley Telhami, eds., *International Organization and Ethnic Conflict,* and David Wippman, ed., *International Law and Ethnic Conflict*) were published in this series in 1995 and 1998, respectively, by Cornell University Press.

The scholars who contributed to this volume were asked to address a topic that has long been overlooked in the literature on development studies, international relations, and foreign aid. We believe that their contributions will expose this complex and important relationship to sustained attention by scholars, practitioners, and commentators.

The editors are grateful to the Carnegie Corporation and to the United States Institute of Peace for financial assistance; to our authors, who have endured and patiently responded to our numerous editorial suggestions; to Ellen McCarthy, our editor at the University of Michigan Press, for her unfailing assistance and support; to Tammy Gardner and Donna Decker for keeping us financially solvent; and to Sandra Kisner for putting this manuscript together for publication.

We have benefited greatly from suggestions offered by the anonymous reviewers for the University of Michigan Press and by friends and knowledgeable scholars who have kindly commented on this manuscript at various stages of preparation. Aiding in the evolution of this project were commentaries from and discussions with Valerie Bunce, Robert Muscat, Susan Woodward, Peter Rutland, John Harriss, Judith Tendler, Bill Rose, Malinda Seneviratne, Jim Scott, Dia Mohan, Crawford Young, Nilan Fernando, Shibley Telhami, Jeffrey Winters, W. Howard Wriggins, Emmanuel Teitelbaum, Kenneth Bush, V. P. Gagnon, Manoj Srivastava, Mick Moore, Barry Preisler, and John Harbeson.

We note sadly that one of the authors, John S. Cohen, did not live to see the publication of this book, to which he made so valuable a contribution.

CHAPTER 1

Projects and Policies, Politics and Ethnicities

Ronald J. Herring and Milton J. Esman

Ethnic conflict[1] has often jarred the international community with its ferocity and durability. The causes are perplexing—clearly multiple and multidimensional, and situationally specific, difficult of generalization. But certainly much ethnic conflict is rooted in or fed by competition for resources. Though no purely materialist explanation can be satisfying,[2] development policy intuitively ranks among the first candidates for investigation. Rapid economic change in either positive or negative direction involves redistribution of opportunity, status, and deprivation in ways that are often inconsistent with deeply held notions of what is fair and what is unacceptable. Reciprocally, ethnic politics intrudes on the apparent technical rationality of development policy; rules are bent, project locations skewed, privatizations distorted. Yet, curiously, the interactive effects of ethnicity and development assistance have attracted little systematic attention.

Despite "aid weariness," the tasks assigned to development assistance have multiplied in number, complexity, and gravity. Discussion of aid in the United States now raises post–Cold War problematics of "chaos," "failed states," "early warning systems," "governance," and "preventive development." Humanitarian assistance in response to horrendous catastrophes takes precedence over traditional development activities, leading to discussions of "development diversion" and mission dilution. Brian Atwood, on retiring as head of the United States Agency for International Development (USAID), criticized the benign neglect of aid in Washington: "What will it take to wake up our political leaders? More failed states? More wars? More south-to-north migration? More transmission of infectious diseases? More terrorism?"[3] The ugly side of globalization stirs fears of broadly gauged threats that substitute for Cold War imperatives as justifications of international aid.

The Asian financial collapse of 1997 found the World Bank not only criticizing its own prior narrowly economistic assumptions about development but assuming a lead role in global crisis management. The president of the bank said in his address to the Board of Governors in 1998: "Today, in the wake of crisis, we need a second framework . . . that includes the human and social accounting, that deals with the environment, that deals with the status of women, rural development, indigenous people, progress in infrastructure, and so on." Mr. Wolfensohn spoke of a mission so broad as "empowering the people, writing the laws, recognizing the women, eliminating the corruption, educating the girls, building the banking systems, protecting the environment, inoculating the children" (Wolfensohn 1998, 11, 12). The World Bank asserts here an extraordinary mandate: global crisis management and local social engineering on a global scale. Whether staff of the World Bank buy into such grand visions operationally remains to be seen; rhetoric tends to outrun both capacity and will.

As expectations have escalated, resources have waned. Until the early 1990s, the volume of international development assistance increased annually. By the mid-1990s, however, it had stagnated at the level of about U.S.$70 billion net of loan repayments (OECD 1996). Though its aggregate volume has stagnated, the impact of development assistance may ironically increase over time. Governments facing fiscal and balance-of-payments crises seek both the hard currency of assistance and the legitimation for foreign direct investment that often follows the lead of development assistance agencies. Many aid-recipient countries depend on foreign assistance to finance their development budgets, to ensure fiscal stability, to balance external payments, and to reassure foreign investors. In the United Nations Development Programme's *Human Development Report* for 1998, 41 countries received aid in excess of 10 percent of GNP. The figure for Mozambique was 72 percent; for Nicaragua, 61 percent. World Bank data for 1998–99 indicate similar patterns.[4] Aid of course constituted a much higher percentage of these domestic budgets than of GNP. Though private resource flows exceed development assistance in some countries, these flows are uneven in distribution and largely avoid the most desperate societies. Aid is especially critical in catastrophes, whether natural or human-made. The Asian financial collapse of 1997 produced at least 20 million poor people very quickly; international development agencies became crisis response managers (Wolfensohn 1998).

Development assistance distributes carrots and deploys sticks to influence regimes and obtain particular outcomes—altered economic policies, democratization, relief of suffering from catastrophes. We believe there are important reciprocal interactions between international development flows—of project monies, loans, grants, policy advice, and conditionality—and ethnic politics, for several reasons. First and most important, aid projects and restructuring policy advice have distributive consequences. Distributive concerns in general, and especially ethnic distributive issues, have been difficult to integrate into the major missions of development agencies; these "soft" considerations remain in unequal competition with the imperative of stimulating growth. This conflict between measurable and soft is not only ideological: if loans do not result in increased productive capacity and thus do not pay for themselves materially, indebtedness rises. Second, however administratively rational the plans of agencies, aid is allocated and administered in a political context; considerations of ethnic territoriality, power relations, and patronage influence the effectiveness of development assistance even when evaluated on narrowly technical grounds. Finally, conditionalities attached to international lending constitute one important point of leverage that the international community regularly uses. Conditionalities began with technical requirements of financial accountability but have expanded to spheres of government performance, political system structure, human rights, poverty alleviation, and other criteria. These broad conditionalities increase the probability that the assistance relationship will cross paths with ethnic politics.

In the prevailing international system of sovereign territorial states, ethnic conflicts are common; most "nation-states" in reality govern multiethnic societies. Their component ethnic communities may be quiescent, or they may coexist peacefully while competing for political, economic, or cultural advantage. Yet the trend is toward overt conflict. Ted Gurr concluded his 1993 comprehensive empirical study with the statement "Every form of ethnopolitical conflict has increased sharply since the 1950s" (316). The 1990s have witnessed an expansion of academic interest in ethnic politics, including a number of explorations of the international and transnational dimensions of ethnic conflict.[5] Development assistance has evoked a library of literature, mostly concentrating on its effects on economic growth; a minor theme has been its implications for political development and more specifically for democratic institutions and human rights.[6] Yet linkages between development assistance and ethnic conflict remain obscure.

The aid relationship—increasingly and optimistically called a partnership—could be implicated in this phenomenon in various ways. Some interventions may be conducive to peaceful coexistence and equity; others may aggravate tensions and precipitate conflict. Some present cruel dilemmas. Food and medical supplies intended to sustain the victims of civil wars may be hijacked by military contingents of their own ethnic community, leading their enemies to interdict all humanitarian assistance. Privatization, intended to enhance economic efficiency, may be perceived as or indeed have the effect of favoring members of one ethnic group over others. Majoritarian elections urged on by the development assistance community may condemn an ethnic minority to structural subordination and discrimination. Pressure for multiparty democracy in societies with no programmatic political parties may result in hardening of primordial loyalties as the only basis for mobilization and competition. Resources provided in the project mode may be diverted by governments to favor fellow ethnics, while reductions in public expenditures may be administered in ways that spare one community while imposing costs on others. But development assistance can be designed to minimize such negative consequences, to mitigate the effects of development projects on vulnerable communities, or to promote positive-sum equity. Fairness can be exemplified as much in the processes of allocation as in the actual distribution of benefits. These are the problematics we seek to explore.

Money Movers and Gatekeepers: Conditionality

Development assistance is constrained and shaped by conditions imposed by donors. *Conditionality* represents a social contract between providers of assistance and recipient governments acting on behalf of societies—a set of expectations on which assistance is premised. Conditionalities have multiplied over the last two decades, growing from accounting requirements and technical and administrative assurances of fiduciary responsibility, to include understandings of preferred—or acceptable—economic policy and sometimes political arrangements. Conditionalities are controversial because the assistance relationship is asymmetric.

By *development assistance* we mean specifically nonmilitary resource transfers on concessional terms from rich to poor countries.[7] *Concessional assistance* denotes resources provided on terms more generous than those available commercially, either as outright grants or as "soft" loans at lower-than-market rates of interest and with longer repayment periods. Providers of development assistance include agencies sponsored by about 20 of the higher-income industrialized countries plus the multilateral development institutions, notably the World Bank, the International Monetary Fund (IMF), the United Nations Development Program, and the regional development banks. There are about 170 aid-recipient states and dependent territories, mostly in Africa, Asia, the Middle East, and Latin America; more recently, Eastern Europe and the successor states of the former Soviet Union have been included.

Governments in recipient nations are inevitably gatekeepers of development assistance. Foreign assistance normally reaches a society through the state as an expression of the latter's sovereignty. Development assistance agencies must negotiate with governments the terms and conditions of the resources they provide. Once governments accept foreign assistance, the resultant projects and policies are administered through their bureaucratic agencies. Yet governments may at their discretion set boundaries for their acceptance of foreign aid or exclude it altogether. Though foreign aid operates mostly as official, government-to-government transactions, some donors have employed universities, private firms, and nongovernmental organizations (NGOs) to implement the projects they finance and may even seek to circumvent governments and deal directly with private businesses, educational and research institutions, local authorities, or NGOs. Given the current hostility to state intervention in economies, NGOs have in many instances become a desired alternative to direct transfers to governments.[8]

Donor agencies have deep organizational interests in this relationship. Officials of agencies are interested in "moving money," in maintaining their programs, and in protecting the creditworthiness of client states. These interests endow host governments with considerable bargaining strength, even in asymmetric relationships. When development assistance agencies choose to work through foreign or indigenous nongovernment organizations, the role of the state may be reduced (Korten and Klauss 1984; Carroll and Montgomery 1987). Yet governments must acquiesce in such arrangements, as they retain the power to proscribe the activities of NGOs or to circumscribe their scope. The shrinkage of government and expansion of marketization now promoted by development assistance agencies can limit but not eliminate the intermediary role of governments.

While some governments may attempt to serve as neutral arbiters among ethnic competitors, often the state serves as agent of the dominant ethnic community or of a ruling coalition of ethnic communities that has captured the state apparatus. Under these conditions, rulers may distribute the fruits of development assistance disproportionately, even exclusively, to their constituents as patronage. When the politically dominant ethnic community is a demographic majority, government can privilege its constituents by formal majoritarian democratic processes. When the politically dominant community is a minority, cruder methods are employed, as is illustrated by John Cohen's account of the machinations of the ruling minority in Kenya in chapter 4. Humanitarian assistance intended to provide relief and sustenance to victims of natural disasters or large-scale collective violence requires on the ground cooperation of governments, which is not always forthcoming. The victims, as in Rwanda and Bosnia, may have been targeted on ethnic grounds. Subsequent efforts at rehabilitation to assist victims, including refugees, to rebuild their lives and to become economically productive and self-sufficient stretches standard development practice and the toughness of conditionalities (Kreimer et al. 1998).

Conditionality may be applied by donors to any flows of assistance. Of particular importance are conditions attached to policy-related transactions. Budget support by the World Bank may be contingent on tax reform; IMF loans to support the balance of payments may be forthcoming only if the country's government agrees to devalue its currency or reduce its budget deficit; consortiums of donors may release development assistance funds only on condition that the host government agrees to allow opposition parties to function and to conduct honest elections, respect human rights, prosecute corruption, or allow freedom of the press.

To enforce conditionality, assistance agencies monitor the performance of governments, releasing funds only in periodic increments, contingent on compliance. Financial flows are normally tied to policy changes. The World Bank and the IMF, for example, may agree to provide resources for a country facing financial stringency, but only after a "policy dialogue" during which the recipient government agrees to implement macroeconomic policy reforms as the condition for loans. Practitioners recognize that achievement of political stability in the process is both a desirable condition for growth and problematic because economic change may induce social disruption (Nelson 1984).

Development assistance provides funds—or more precisely, supervised lines of credit—to implement projects or policies. Projects run the gamut of activities involving the "productive" sectors (agriculture and industry), physical infrastructure (roads, dams, water-supply systems, airports), and social infrastructure (education, health, family planning, public administration). They may be very large, "lumpy" investments, such as hydroelectric power systems, or relatively small, divisible facilities, such as community health services.

In contrast to projects, policies are governmentally enforced measures that affect the entire society or particular sectors of the economy. The most obvious are macroeconomic policies associated with economic stabilization and structural adjustment—increasing revenues, cutting back public expenditures, devaluing the currency, privatizing the ownership and management of public enterprises, reducing protectionism, removing obstacles to foreign private investment, shrinking the role of government in the economy and society. Of growing importance are macropolitical conditionalities relating to democratization and human rights; these include freedom of expression and of political organization, free and fair elections, the rule of law, and protection of minorities.

There are reasons to expect implications for ethnic dynamics in both project assistance and policy lending. Distributive consequences of projects are more direct and transparent but less far-reaching than those resulting from policy reforms required by structural adjustment and stabilization.

Project Lending: Patronage, Territoriality, Efficiency, and Fairness

The introduction of new resources into any social equilibrium presents potential for competition and conflict. To the extent that plausible ethnic interpretations of winning and losing are activated—that the Hausa are benefiting or the Yoruba are losing, for example—project assistance may actively threaten the balance of ethnic power. Even in an expanding-sum game, relative gains may be more important than absolute gains.

It is reasonable to expect most governments in ethnically politicized societies to channel benefits of external assistance to their constituents or to administer policies in ways that protect the interests of their political base. We expect this dynamic to be strongest where the political significance of ethnicity is established and recognized in daily practice and perception and where ethnic territoriality is clearly understood. It will also be increased to the extent that the government normally operates in a patronage mode and when particular projects lend themselves to patronage. John Cohen's treatment of Kenya in this volume is archetypal: it is clear that ethnicity influenced the allocation of aid resources, that the resultant patterns of benefits were known and contested, and that these dynamics threatened the stability of the ethnic equilibrium in the political system.

Where the benefits of development assistance are systematically skewed in favor of a particular ethnic community, or if such skewing is widely perceived to occur, resentment and grievances will certainly ensue among those who believe they have been cheated or left out. Hostility resulting from scenarios of this type may be the result of deeply held conceptions of justice and discrimination and may undermine the legitimacy of a state that claims to rule for the benefit of all. Large projects may induce "defensive reactions" from those groups whose interests or survival strategies are threatened by change. Among projects, schemes involving involuntary displacement or resettlement stand out as having especially great potential for a dynamic impact on ethnic politics. Dams, for example, drown forests, farms, villages, and burial grounds and globally uproot millions of people.[9] In one of the most important cases of successful protest, the Narmada Bachao Andolan in India organized to oppose a series of dams on the Narmada River. This mobilization achieved wide international attention and forced a review of project support by the

World Bank, leading to the bank's withdrawal of funding of the Sardar Sarovar dam. But downstream beneficiaries of dams may equally employ ethnic mobilization in reaction; in the Narmada case, downstream Gujarati farmers in a drought-prone area effectively mobilized to press the government of India to continue the project after the World Bank's withdrawal. Gurr (1993, 132) notes more generally that political reactions "have been especially sharp in response to the alienation of the lands, forests, and natural resources on which they [indigenous peoples] are culturally as well as materially dependent."

Defensive reactions often pit ethnically defined groups against the state. At the other end of the continuum, projects may simply expand opportunities without directly harming any interests, if external flows create an expanding-sum game. In these cases, ethnic tensions will be a function of perceptions of fairness—the perception that winners are exclusively or disproportionately from one group as opposed to another. Such projects conform to the notion of "pork-barrel politics," used in political discourse in the United States to refer to particularistic criteria used for the distribution of jobs, perquisites, and subsidies and for the location of projects and letting of contracts, as well as to selective eligibility criteria that advantage some communities over others. Whereas managers of aid tend to emphasize economic efficiency, local politicians and administrators are more concerned with distributive effects—with who benefits. Not all patronage is ethnic; party affiliation, extended family or kinship, faction, old school ties, and other particularistic criteria may come into play. The extent to which ethnic tensions are exacerbated will vary with the extent to which allocative criteria or consequences are perceived to be primarily ethnic, and it will also depend on the frequency in which there is not enough to go around.

Large-scale colonization schemes providing new lands for settlers from poor agrarian economies would seem to be an example of an expanding-sum game, but only if resettlement is not on territory claimed by another ethnic community. Israeli development of the West Bank is not ethnically neutral, nor is resettlement ("transmigration") from Java to the outer islands of Indonesia. But even under conditions of expanding pies, communities disproportionately excluded from benefits may add a grievance to their collective list, as certainly was the case with the massive development project in the Mahaweli River valley in Sri Lanka: Sinhalese settlers were established on ground considered Tamil territory by minority Tamils.[10]

Territoriality in general marks a turbulent intersection of aid and ethnicity. The extent to which people perceive terrain to be ethnically divided matters fundamentally. Lumpy, nondivisible aid projects tend to benefit particular areas and hence some groups but not others. Aid projects offer evidence that some particular group is privileged, has power, or is being coddled. Real—as opposed to proclaimed—power structures become manifest in aid allocations. These allocations differ from politics as usual because they are perceived as gifts and are not subject to the very terms of developmental rationality (efficiency, cost-benefit ratios, etc.) that development agencies assume (and believe to be widely shared).[11] The two logics clash: agencies assume there are defensible objective criteria for allocating boons (criteria that maximize development impact), but the political culture sees the same resources as windfalls to be distributed in a way that is somehow fair or at least in accord with existing rules of the game.

One possible conclusion from this discussion is that in the world of projects, small is indeed beautiful (Schumacher 1975), or at least large is not. Large projects have the potential for doing great harm, both directly and indirectly. Norman Uphoff's chapter in this volume traces the beneficial effects of a project in Sri Lanka in which there could be no conflict over new resources because they were not there; instead, the project was premised on building local participation and local contributions. The scale was appropriate for face-to-face resolution of conflicts; the common interests of farmers overcame alternative identifications as members of ethnic groups, even as civil war raged all around. Is the implication that downsizing in scale is the surest formula to ensure that project aid does minimal harm? This conclusion runs contrary to the traditional logic of foreign aid (Tendler 1975). Aid agencies prefer large scale to small; the dominant pressure is to move money, to produce highly visible results, and to utilize the goods and services of firms championed by the nations providing aid. The search for appropriate project scale runs counter to this logic but should and could incorporate an ethnic sensitivity.

Program Lending and Policy Intervention:
Neoliberal Pressures

A more problematic set of donor influences comes as a package once characterized as the Washington consensus (Williamson 1990). Its general thrust seeks to give markets more allocative authority at the expense of politics and public administration, working under such labels as structural adjustment, liberalization, stabilization, marketization, deregulation, privatization, and state shrinking (Walton and Seddon 1994, chap. 1). The consensus was never monolithic and has shown more cracks since the development of disagreements between the IMF and the World Bank following the Asian financial crisis that began in 1997; nevertheless, a preference for enhancing the allocative authority of markets remains central to the agenda.

Compared to projects, the effects of neoliberal packages of carrots and sticks must be more indirect and less transparent to political actors as well as analysts. Effects are ambiguous and difficult to trace, leaving vast space for interpretation by political entrepreneurs and mass publics. Nevertheless, the effects are almost certainly more profound. Projects have limited effects over space and economic structure. Neoliberal packages are meant to alter entire political economies in significant ways.

Marketizing reforms inevitably advantage some groups while imposing pain on others, whether or not the national economy expands at a higher rate in the aggregate (Dell 1984; Girvan 1980). The term *IMF riot* appeared in the literature because violent protest was frequently the result of insecurity and deprivation from austerity packages imposed as conditionality by the IMF. The empirical link between stabilization and mass protest cross-nationally is strong (Walton and Ragin 1990).

Neoliberal policies ramify throughout societies along numerous dimensions. Challenges to neoliberal reforms constitute an important part of the context for new mobilization of identities recently observed among many Amerindian communities in South and Central America (Veltmeyer 1997). To the extent that opening to transnational corporations and foreign direct investment is part of the package, the contentious dynamics of natural-resource extraction may be intensified. Such extraction frequently confronts an ethnically defined landscape.[12] Likewise, trade liberalization exposes specific sectors to international competition. Where specific ethnic communities occupy niches harmed by imports, protest may take an ethnic coloration, as in the Chiapas revolt in Mexico (McMichael 1996, 234–37). Even privatization of public sector enterprises, urged on states for efficiency reasons, often either enhances the prospects of some communities over others, as chapter 4 illustrates for Kenya, or is perceived to do so, as in the ethnonationalist attacks on Jewish "oligarchs" in Russia discussed by Stephen Shenfield in chapter 7.

Fiscal retrenchment and deflationary stabilization policies have been implicated in general in significant political turmoil (Walton and Seddon 1994); the ethnicization of protest depends on the pattern of pain imposed. In Ecuador, for example, mandated fiscal retrenchment reduced funds for bilingual education, which primarily affected speakers of Quechua and other Indian languages; subsequent protest employing indigenous identities rolled back some IMF agreements, but turmoil broke out again in early 2000 with mobilization around demand for restoration of cuts in the social sector and a "plurinational and multiethnic state."[13] For exactly this reason, states undergoing bouts of adjustment and restructuring may be prone to employ repressive measures to quell popular discontent (Sheahan 1980). To the extent that exclusion and repression are perceived in ethnic terms, an additional source of conflict between the state and ethnic groups emerges.

External demands for fiscal austerity often produce conflict between the center and periphery of a nation or across regions, over how the pain will be distributed; international financial institutions (IFIs) deal by contract with centers—national governments. Susan Woodward's 1995 analysis of the disintegration of Yugoslavia (especially 200–204, 232) provides an illustration of confluence of these ethnic and developmental factors. Adjusting the mix of program cuts and tax burdens accentuates, if not creates, regional conflicts with the center and among regions, which in the Yugoslav case had predominantly ethnic definitions. Simultaneously, at the popular level, economic distress blamed on the government laid the groundwork for intensifying mobilization of subnational identities. Woodward argues that the terms of IFIs created "a constitutional crisis over the functions and jurisdiction of the federal government" (201). Banking was the most immediate manifestation; this phenomenon is especially likely in those nations in which regions differentially produce hard currency and have different profiles of exports, imports, and fiscal health. Serbia's call for more centralized state authority was consonant with IFI preconditionality but alienated the richer republics, Slovenia and Croatia. The consequence was additional pressures for dissolution of the Yugoslav state along lines that largely but imperfectly coincided with ethnic identities. Disintegration of the composite state resulted in ethnic wars of remarkable ferocity and obduracy.

Aid has implications for which regimes will survive and which will not and for how surviving regimes will govern. The state backed by foreign resources has less incentive to share power (Moore 1998). This phenomenon is sometimes termed the *political substitution effect,* meaning that the regime substitutes external props for domestic support. Politicians come to believe that support of the international financial institutions is more important than, and can substitute for, building domestic coalitions for governance.[14] Foreign support may then produce increased intransigence, relieving the government of the necessity of seeking legitimacy through accommodation with ethnic grievances. Aid agencies have strong incentives to ensure the success of client states and are thus constrained in using conditionality leverage on issues of human rights abuse or democratization. There often develops a "mutual dependency" between donors who want the economy to do well and ruling elites who would have trouble surviving without external flows (Moore 1990, 357).

Finally, the globalization promoted by neoliberal policy packages typically involves cultural challenge. Economic decline is humiliating. Ethnonationalism in the form of lashing out against those undermining the "nation" (i.e., the majority ethnic group) is a common response; in the chapters that follow, instances from Russia and Sri Lanka are analyzed. Modernism as a publicly proclaimed good denigrates cultures rooted in particular ethnicities. State leaders, entrepreneurs, and bureaucrats adopt the suit-and-tie garb of international status; "backward" modes of behavior and attire are threatened symbolically as well as economically. Newly valorized patterns of consumerism carry potential for creating "unfulfilled dreams [and a] profound sense of alienation and deprivation" (Rupesinghe 1992, 5). "Handicrafts" and artisan production identified with ethnicity may be swamped by market determination of production technologies and product mix. Culturally meaningful landscapes are scarred. International investment spurred by policies that are more open may produce new threats to sacred or otherwise valued terrain. In reaction, new assertions of "traditional" identity may emerge to contest the pervasive assault on a passing world. In some cases, ethnic market niches appear as alternatives to homogenization, as Brysk's chapter on Ecuador illustrates. But where cultural alienation and deprivation are deepened, they provide fertile grounds for the envy, rage, and scapegoating ideally suited to ethnic mobilization.

The Dynamics of Ethnicity

Our overview suggests that much hinges on two system parameters: the extent to which the political economy is or is believed to be ethnically differentiated, and the extent to which the state pursues ethnic strategies in allocation. Another question involves a dynamic element: the formation or reformation of ethnic identities, generally termed *ethnogenesis.*

Where ethnicity is an established base for contesting politics, ethnic competition is likely to be influential in the politics surrounding any policies that have distributive consequences. The Kenyan case discussed in chapter 4 is archetypal in many ways. Less well understood is the dynamic process of interactive formation or reformulation of ethnic identities and strategies resulting from economic change.

Much contemporary analysis of ethnicity stresses porous boundaries, socially constructed identities, and state-cued behavior rather than primordial identities.[15] There is general agreement that ethnic identities do not connote fixed essences but are modified over time by internal dynamics or by influence from the external environment, including the state. Public policy may provide the cues and frames for reformulation of identities. The Sinhala-Tamil conflict that continues to bleed Sri Lanka cannot be understood without understanding the changes in official language policy beginning in the 1950s (Wriggins 1960) or the symbolic celebration of one narrative of ethnic history promulgated by a developmentalist regime in the late 1970s (see chap. 6 of this volume). In chapter 2, Dan Gibson finds ethnogenesis as one response to displacement of peoples by development projects: previously uncooperative or segmented groups found a common identity in the developmental threat to their landscape and well-being.

Data are scarce on many of the important questions already suggested—for example, on numerical distributions of ethnicity across economic niches. Indeed, to the extent ethnicity is a charged issue, objective indicators may prove particularly distorted. Ethnic considerations in Kenya's privatization, for example, caused false names of ethnically acceptable front men to be used for transactions. Minority-fronted firms created to take advantage of affirmative action in the United States likewise distort appearances of real economic control. The objective picture is clouded—by governments that seek to downplay ethnicity, by ethnically blind categories of data collation, and by adaptive subterfuges of entrepreneurial individuals.

Social scientists often lack access to the objective ethnic structure, but so, too, do mass publics, except through myth, stereotype, rumor, and anecdote. These are the real stuff of mass politics, the substrate on which politicians build strategies. For aid analysts, it is more important to know the extent to which the economy and its attendant privileges and deprivations are intersubjectively *interpreted* as ethnically differentiated. The word in some low-income neighborhoods in the United States is that "the Asians own everything." This statement may be more important for understanding patterns of looting and violence than might be any quantitative account that claims to be objectively accurate. Likewise, if people believe that "the Jewish lobby controls U.S. policy in the Middle East," objective indicators of power and influence matter little politically. The operative understanding of ethnic power and influence is more important than its problematic measurement. The methodological implication is that development analysts need to pay more attention to grounded qualitative assessments of ethnic dynamics.

Episodes of economic change, such as those prompted by development assistance, can trigger resurrections of long-standing stereotypes or create raw material from which new stereotypes may emerge. A real-estate boom in the capital city of Sri Lanka—fueled by both trade liberalization and IFI activities—was widely interpreted to disproportionately enrich Tamils in the period leading up to the pogrom against them in 1983. Dam projects and development displacement in general have been important for the emergence of a genuinely new all-India "tribal" *(adivasi)* identity that challenges both the legitimacy of existing authority relations and the operative values of "development" (Kothari and Parajuli 1993).

Crisis seems to spur the search for scapegoats, which ethnic lore provides. Attacks on Chinese citizens in Indonesia in the wake of the economic collapse of 1997 were widely reported in an almost naturalized fashion, like the periodic weather disasters that visit Asia. Yet ethnic conflict is nowhere continuous; there are triggers of specific episodes, though episodes may escalate to produce a quite durable conflict structure. Inflation implicates ethnic middlemen who become its bearers, whatever its origins; their passing on of higher costs is interpreted as price gouging, in violation of local moral economies. Anti-Semitism in Russia reappeared in especially virulent form after the financial crash of 1998; Jews were accused of profiting from marketization urged on by development experts and assistance agencies.[16] Leader of the Communist Party Gennady Zhuganov argued:

> Our people are not blind. They cannot fail to see that the spread of Zionism in the government is one of the reasons for the current catastrophic conditions of the country, the mass impoverishment and the process of extinction of its people. (Engel 1999)

Viktor Ilyukhin, head of the Russian Parliament's security affairs committee, said in his testimony urging impeachment of President Yeltsin (*New York Times,* December 16, 1998): "The large-scale genocide wouldn't have been possible if Yeltsin's inner circle had consisted of the main ethnic groups, and not exclusively of one group, the Jews."[17] The fusion of ethnic architects and beneficiaries of reform is reflected in the use of the term *zionacrats.*[18] Nikolai Kondratenko, a Communist-Nationalist elected governor of the Krasnodar region along Russia's southern border, found evidence for his region's collapse in the machinations of zionacrats; his scapegoats extended to other ethnic minorities—Armenians, Turks, Chechens—but he explicitly associated Jews with economic reforms.[19]

The collapse of state planning and the externally supported rapid marketization has increased perceptions of an ethnic economy in Russia—perceptions that the Chechens control some markets, for example, or that Jews are beneficiaries of policy changes that Jews implement with backing from Western experts and agencies. Given the extreme hardships of economic change in Russia, scapegoating and victimization are predictable consequences. Stephen Shenfield's analysis of reactive ethnonationalism of Russians in chapter 7 focuses on the rise of anti-Semitic interpretations of power and wealth, but similar dynamics apply to other ethnic groups and other ethnonationalisms—the Chinese in Indonesia, for example.

At the other end of the social spectrum, the convergence of the propositions presented in this section is explored by Alison Brysk in chapter 8. At the bottom of Ecuador's social system, Indians represent an *eth-class*, a social formation in which subordinate social standing coincides with inferior class position. IMF conditionality resulted in decreases in government subsidies and services, as well as deceleration of land reform. A fiscally strapped government did not compensate these losses, resulting in three responses. The first, passive acceptance, or migration, diluted the potential for ethnic mobilization. Under those conditions, political mobilization and resistance were more effective when NGOs were available for assistance. Second, defensive reactions to economic reform were significant. Intrusion of oil firms in the Amazon spawned active mobilization and resistance; in the highlands, protests and national coalitions were also direct responses to adjustment policies regarding land, subsidies, bilingual education, and other social welfare issues. Finally, there was the path of economic mobilization, where cooperatives, tourism, and market strategies were developed to take advantage of ethnic niches in the global economy. In response, there was a backlash from mestizos, who resented the help that international NGOs targeted toward Indians on ethnic grounds. Thus, while adjustment pressures further marginalized indigenous eth-classes, they also stimulated countervailing mobilization that altered the political and institutional landscape and created the basis for future resistance. The resultant political configuration of Ecuador was thus restructured by divergent responses to economic changes set in motion by standard stabilization policies of the IMF, even as those policies were altered by popular mobilization.

The Policy Logics of Development Institutions

How do development agencies incorporate possible ethnic complications in their policy logic? It is conceivable that interventions could be ethnically neutral or could even dampen conflict by expanding the pie. It is possible that aid permits the targeting of traditionally neglected regions or groups that have distinct ethnic identities, thereby averting conflict. Might such targeting cause the inefficient use of scarce economic resources? In a parallel to emergent concerns for environmental consequences, does the potential ethnic impact of policy recommendations enter into calculations?

Thinking instrumentally, no one believes that civil war is good for growth. But is passive suffering by ethnic groups without the resources to mount meaningful protests against overwhelming state power acceptable? The question is both developmental and ethical. Policies that provoke effective resistance do not further the objectives of development assistance agencies in either the long or the short term. In Brysk's treatment of Ecuador, structural adjustment inflicted pain that was ethnically differentiated, primarily because class was ethnically differentiated; popular mobilization and rolling back of adjustment conditionalities followed. But it is unlikely that a sustainable and capable political system can be built on exclusion and injustice, whether or not the resources for resistance are mustered.

Proponents of structural adjustment would argue that induced pain may be no more conducive to ethnic conflict than would be continued scarcity, crisis, and collapse—which the IMF sees as a possibility in crises of contemporary poor countries. The counter case is always Weimar— social disintegration brought on by hyperinflation and economic collapse, enabling a genocidal regime to take power. Thus, much hinges on economic theory: the IMF says sharp pain now is necessary to avoid a worse trajectory of economic collapse; the World Bank says pain needs alleviation through safety-net programs. This is the evolving de facto consensus in Washington. The dispute in economic theory cannot be settled here. Ethically, the burden of proof is on those who would put others at risk, but that determination is by no means easy.

Ethnic considerations have not in practice been fundamental to considerations of development assistance. The dominant worldview in international development organizations has been that technically correct policies produce macroeconomic results that are desired by and eventually benefit all citizens in all countries. Yet if consequences are not ethnically neutral or uniformly beneficial, new ways of incorporating ethnic consequences become important for policy success. Getting the prices right has little chance of stimulating investment and growth in a society torn by ethnic conflict.

The logic of institutional policy is complicated; what may appear to the outside observer to be unintended consequences may instead be a second-best scenario within an institution with considerable policy-analysis capacity. Moreover, understanding of consequences often differs across the field staff, headquarters, and government. Agency headquarters are more likely to operate in a technical/rational mode removed from ethnic politics, pursuing seemingly unrelated goals, such as improving the balance of payments, with little attention to the ethnic implications of economic changes they are promoting. Staff on the ground typically operate in quite a different milieu, with the kind of understandings John Cohen explains in his chapter on Kenya.

Locally based operatives of development agencies may also recognize the ethnic consequences of policy but consider the costs unavoidable or acceptable given the aggregate effects. Reflecting back on the ethnic fallout from the massive development project in the Mahaweli River valley in Sri Lanka, the then U.S. ambassador Howard Wriggins recalled with regret his efforts to persuade the government to "do half as much" as the accelerated grand scheme projected, to consider small-scale projects crowded out by Mahaweli, and to reassure Tamils that adequate lands would be available to them despite the influx of Sinhalese settlers.[20] In the event, the project came to be seen as an expression of ethnonationalist Sinhalese expansion on territories claimed by militant Tamil political groups. Nevertheless, Ambassador Wriggins believed at that time, as conventional development logic validates, that the aggregate gains in national production promised enough welfare gains to justify overlooking what were then thought of as short-term ethnic tensions. The discourse of development professionals and aid agencies is aggregate in nature: the nation-state is the unit of analysis. The personified nation has needs, which demand satisfaction; the nation is said to be doing well or badly, to be sick or healthy. Thus, a nation may need rice self-sufficiency or a higher growth rate. Imagining this economic person as object of policy obscures internal differentiation experienced by real people on the ground, but is central to the abstractions of development discourse.

To the extent that noneconomic criteria are being incorporated into the calculations of international development institutions, concerns for environment, gendered deprivation, good governance, human rights, and democracy have made sequential appearances, at least rhetorically. The problems for agencies are that not all good things may go together and that too many objectives piled on the same policy may be immobilizing, as Heather McHugh illustrates in her analysis of USAID in chapter 3. Global concerns for human rights and cultural survival have buttressed resistance to people-displacing projects; giant dams in particular seem to have fallen from favor within the World Bank, dramatized by withdrawal from the Sardar Sarovar project on the Narmada in India. In chapter 2, Dan Gibson analyzes the internal logic of the World Bank by examining disputes about displacement of peoples by development projects and their resettlement. Consideration of environmental externalities has aided in the redefinitions of development in ways congruent with "sustainability" (Sachs 1993). How do, or how could, these broadenings of the notion of "development," including implications for ethnic conflict, enter into the institutional logic of moving money efficiently?

Even if the consequences of development projects or policies are ethnically differentiated and raise new tensions in society, ethnic conflict is by no means inevitable. Government policy choices, with or without conditionality, remain crucial. Compensatory policies may successfully reduce some of the pain by compensating losers if regimes seek to accommodate ethnic grievances and mitigate tensions. Regimes may be discouraged from treating aid as spoils to be distributed to consolidate or expand their political base. The extent to which the latter policies work politically will depend on the strategies of mobilized ethnic groups. Further complicating the causal connection is the fact that ethnic communities may pursue confrontational or accommodative strategies, ranging from quiescence to violence. Cleavages within ethnic communities often lead to disputes over strategy and produce unlikely alliances across ethnic boundaries (Bush 1994).

That ethnic conflict is difficult to understand in simple causal terms is one complicating factor for policy and policy makers; path dependency is another. One can think in terms of tipping points around fragile equilibria. Small changes alter the path of ethnic politics, which seem uniquely capable of producing mirror images that escalate in a self-reinforcing logic of confrontation. A single murder, rape, or desecration is quickly turned by the rumor mill into a general assault on an ethnic group or evidence of a government's failure to protect. Retaliations are likewise interpreted and magnified. Weak states either utilize such conflict for their own purposes or are incapable of stopping the escalation. Triggers need not be large to have large effects; the metaphor is straws that break camels' backs. The accumulation of evidence that the regime is unfair, that one's people will forever get the short end of the stick, produces social dynamite. The use of development assistance or the distribution of the pain it inflicts can contribute to the accumulation of evidence of unfairness or offer mechanisms of diffusion.

The implication, then, is not that development agencies should run from or ignore ethnicity. Indeed, an argument can be made that social progress frequently involves ethnic confrontation to alleviate oppression and that ethnic groups are functional for development.[21] Development policy should be constructed with one eye on facilitating these positive outcomes and with the other on possible calamities. Early warning and prevention could return large dividends; local knowledge and sensitivity to social variation take precedence over generic models.[22] The stakes are high. Once ethnicity becomes a base of conflict, the dynamics of us-them politics generate their own logic of mirror-image perceptions, escalation, violence, even civil war. At that point, peaceful accommodation is excruciatingly difficult; it requires astute statesmanship domestically and judicious support by outsiders, including development assistance institutions.

The Structure of This Book

In the remainder of this book, seven case studies provide the empirical base for addressing the questions suggested in this chapter; a concluding analysis contemplates implications of their findings. Five of the chapters are country or regional studies; two analyze recent initiatives by major development assistance agencies (USAID and the World Bank). In the selection of cases, we made no pretense of representativeness. Indeed, it would be difficult to know what would constitute a representative sample. There is enough variation in the cases to permit exploration of the complex issues presented in this chapter and to provide points of departure for future research.

The final chapter identifies and elaborates on three simple but convenient categories that emerged from these cases: projects, policies, and institutions. These categories crosscut the individual country cases and provide ingredients for initial generalization. The scope and coverage of projects provide more easily accessible results than do macroeconomic or macropolitical policies; their consequences are more easily traced and controlled than those resulting from policy reforms. The institutions that deliver development assistance have distinctive personalities resulting from their charters and their sources of support. These personalities determine the types of conditions they are disposed to require and the methods employed to enforce them, including present or prospective conditions regarding ethnic conflict. How do projects, policies, and institutions separately and jointly constrain and facilitate the ability of foreign aid to influence the course of ethnic conflicts?

It is our hope that these empirical and analytical results might enable foreign aid officials to become more aware of relationships between the resources and advice they provide and ethnic relations in the countries in which they intervene. If development assistance can and does make a difference, and if the differences affect political stability and domestic tranquility on which economic development depends, denying or overlooking the ethnic dimensions of aid intervention is unwise even when using the most instrumental meanings of the term *development*. Incorporation of ethnic consequences into assessments of prospective projects or policy interventions and evaluations of performance inevitably will rest on indeterminate theory, but the exercise itself should improve consequences, much as assessments of environmental impact draw attention to risk even in the face of uncertainty about precise dynamics of ecological change.

The application of this knowledge, however, raises difficult questions of context, criteria, and the most fundamental social values. Assuming one learns to estimate more adequately ethnic consequences of interventions, what goals are appropriate? Should agencies use their influence to achieve interethnic fairness and equity, so that members of all component communities are treated equitably by governments—so that all start out on a level playing field, with no discrimination and no preferences, and with all allocations based on fair competition according to objective criteria? Or should they aim for rough similarity of results, which might require institutionalized preferences for members of ethnic communities that are deemed to be collectively disadvantaged? What should be the scope of external concerns? Should they be limited to economic opportunities and educational entitlements, or should they extend also to terms of political participation and to cultural issues, such as language rights? Should special measures be prescribed to ensure the security of minorities, such as territorial or cultural autonomy or proportionality in allocating political and economic values?

An alternative to proactive ethical concerns from outside—which undoubtedly will be perceived as a new dimension to neocolonialism—is confinement to narrow objectives traditionally considered in growth theory. Should considerations of equity yield to political pragmatics—that is, to whatever measures promise to moderate grievances or manage conflict under particular circumstances, thereby contributing at least in the short run to peaceful interethnic coexistence? Are there trade-offs between short-term and long-term objectives? Whether the goal is greater fairness or simply conflict avoidance, would it be prudent for aid agencies to employ the insights gained from this and future research to calculate the distributional effects of their activities along ethnic lines, as they have begun to do for income distribution, gender, and environmental considerations? The final chapter returns to these considerations.

NOTES

1. By the term *ethnic conflict*, we mean tensions between two or more mobilized communities whose collective identities are based on perceptions of common ancestry, history, culture, nationality, or destiny. The term can also denote conflict between mobilized ethnic communities and a government, when, as is frequently the case, two or more such communities dwell within the borders of a single state.

2. Donald Horowitz's compendium (1985) explains succinctly the varieties of economic factors implicated in ethnic conflict and the theorists who give greater weight to these factors than does Horowitz (105–35). Simultaneously, his discussion develops the limits of materialism as an explanation of ethnic conflict by laying out what seem to be phenomenologically stronger motivations for collective action.

3. "Retiring AID Head Vents Frustration," Associated Press/AP Online, June 30, 1999. Heather McHugh's chapter in this book (chap. 3) treats these shifts in detail.

4. The World Bank's *World Development Report* for 1998–99 (table 21, pp. 230–31) reports that 30 nations received aid in excess of 10 percent of GNP; the figure for Mozambique was 60 percent; for Nicaragua, 57 percent; for Rwanda, 51 percent.

5. For example, Esman 1994; Wippman 1998; Brown 1996; Smith et al. 1991; Schechtermann and Slann 1993; Ryan 1990; Moynihan 1993.

6. See, for example, Montgomery 1962; Diamond 1995; Carothers 1991; OECD 1996, 25–34; and works cited in the substantive chapters.

7. The relatively large military transfers often bundled with aid budgets may obviously have an independent and important effect on the course of conflict and its human costs. Our purpose is to consider the less obvious implications of non-military transfers.

8. In the New Partnership Initiative, USAID was mandated to spend 40 percent of its funds on NGOs. Clearly this move reflects the budget crunch and USAID's weak domestic constituency coupled with the power of domestic NGOs in the United States, but it also reflects the current Zeitgeist that holds rent seeking and inefficiency to be characteristic of public authority (an early influential statement of which may be found in Krueger 1981). See chapter 3 for elaboration.

9. Kothari (1995a, 1995b) has summarized the extensive literature on development displacement and protest in India, where dams have been a central issue. Gurr (1993, 132) notes more generally: "The worldwide impetus to industrialize and to exploit under-utilized human and natural resources has benefitted some ethnic and communal groups and harmed others." Gurr concludes that in this process, "indigenous peoples have been most adversely affected."

10. As in the long-standing conflict over ethnic ratios in colonization schemes in the dry zone of Sri Lanka (Peebles 1990; Gillies 1992). See also Herring's treatment of the macrolevel consequences in chapter 6 of this volume, in contrast to Uphoff's countervailing microlevel story in chapter 5.

11. Prime Minister Apolo Nsibambi of Uganda (personal communication, Ithaca, New York, September 7, 1999) made these points about aid and ethnicity in his experience.

12. Oil exploration and Indian protest in Ecuador is representative; see Alison Brysk's chapter in this volume (chap. 8). More generally, the confluence of ethnic identity with particular landscapes renders natural-resource development (often meaning destruction) a cultural threat and possible agent of regenerating identity and political mobilization. See Gibson's contribution to this volume (chap. 2); Watts 1996; Sachs 1993.

13. The *New York Times* of January 27, 2000 (A3), reported on the recent Indian uprisings that contributed to Ecuador's regime crisis of early January, resulting in replacement of the president. It concluded that rural smallholders have been pauperized by the recent inflation and collapse of the Ecuadorian currency; "struggling to fulfill the austerity measures they have had to agree to in order to secure

loans abroad," reported the newspaper, "successive administrations have also reduced support for bilingual education programs for speakers of Quechua and other Indian languages." Bishop Raul Lopez, of Latacunga in the Andean highlands, said: "The situation is truly tragic. . . . The government has cut the budget for everything in the social sector in order to satisfy the demands of the International Monetary Fund and to make payments on our foreign debt." Collective action around the Indigenous Parliament has included demands for a plurinational and multiethnic state. For a treatment of the longer run of politics around aid and ethnic mobilization, see Brysk's chapter in this volume (chap. 8).

14. Peter Rutland (1995) argues that this effect was especially important in the abortive stabilization programs of Yegor Gaidar (Russia, 1992) and Leszek Balcerowicz (Poland, 1990).

15. For example, Ted Gurr writes in this vein (1993, 89): "Communal identities in all plural societies have a transactional character: they change with time as a result of interactions within the group and between groups."

16. Matthew Engel (1999) attributes some of this resurgence of anti-Semitism to the "swaggering excesses" of the "oligarchs" who were associated with economic reforms both as policy makers and beneficiaries.

17. In a reciprocal controversy on "genocide," the Duma refused to censure one of its members, General Albert Makashov, who advocated on television the extinction of the "Zhids"—a term that Engel (1999, 3) says "in Russian has always conveyed more venom than the English 'Yid.'" In defending his colleague, another deputy, Alexander Saley, argued: "It is the result of the unstable situation. . . . When certain groups defend their own selfish interests that is what happens. This was Makashov's point. He is reflecting the sentiments of the whole society."

18. *Zionacrat* is glossed by *New York Times* reporter Celestine Bohlen (November 15, 1998) as "a new code word for Jews in government, finance and the news media."

19. Deputy Governor Nikolai I. Kharchenko argued more specifically that the distress of the region's agriculture was a result of economic reform and that "[n]ative Russians never would have allowed all these reforms to happen" (*New York Times*, November 15, 1998).

20. Personal communication, December 1995. The case is treated in more detail in chapter 6. What makes the case more poignant is that Wriggins is a major scholar of Sri Lanka, including its ethnic politics (Wriggins 1960).

21. Robert Bates writes (1999, 42): "Ethnic violence, when it occurs, is destructive beyond all imagining. But it occurs rarely, whereas ethnic groups daily foster the education of the young and their movement to places of opportunity, and, while uttering the rhetoric of tradition, promote the process of development."

22. James Scott, in *Seeing like a State* (1998), makes a systematic critique of schematic, formal models that do violence to complex social interdependencies. What Scott says of states applies with even greater force to development institutions with global vision.

REFERENCES

Bates, Robert H. 1999. "Ethnicity, Capital Formation, and Conflict." Working Paper, Weatherhead Center for International Affairs, Harvard University, Cambridge.

Brown, Michael, ed. 1996. *The International Dimensions of Internal Conflict.* Cambridge: MIT Press.

Bush, Kenneth D. 1994. "The Intra-group Dimensions of Ethnic Conflict in Sri Lanka and Northern Ireland." Ph.D. diss., Cornell University.

Carothers, Tom. 1991. *In the Name of Democracy: U.S. Policy Toward Latin America in the Reagan Years.* Berkeley: University of California Press.

Carroll. T. J., and John D. Montgomery, eds. 1987. *Supporting Grass Roots Organizations.* Cambridge, MA: Lincoln Institute for Land Management.

Dell, Sidney. 1984. "Stabilization: The Political Economy of Overkill." In *The Political Economy of Development and Underdevelopment,* ed. Charles K. Wilber. New York: Random House.

Diamond, Larry Jay. 1995. *Promoting Democracy in the 1990s.* Washington, DC: Carnegie Commission on Preventing Deadly Conflicts.

Engel, Matthew. 1999. "A History of Hate." *Guardian,* August 16, sec. G2, pp. 2–3.

Esman, Milton J. 1994. *Ethnic Politics.* Ithaca: Cornell University Press.

Ferguson, James. 1990. *The Anti-Politics Machine: "Development," Depoliticization, and Bureaucratic Power in Lesotho.* Cambridge: Cambridge University Press.

Gillies, David. 1992. "Principled Intervention: Canadian Aid, Human Rights and the Sri Lankan Conflict." In *Aid as Peacemaker: Canadian Development Assistance and Third World Conflict,* ed. Robert Miller. Ottawa: Carleton University Press.

Girvan, Norman. 1980. "Swallowing the IMF Medicine in the Seventies." *Development Dialogue* 2.

Gurr, Ted Robert. 1993. *Minorities at Risk: A Global View of Ethnopolitical Conflicts.* Washington, DC: U.S. Institute of Peace.

Horowitz, Donald L. 1985. *Ethnic Groups in Conflict.* Berkeley: University of California Press.

Korten, David C., and Rudi Klauss, eds. 1984. *People-Centered Development: Contributions toward Theory and Planning Frameworks.* West Hartford, CT: Kumarian Press.

Kothari, Smitu. 1995a. "Whose Nation Is It? The Displaced as Victims of Development." *Lokayan Bulletin* 11, no. 5 (March–April): 1–8.

———. 1995b. "Developmental Displacement and Official Policies: A Critical Review." *Lokayan Bulletin* 11, no. 5 (March–April): 9–28.

Kothari, Smitu, and Pramod Parajuli. 1993. "No Nature without Social Justice: A Plea for Cultural and Ecological Pluralism in India." In *Global Ecology: A New Arena of Political Conflict,* ed. Wolfgang Sachs. London: Zed.

Kreimer, Alcira, et al. 1998. "The World Bank's Experience with Post-conflict Reconstruction." Washington, DC: World Bank.

Krueger, Anne O. 1981. "Loans to Assist the Transition to Outward-Looking Policies." *World Economy* 4, no. 3.

McMichael, Philip. 1996. *Development and Social Change.* Thousand Oaks, CA: Pine Forge.

Montgomery, John D. 1962. *The Politics of Foreign Aid.* Boulder: Praeger.

Moore, Mick. 1990. "Economic Liberalization versus Political Pluralism in Sri Lanka." *Modern Asian Studies* 24, no. 2: 341–83.

———. 1998. "Death without Taxes: Democracy, State Capacity, and Aid Dependence in the Fourth World." In *The Democratic Development State: Politics and Institutional Design,* ed. M. Robinson and G. White. Oxford: Oxford University Press.

Moynihan, Daniel Patrick. 1993. *Pandaemonium: Ethnicity and International Politics.* New York: Oxford University Press.

Nelson, Joan M. 1984. "The Political Economy of Stabilization." *World Development* 12, no. 10.

Organization for Economic Cooperation and Development (OECD). 1996. *Development Cooperation: Efforts and Policies of the Members of the Development Assistance Committee.* Paris: OECD.

Peebles, Patrick. 1990. "Colonization and Ethnic Conflict in the Dry Zone of Sri Lanka." Journal of Asian Studies 49, no. 1 (February).

Rupesinghe, Kumar, ed. 1992. *Internal Conflict and Governance.* New York: St. Martin's.

Rutland, Peter. 1995. "The International Economy and Ethnic Conflict in the Transition from Socialism: The Russian Case." Paper presented at the conference "Development Assistance and Ethnic Conflict," Einaudi Center for International Studies, Cornell University, October 6–7.

Ryan, Stephen. 1990. *Ethnic Conflict and International Relations.* Aldershot: Dartmouth.

Sachs, Wolfgang, ed. 1993. *Global Ecology: A New Arena of Political Conflict.* London: Zed.

Schechterman, Bernard, and Martin Slann, eds. 1993. *The Ethnic Dimension of International Relations.* New York: Praeger.

Schumacher, E. F. 1975. *Small Is Beautiful: Economics as if People Mattered.* New York: Harper and Row.

Scott, James C. 1998. *Seeing like a State: How Certain Schemes to Improve the Human Condition Have Failed.* New Haven: Yale University Press.

Sheahan, John. 1980. "Market-Oriented Economic Policies and Repression in Latin America." *Economic Development and Cultural Change* 28, no. 2.

Smith, Paul, et al., eds. 1991. *Ethnic Groups in International Relations.* New York: New York University Press.

Tendler, Judith. 1975. *Inside Foreign Aid.* Baltimore: Johns Hopkins University Press.

United Nations Development Program. 1998. *Human Development Report.* New York: Oxford University Press.

Veltmeyer, Henry. 1997. "New Social Movements in Latin America: The Dynamics of Class and Identity." *Journal of Peasant Studies* 25, no. 1:139–69.

Walton, John, and Charles Ragin. 1990. "Global and National Sources of Political Protest: Third World Responses to the Debt Crisis." *American Sociological Review* 55 (December): 876–90.

Walton, John, and David Seddon, eds. 1994. *Free Markets and Food Riots.* Oxford: Basil Blackwell.

Watts, Michael. 1996. "The Shock of Modernity: Petroleum, Protest, and Fast Capitalism in an Industrializing Society." In *Exploring Human Geography: A Reader,* ed. Stephen Daniels and Roger Lee. London: Edward Arnold.

Williamson, John. 1990. "What Washington Means by Policy Reform." In *Latin American Adjustment,* ed. John Williamson. Washington, DC: Institute for International Economics.

Wippman, David, ed. 1998. *International Law and Ethnic Conflict.* Ithaca: Cornell University Press.

Wolfensohn, James D. 1998. "The Other Crisis: Address to the Board of Governors." Washington, DC: World Bank Group.

Woodward, Susan. 1995. "Redrawing Borders in a Period of Systemic Transition." In *International Organizations and Ethnic Conflict,* ed. Milton Esman and Shibley Telhami. Ithaca: Cornell University Press.

Wriggins, Howard. 1960. *Ceylon: Dilemmas of a New Nation.* Princeton: Princeton University Press.

CHAPTER 2

The World Bank and Displacement:
The Challenge of Heterogeneity

Daniel R. Gibson

Displacement: Recognizing Losers in Development

International development agencies have become sensitive to potentially adverse social consequences of their projects. But mere recognition of potential problems ensures neither avoidance nor mitigation. Project-related population displacement is one such source of problems, including ethnic conflict in some instances.

Since 1980, World Bank policy has sought to restore people displaced by bank-supported projects to their previous standard of living. This chapter explains why this policy often fails to achieve its purposes in project areas inhabited by an ethnically mixed population. Especially with regard to indigenous peoples, the policy explicitly recognizes the inadequacy of ethnically neutral economic criteria. But the policy does not provide a means for restoring standards of living in project settings where affected populations adhere to different standards. These problems are inordinately complex, as will be discussed shortly. They often become even more difficult because the bank and its borrowers fail to recognize varying ways in which displacement can affect the salience of ethnic identity, perception, and behavior.

The World Bank's experience illuminates the interactive theme of this volume. Just as the impact of development projects on affected populations varies, the varying responses of affected groups can determine the success or failure of development projects and can expose incoherent principles at work within development agencies themselves.

Distributive equity provides a case in point. International concern for the losers in development is relatively new. Development assistance typically has been provided through the medium of development planning to spur aggregate economic growth. People suffering losses were asked to bear this sacrifice to support planned growth and national progress. With state building high on the agenda, many in international development circles advocated forceful governmental action to make development plans stick (Heilbroner 1962; Huntington 1968).

Stung by international criticism regarding the debilitating impacts of some projects on some people, as well as by their own project failures, development agencies initiated reforms in the 1970s designed to curb distributive inequity. This trend accelerated in the 1980s, with demands for social and environmental safeguards leading to a proliferation of development policy concerns.[1] The World Bank began to question the efficacy of state planning (originally undertaken in some countries at the bank's behest), acknowledging that interests imputed to states often varied from those of many people residing within them. Planned development has lost favor to participatory development. As the presumed validity of state-imposed sacrifice began to ebb, opposition from people facing the costs of development began to flow. Displacement has been a major source of such opposition.

The Problem of Displacement

Governments worldwide invoke eminent domain to pursue objectives they deem socially beneficial. International development agencies frequently support projects—dams, roads, ports, urban improvement, parks and reserves, and so on—that displace people from homes, communities, or means of subsistence. Some projects displace no one; others displace hundreds of thousands. The partial land acquisition required for improvements of existing roads, for example, usually produces relatively minor inconvenience; construction of new reservoirs, by contrast, can require relocation of whole communities and can wreak widespread economic devastation.

Until 1980, international development agencies left displacement issues to the discretion of borrowing governments. It was generally assumed that displaced people would adapt to opportunities presented by the growth and economic diversification that the projects would spur. When considered at all, planners commonly underestimated (or even deliberately deflated) by wide margins the number displaced and their losses (World Bank 1994, 5/3; Cernea 1990, 6–7). Furthermore, they erred in assuming that the adaptability associated with voluntary economic behavior would accompany involuntary displacement.

But by 1980 field studies had demonstrated that the very human costs of displacement often went unrecognized, much less mitigated (Chambers

1970; Colson 1971; Scudder 1973; Guggenheim and Cernea 1993; Cernea 1993, 1991). In addition to loss of land or physical assets, these costs frequently included ills associated with social disintegration, as well as costs of adjustment to alien or distasteful environmental or social conditions following relocation. Also overlooked in many cases were the secondary displacement costs borne by "hosts" already residing in areas chosen for relocation.

Two World Bank–supported projects were prominent in the catapulting of displacement issues to international notoriety. In the Sobradinho Dam project in Brazil, some 60,000 people were displaced with little advance planning, leading to chaos as floodwaters began to rise. Because they lacked formal land titles, as many as two-thirds of the households received no compensation. And more than half of the land provided for resettlement proved unsuitable for agriculture. The lesson was that "development" projects were reducing thousands of self-sufficient families to utter destitution. In the Philippines, meanwhile, plans to build four dams along the Chico River promoted ethnic amalgamation among traditional tribal rivals, culminating in support for a communist insurgency and eventual project cancellation. The lesson was that "backward" indigenous groups could unite, resist, and prevail, even over the strong-arm tactics of the Marcos regime.

As attention to displacement issues has accelerated, estimates of worldwide displacement associated with development projects have grown apace. In 1993, extrapolations suggested that 2–3 million people were displaced each year (Gibson 1993; Guggenheim and Cernea 1993). But a 1994 study led the bank to conclude that as many as 10 million people are displaced annually from dam construction, transportation, and urban projects alone (World Bank 1994, 1/3). In aggregate terms, the number displaced by planned projects far exceeds international refugee flows attributed to civil conflict and natural disaster (Cernea 1993).[2]

Some official organizations, nongovernmental organizations, and World Bank critics now call for an end to displacement—especially of indigenous peoples.[3] Meanwhile, rising population densities, along with rising expectations, increase the demand for water, energy, roadways, sanitation systems, and other infrastructural projects even as they exacerbate displacement and its associated problems.

So how should development projects be selected? While projects continue to be justified through cost-benefit analysis, it is becoming increasingly evident that some costs and benefits cannot be known in advance. Some, including many associated with displacement, are contingent on the responses of project-affected people. Displaced people may fail to adapt to new surroundings, rejecting new techniques or failing to cooperate in activities essential to achievement of project benefits. Or people facing displacement may resist, creating costly delays or even project cancellations. Displacement, then, presents a paradox: displacement is involuntary, yet the choices made by displaced people often have a profound effect on project outcomes. Devising methods for the equitable treatment of displaced people now presents one of the more vexing development challenges.

The World Bank and Involuntary Resettlement Policy

The first involuntary resettlement policy adopted by the World Bank in 1980 went beyond demanding fair compensation for lost assets to also ensure that displaced people regained previous living standards.[4] The policy represented a major departure from orthodox development economics, requiring actual Pareto efficiency: the bank vowed not to support projects requiring losers to subsidize projects through displacement.

From the beginning, the policy further politicized the relationship between the World Bank and its borrowers, as well as decision making within the bank itself. As with other attempts to extend policy conditionality, the bank has found that it must bargain for influence (Mosley, Harrigan, and Toye 1991). That bargaining is asymmetrical. World Bank bargaining power is front-loaded: government policy makers seeking World Bank assistance have *ex ante* incentives to prepare resettlement plans in accordance with the bank's terms, but the bank frequently has been unwilling or unable to sanction *ex post* noncompliance, particularly by larger borrowers (Gibson 1993). Moreover, the bank often finds it difficult to tell whether noncompliance reflects borrower incapacity or strategic dissembling. The bank typically responds with *constructive engagement*— avoiding punitive sanctions in the hope that policy dialogue can coax borrowers to improve resettlement implementation.

By the mid-1980s, meanwhile, policy proponents noted slippage in internal World Bank compliance with displacement policy, which remained at odds with the bank's economic orientation and its practical imperatives. While the front office preached deregulation and economic liberalism, the bank's displacement policy attempted to regulate the distribution of costs and benefits. In terms of operations, the new policy slowed project approval, interfering with powerful incentives to "move money." While critics often portray the bank as monolithic, internal compliance and controversies over policy interpretation remain among the major concerns of policy supporters (Cernea 1993).

In subsequent revisions, more expansive policy objectives have generated controversies within the World Bank, as well as between the bank and its borrowers. For example, restoring assets and incomes is now portrayed as a minimum objective; policy rhetoric now emphasizes that displaced people should be targeted to become beneficiaries, with improved incomes and living standards following resettlement. Furthermore, the revisions have sought to reduce the scope for technical and administrative criteria in favor of more participatory processes of resettlement planning, implementation, and monitoring.

Policy revisions also have led to increased emphasis on the particular needs and vulnerabilities of displaced groups. In most project settings, the range and salience of these particularities are constrained by relatively great degrees of social and economic integration. If differing groups of people are all to regain their previous living standards, however, resettlement needs to be culturally appropriate. For example, the 1980 policy paid virtually no attention to issues involving ethnicity or conflicting property claims. The policy did not explicitly require resettlement assistance for those lacking formal title to property, did not recognize the importance of communally managed resources, and provided no safeguards for unacculturated or partially acculturated indigenous groups inhabiting the resource frontier.

World Bank project reviews and outside analyses showed such problems to be continuing sources of debilitation, even in projects initiated after 1980. Policy revisions specifically recognized the validity of customary claims to property, required assistance for displaced but landless people, required replacement or compensation for loss of common property, and required special protections for tribal peoples.

Over the years, then, the World Bank's policy demonstrated an increasing sensitivity to both ethnic and socioeconomic diversity. As the resettlement agenda grew more complex, however, policy hurdles sometimes grew steeper inside and outside of the bank. Some policy provisions—such as requiring that those lacking legal claims be eligible for resettlement—were at odds with borrowers' legal systems.[5] And determining what is culturally appropriate often proved less than straightforward in ethnically diverse areas. The insistence on culturally appropriate resettlement provisions, for example, proved burdensome where land was scarce and where affected populations—especially rotational agriculturalists, forest gatherers, and pastoralists—employed land-intensive practices.

In sum, some World Bank projects appear caught between integrationist and preservationist goals and between technical planning criteria and participatory processes. Policy revisions have promoted preservation of customary institutions, for example, while simultaneously urging socioeconomic integration into host communities. But the policy does not state how hosts and resettlers are to be integrated while preserving distinctive institutions of each. Similarly, stating that affected people should have a voice in their resettlement does not indicate how much of a voice they should have or what to do when their voices are discordant with those of planners or with each other. Whenever it becomes politically salient, socioeconomic heterogeneity reveals policy incoherence; it proves impossible to fully restore previous living standards for all when affected groups embrace fundamentally different standards.

Heterogeneity, Ethnicity, and Displacement

Since World War II, Marxians, modernization theorists, economists, and planners alike have sounded the knell for ethnic identity, believing that the benefits of development would induce individuals to discard "primordial attachments." Instead, state-sponsored development processes often have had the opposite effect (Newman 1991; Horowitz 1985). As with the Chico Dam experience, some cases even contributed to ethnogenesis—spurring ethnic amalgamation among previously hostile peoples.

Though development interventions produce a wide array of ethno-political responses, development practitioners remain remarkably insensitive to sources of variability in both interethnic and intra-ethnic behavior. Interethnic conflict plainly is neither constant nor reflexive. While the salience of intergroup relations may be slower to fall than to rise, even the most ancient animosities are punctuated by swings in intensity and long periods of dormancy. Similarly, intragroup behavior varies. The ascriptive ties that anchor ethnic affiliation—race, ancestry, place of origin, religion, language—are generally constants and as such cannot explain the varying salience of ethnicity. Many scholars have observed that ascriptive ties can be more perceived than real (Anderson 1983; Connor 1969, 1991). Even where real blood ties exist, the dynamics of ethnic behavior are relational and situational (Young 1976). When ethnic identification is highly salient, the ethnic boundaries seen by Barth (1969) assure extraordinary levels of conformity. As salience declines, however, boundaries become porous, with many individuals failing to conform to ethnic expectations. Where salience is low, ethnic behavior manifests in an intermittent and sometimes simply opportunistic fashion.

Exploring this variation in behavior within and among groups requires attention to ethnicity as institutionalized behavior (Horowitz 1985, 77). Situated within or among widely varied ethnic landscapes, development projects and policies often impose unwelcome institutional change, yet the relationship between ethnic behavior and institutional change is typically overlooked (Van Arkadie 1990). In some project settings, ethnic groups may compete within integrated socioeconomic or political institutions. In other settings, ethnic groups adhere to distinct and different institutions. Ethnic conflict, then, varies by form as well as intensity.

Ethnic competition for jobs, votes, or educational opportunity reflects relatively great institutional integration—competing groups desire scarce resources for similar reasons. Under such circumstances, ethnic conflict is largely distributive (Bates 1983; Rothschild 1981), often reflecting the dynamics of "ranked" or "unranked" systems of ethnic stratification (Horowitz 1985).

However, frontier regions of many countries remain peopled by "socially or culturally defined collectivities demarcated by wholly separate and autonomous institutional structures" (Young 1976, 17). Writers since Boeke (1942), Furnivall (1956), and M. G. Smith (1965) have emphasized the peculiarities of development in nonintegrated plural societies. In such settings, development disputes may involve groups employing strikingly incommensurate valuation of resources or incompatible mechanisms for dispute resolution, generating *valuative conflict* (see fig. 1). At stake are the terms of integration, or the very definition of development, from which the ascent into dominance of one group threatens another with social disintegration.[6]

The drive toward national integration has been seen as "the central political and social drama of recent history" in the developing areas, in which disparate groups vie over "who will make the rules, and who will determine the property rights that define the use of assets and resources in the society" (Migdal 1988, 27–28; see also Geertz 1963; Connor 1972). Policy makers intent on state building almost uniformly define development in ways that favor integration or promote dissolution of obstacles, including the noncompatible institutions of others. They justify plans and projects by reference to national or social welfare. Such collective concepts imply socioeconomic integration, so that the interests of individuals and groups can be treated as comparable and measurable. But, as Arrow (1983, 28) reminds, collective measures are "the end product of certain values assumed to be unanimously held rather than a method of reconciling divergent value systems."

Displacement often generates severe and unwelcome forms of institutional change. Even in relatively homogeneous settings, displacement generates difficulties in apportioning costs and benefits. In ethnically mixed areas, however, projects can produce forms of institutional change that promise to generate an ethnic distribution of costs and benefits, in which future benefits will accrue disproportionately to one or more ethnic groups, while foregone opportunities or other adverse impacts are borne disproportionately by others. Of course, development projects exist to accelerate

1. *Legal Structure:* Tribal groups emphasize customary limits to behavior while national systems utilize formal codes. The latter emphasizes rule of law while the former emphasizes judgment of individuals.

2. *Property Rights and Land Tenure:* Tribal groups typically hold customary communal claims to property and view land as inalienable. Government policy favors formal private titling to property (or state ownership) and views land as a commodity.

3. *Factor Valuation:* Swidden agriculture is land-intensive, maximizing return to labor. Integrated development policy favors maximizing return to available territory. Often, displacement follows policy maker's determination that land has a higher social value as inundated water storage.

4. *Product Valuation:* Many tribal groups use minor forest products with no established market value. Development promotes marketable commodities. Cost-benefit analysis in general and displacement-related compensation formulas assign little or no value to nonmarket resources.

5. *Mode of Compensation:* Nonmonetized or partially monetized tribal groups typically favor compensation in kind. Where replacement land is scarce, governments favor cash compensation. No objective compensation value exists for loss of inalienable property or of ancestral shrines, burial grounds, or other sacred sites.

6. *Discount Rate:* Inalienability encourages a very low discount rate on future value of resources. Development policy often encourages higher present consumption, especially where poverty or overpopulation is prevalent.

7. *Mode of Production:* Many tribal groups rely heavily on subsistence production, often with some trade in commodities as a secondary endeavor. Revenue-dependent governments typically favor production of surplus.

8. *Mode of Exchange:* Many tribal groups engage in labor reciprocity and pooled insurance schemes to produce consumption goods relatively invariant and nonfungible in value. Government promotion of markets favors accumulation of profit through trade of commodities of highly variable value. The commoditization of labor commonly assigns little or no value to the traditional tasks of women and children.

Fig. 1. Problems of incommensurate valuation

change. But the rate of change, as well as the distributive effects of change, can heighten the salience of ethnic identity (Olson 1963).

Where projects produce an ethnic distribution of costs and benefits within institutionally integrated settings, an increase in ethnic salience may shift attention to relative gains, by which displacement becomes a zero-sum activity; even if compensated for their losses, members of an ethnic group may be acutely aware that they were dislocated against their will for the benefit of others.

Where institutional heterogeneity accompanies ethnic heterogeneity, as is commonly the case in frontier areas, displacement can produce a sharply identifiable ethnic distribution of present and future opportunity. Because many projects are intended to develop a country's resource frontier, indigenous peoples bear a disproportionate risk of displacement. Many of the most controversial episodes of failure of displacement policy occur in projects affecting indigenous groups. A major policy obstacle has been operationalizing ethnic terms. The concept of indigenous peoples captures reasonably well the distinctiveness of the most remote and isolated frontier groups. But because ethnic groups more commonly vary by degree of acculturation and integration, project officials frequently find it hard to categorize reliably. Or, alternatively, they categorize to suit their purposes.

Ethnic categorization aside, the costs indigenous groups bear are more likely to go unrecognized and uncompensated. They are more likely to face displacement not because they lack resources but because their property rights are not acknowledged or because they use resources in ways adjudged suboptimal by policy makers. Resources of low-yield producers will be targeted for infrastructural development or for more intensive utilization. Not uncommonly, project-related displacement leads to secondary displacement of indigenous peoples as planners search for "undeveloped" resettlement areas.

If displaced people adhere to institutions distinct from those dominant in the resettlement area, moreover, adaptation is more likely to be stunted. Replacement land, if provided, may not be sufficient to allow affected groups to move en masse. Resettlement programs are likely to undermine traditional leadership or decision rules or to impose unfamiliar production methods. Meanwhile, labor exchanges, marriage circles, or other customary institutions may be damaged beyond repair (Behura and Nayak 1993).

Anthropologists have emphasized that involuntarily displaced groups frequently either fail to adapt or adapt very slowly to new environments (Scudder 1991). Contingent costs of maladaptation and nonresponsiveness arise in the form of lost productivity, failure to adopt preferred production methods, desertion of resettlement facilities and encroachment into nearby forests or migration to urban slums, and prolonged lack of social integration into the broader community. At the extreme, displacement-induced cultural disintegration leads to pronounced increases in morbidity and mortality.

In many cases, however, indigenous groups resist, seeking better resettlement terms or hoping to escape displacement altogether (Oliver-Smith 1994, 1991). The collective threat of displacement can strengthen ethnic bonds and promote ethnic amalgamation among groups similarly situated. This resistance only sometimes spurs anything more than sporadic ethnic violence (Scudder 1990; Gibson 1993). But even at lower levels of intensity, resistance creates high contingent costs, producing costly project delays or even cancellations,[7] as well as the potential for international controversy.

Despite the wide spectrum of observed resettlement-related outcomes and their significance for project success and the public image of the World Bank itself, the bank in practice often appears to respond ineffectively to even the most evident differences in a project's socioeconomic context. In some cases, bank officials prefer to drop proposed projects altogether rather than to engage contentious and culturally complex resettlement issues, when they are foreseen. In others, however, even elaborate screening exercises have failed to alert the bank to the potential for social conflict or project failure. The remainder of this chapter argues that, despite the bank's economic orientation, an inattentiveness to incentives and institutionalized behavior frequently misleads project analysis and design when projects involve ethnically mixed populations inhabiting the resource frontier.

Placing Displacement in a Comparative Framework

Especially in frontier regions, displacement is likely to confront two dimensions of heterogeneity. *Institutional heterogeneity* refers to settings in which people lack mutually accepted laws, rules, norms, customs, or other rights and obligations. Institutional heterogeneity may or may not be congruent with *ethnic heterogeneity,* which refers to the relationship between or among two or more groups basing collective identities on real or perceived ascriptive ties.

For illustrative purposes, the range of institutional relationships can be formulated as ideal types in a 2 × 2 table. Figure 2 categorizes development projects by reference to the level of institutional heterogeneity and the salience of ethnic heterogeneity in the project setting.[8] No systematic testing of World Bank projects has been attempted.[9] Nonetheless, available project documents and secondary literature support the view that the World Bank's displacement policy will be least effective when institutional heterogeneity is present and ethnic heterogeneity is salient.

Low Ethnic Heterogeneity and Low Institutional Heterogeneity

The right lower cell in figure 2 portrays a relatively homogeneous setting. In such cases, displacers and displaced are likely to share cost and benefit

Salience of Ethnic Heterogeneity

High	Low
Thailand (Khao Laem) Indonesia (Irian Jaya)	Indonesia (dam projects in Java)
Sri Lanka (Mahaweli) Sri Lanka (Gal Oya)	China (projects in Han areas) India (Maharashtra Irrigation II)

Note: Variation is continuous rather than discrete, changing in intensity over time.

Fig. 2. Some World Bank–supported projects causing displacement, sorted by two dimensions of heterogeneity

categories, and distributive conflict is likely to be muted by mutually legitimated arbitration rules. When resettlement-related delays occur, they are likely to reflect disputes over compensation rates or other mitigative measures, rather than rejection of displacement or the project altogether.

Displacement and resettlement in China. The World Bank touts resettlement in Chinese projects as among the most successful and upholds Chinese resettlement policy as a model to be emulated by others. In the Shuikou Hydropower project in Fujian Province, for example, advanced planning with the participation of local leaders helped to ease resettlement for 68,000 people. World Bank evaluations indicated that, on average, the people displaced now enjoy higher incomes, more living space, and more social amenities. On balance, most Shuikou resettlers reported satisfaction with their new lives (World Bank 1994, 1/6–7).

Despite the overall upbeat assessment of Chinese projects, the World Bank observes that displacement continues to generate an ethnic distribution of costs and benefits. The projects singled out for praise affect predominantly Han Chinese. Conversely, resettlement problems appear to plague projects affecting indigenous minorities (ibid., 4/5). The Daguangba Multipurpose Dam project in the island province of Hainan, for example, affected predominantly Li and Miao peoples. Failure to consult with them led to "a near-universal rejection of the contractor-built housing" in favor of traditional styles (ibid., 6/11). While moving the affected people into closer proximity to Han Chinese, the project failed to give displaced groups the education or training necessary for successful economic integration.

The Chinese experience, in sum, would appear to support the World Bank's view that detailed planning, adequate financing, and political commitment can produce better resettlement outcomes. Even in this most successful of country cases, however, ethnic and socioeconomic heterogeneity complicate resettlement, generating a greater likelihood of hardship for indigenous peoples.

Maharashtra Irrigation II project, India. Resettlement episodes may appear successful when planners and evaluators fail to evaluate disparate effects on a heterogeneous population. In the Maharashtra Irrigation II project in India, for example, the World Bank rated the resettlement experience as generally satisfactory (1993a, 40; 1993c, 34). The bank credited the government of the Maharashtra State with "a strong commitment towards a satisfactory resettlement outcome" (1993a, 40). Indeed, among those surveyed following resettlement, most were better off and three-fourths were satisfied with their new lives.

The study indicated, however, that gains accrued primarily to members of the locally dominant Maratha caste. The politically influential Maratha "used their bargaining power effectively" (ibid., v). The government tended to resettle Marathas in nearby areas, preserving and sometimes extending their social advantages. Actual resettlement sites were in areas in which non-Marathas were more numerous—the government "avoided villages where there were large landowning populations with strong political connections" (ibid., 9). Several years later, a survey found that the resettled people (70 percent of whom were Maratha) enjoyed higher incomes than their "hosts" (many of whom were not).

The project produced no widespread ethnic violence. But the bank noted that conflict over land broke out on several occasions between resettlers and host households. Still persisting, the study reported, was conflict in villages where common grazing areas—vital to landless, lower-caste villagers—was taken by the government to resettle the displaced people (ibid., 15 and n. 15). Other minor disputes arose when lower castes found themselves excluded from new village amenities, such as cremation sites (Sawant 1985).

Meanwhile, as many as 45 percent of the displaced people—mostly landless and more likely to be members of lower castes—were officially ineligible for resettlement programs, including replacement fields or house lots. They were forced to fend for themselves, which caused many to move away. The study indicated that their welfare and their whereabouts are simply unknown. "The benefits of belonging to the same ethnic and political system worked in favor of those who were deemed eligible by government for replacement land," the bank observed (ibid., 9).

High-Low Cells

The two intermediate categories, reflecting a majority of cases and a wide array of outcomes, will be considered very briefly. In the right upper cell of figure 2, the salience of ethnic heterogeneity is relatively low while socio-economic heterogeneity is somewhat more significant. Some displacement episodes in Java, the economic and cultural core of Indonesia, fit within this cell.[10] As a consequence of chronic confusion over conflicting claims to property, many costs of displacement go unrecognized and uncompensated, even in urban improvement schemes in Jakarta.

In the left lower cell of figure 2, ethnic heterogeneity is salient within a socioeconomically integrated area. Such distributive ethnic conflict arises when ethnic groups desire the same scarce resources—land, water, licenses, educational opportunity, jobs, votes, appointment to public office—for generally the same reasons. For example, the Accelerated Mahaweli Development Program in Sri Lanka, supported by the World Bank and several other aid agencies, has been associated with recurrent ethnic violence. In large part, the violence has been fueled by a Tamil perception that the project is an effort to extend Sinhalese dominance over traditionally Tamil areas (Scudder 1992, 1990; Hannum 1990, 284; Tambiah 1986; Herring, chap. 6 in this volume). Only in a symbolic sense is the project connected to religious or cultural cleavages. At stake is access to mutually desired irrigated land. Within the program, far fewer Tamils were selected for participation than the announced ratio, and less investment occurred in program areas peopled by Tamils (Scudder 1992, 6–7; 1991, 173). Resistance has slowed or halted some aspects of the program and has altered plans in others.[11]

High Ethnic and Institutional Heterogeneity

Contingent costs rise dramatically in the left upper cell of figure 2. Here displacement occurs in areas characterized by both ethnic heterogeneity and institutional heterogeneity. In this cell, conflict is more likely to be valuative—the definition of development and the ensuing determination of future opportunities are at stake—and hence conflict is likely to heighten the salience of ethnic identity. Note that the World Bank's displacement policy applies to projects in all four cells, but its only explicit ethnic policy provisions—safeguarding the interests of indigenous peoples—are directly tested in this cell.

Indonesian transmigration. The Indonesian government has subsidized the transmigration of roughly four million people from densely populated Java and nearby islands to develop frontier regions. Most transmigrants voluntarily join the program, and many fare well. But the program has produced displacement and dispossession among institutionally distinct Outer Island groups. Confusion regarding formal and informal property rights has sparked episodic violence between unwilling host populations and transmigrants in Sumatra, Sulawesi, Kalimantan, and elsewhere. Other contingent costs include large-scale encroachment into adjacent forests and abandonment of sites in inhospitable or unsustainable settings.

While lending about $1.6 billion for transmigration-related projects, the World Bank applied neither its resettlement policy nor its separate indigenous peoples policy. Regarding the resettlement policy, the displacement of host populations sometimes went unacknowledged by Indonesian authorities. Where displacement was acknowledged, the bank accepted the Indonesian policy position that land compensation would make projects unaffordable (World Bank 1988, 92). Regarding indigenous peoples, the bank sometimes suggested that it did not assert its own policy because Indonesian policy was so similar (ibid., 95). Yet Indonesian policy explicitly discounts the validity of customary land claims and often has sought to forcibly impose cultural assimilation.

In the sparsely populated province of Irian Jaya, for example, the roughly one million Melanesian indigenous people are racially as well as institutionally distinct from the rest of Indonesia. By the mid-1980s, transmigration accounted for nearly half of provincial population growth, and the government announced plans (since curbed) to settle roughly 700,000 more people there by 1989. Furthermore, the government claims that 99 percent of the vast province is state-owned forest, meaning that little or no compensation was given customary property holders when tracts of land were taken for transmigration or other purposes. The introduction of transmigration, mining, plantations, forestry, and other ventures, combined with programs of forced assimilation and racial and cultural disparagement from Javanese officials, has contributed to an amalgamated Papuan nationalism and separatist revolt that has continued sporadically throughout the 1990s. Meanwhile, as a response to international cultural and environmental controversies, the World Bank ceased support for transmigration rather than seeking to bring its policies to bear on the program.

Sardar Sarovar project, India. Few projects can match the notoriety of the Sardar Sarovar Dam in the Narmada River basin. Under pressure from environmental groups, human rights advocates, and legislative delegations from several countries, the World Bank withdrew from the project in March 1993 at the official request of the government of India. Given the acrimony over displacement and environmental issues, the potential impact on tribal peoples drew relatively little attention.

The bank's project appraisal noted that more than half of the people to be displaced were considered tribal people, but the bank's indigenous peoples policy was not incorporated into project agreements. That failure represented, in part, confusion over the definition of tribal people. The ethnic mosaic of the project area, like that of India in general, is inordinately complex. Groups identified as tribals, or identifying themselves as tribal, vary widely in their degree of assimilation into the Hindu caste system. Some remote groups live relatively autonomous lives, while others move selectively between tribal and caste worlds.

A similar complexity attends institutional arrangements, such as property rights, in the project area. Some tribal groups are subsistence agriculturalists; some engage in wage labor. Much of the project-affected area is customarily claimed by tribals but officially considered state forest, so many people were officially labeled encroachers and stood to receive little or no compensation (Morse and Berger 1992).

The actions of the government of Maharashtra (one of three Indian states most affected by the project) in relation to the Sardar Sarovar project appear strikingly different than those taken in the Maharashtra Irrigation II project (already discussed). While the prevalence of higher-caste Marathas spurred government responsiveness in the latter, the prevalence of tribals spurred no such response in the former.

Before project approval, a World Bank consultant noted that tribal people displaced in Maharashtra would need special protection to avoid dispossession or impoverishment (Scudder 1983). But the independent panel of experts established by the bank to assess project controversies concluded that tribal peoples officially viewed as encroachers continued to face partial or total dispossession (Morse and Berger 1992, 137–40).

At the bank's urging, the state agreed in 1991 and 1992 to resettlement terms that were more generous, deciding that "encroachers" might be allotted up to one acre of replacement land if available land were to be found (ibid.). Those with recognized title to land, however, were assured of far more generous terms, and, predictably, available land proved difficult to find for others, which only furthered claims that the project promoted tribal dispossession. In the face of continued opposition and growing international controversy, the bank withdrew from the project in 1993 and subsequently has ceased almost all lending for dam and reservoir projects.

Khao Laem Hydroelectric project, Thailand. The World Bank–supported Khao Laem Hydroelectric project displaced roughly 12,000 people, yielding an ethnic distribution of dispossession in a remote area subject to contending property claims. Government policy provided replacement land only to roughly 50 percent of the displaced people, those with documented land rights, typically ethnic Thais. Registered aliens without documented land rights—25 percent of the total number of displaced people—were provided a house lot but no agricultural land. Another 20 percent—unregistered alien members of hill tribes—received neither compensation nor resettlement assistance.

Survey results published in 1993 showed that after displacement, all families surveyed enjoyed higher incomes, spurred largely by rapid growth in the Thai economy. Nonetheless, 80 percent of the affected people indicated that their living standards had deteriorated, voicing dissatisfaction with the loss of agricultural self-sufficiency. The World Bank report seemed to question the rationality of this discontent.

> Although income sources have diversified, these families continue to view themselves primarily as farmers and thus consider their access to land as determining their standard of living, whether this is in fact the case or not. The rapid economic growth which has characterized Thailand over the past decade has in turn affected rural communities, with many families looking back to their former life with nostalgia. (World Bank 1993b, v, 29)

Why did these beneficiaries in terms of income count themselves as victims in terms of their own living standards? There is a tendency among development practitioners to treat income as a common-denominator yardstick for living standards, with income viewed as generally fungible within an integrated and commoditized economic system. But income gains from the hiring out of personal labor are susceptible to decisions of others and to broader economic trends, and in this case they often required seasonal migration. The dissatisfaction of the displaced people reflects a belief that income gains did not compensate for the loss of agricultural land, which, prior to their displacement, most had ranked as their most highly valued resource. In the case of ethnic groups counted as nonregistered aliens, income gains did not erase the fact of simple dispossession without compensation.

Even in this relatively benign case, contingent costs arose as many displaced people failed to adopt intensified agricultural methods or chose instead to encroach on nearby forests. The World Bank attributed these behaviors in part to a lack of integration: "The lesson is that clear rights and responsibilities based either upon legal codes or agreed principles conferring rights would result in a more satisfactory outcome" (ibid., 15).

Displacement and the ensuing dissatisfaction, however, did not spawn resistance beyond sporadic protests over compensation levels. Why did intensive ethnic mobilization not occur? The general pattern of economic growth undoubtedly blunted some of the hardship. Also, the availability of forest reserves for encroachment gave many non-Thais a low-cost "exit" option. But a World Bank review suggested that other factors also may have encouraged acquiescence. Project officials actively solicited the cooperation of traditional leaders, agreeing, among other things, to relocation of temples. Widespread provision of other benefits—access to education, health care, electricity, roads—typically benefited Thais and non-Thais alike. Those people affected made it clear that such benefits were no substitute for lost lands, but extension of individual and collective benefits to many non-Thais nonetheless appears to have diluted the potential perception of collective cost.

Conclusion

As chapter 1 in this volume observes, "schemes involving involuntary displacement or resettlement stand out as having especially great potential for a dynamic impact on ethnic politics." While the potential for conflict from demolition of homes, disruption of incomes, and relocation of communities is high, the actual impact is highly variable, contingent on the kind and intensity of political responses among those people affected. Though conflict occurs, one might well wonder why conflict does not occur far more often or in more intense forms.

Most projects, including most of those sketched in this chapter, generate mixed results and partial successes, reflecting neither the costless progress imagined by development planners nor the cultural collapse or violent resistance predicted by development critics. That displacement can impose hardship on the most vulnerable segments within many national populations is an appreciated fact. How some of the most vulnerable groups—indigenous peoples small in number and divided by rivalry or enmity—can have such a tremendous impact on some project outcomes (as also sketched in this chapter) is less well understood. Also far from obvious are the policy prescriptions that may prevent or further reduce ethnic conflict associated with displacement.

The World Bank's 1980 displacement policy and its revisions have produced improvements. At minimum, the bank is unlikely to approve future projects without serious attention to resettlement planning (World Bank 1994, 5/1–15). As a consequence, displacement has been reduced or avoided altogether in some projects, while resettlement has been handled more effectively in others. Meanwhile, the bank's policy has induced international normative change, with similar displacement policies now adopted by most other development agencies and by many government agencies in developing countries.

The policy nonetheless continues to complicate the bank's relationship with its borrowers. As World Bank policy attempts to internalize more of the costs of displacement, the economic, social, and political issues appear to grow in complexity. While highly specific or formulaic policy terms are advanced to prevent the gross abuses of the past, they simultaneously limit the flexibility and innovation that may be essential when displacement affects heterogeneous areas. If borrowing government officials do not support World Bank policy goals, formulaic approaches are unlikely to eliminate selective noncompliance. Government policy makers intent on "developing" the resource frontier intend institutional change. Unless they foresee significant problems of maladaptation or resistance, they have little incentive to comply with a World Bank policy that they see as reinforcing the status quo.

The World Bank, for its part, has been unable to confront either the political or the methodological challenges of institutional heterogeneity. The bank's policy statements are ambivalent or contradictory regarding indigenous peoples. On one hand, they champion tribal political autonomy and preservation of cultural diversity. On the other hand, the bank explicitly promotes processes of national and international economic integration that logically promote encroachment on indigenous peoples' resources and prerogatives. How to provide incentives and options so that ethnic groups only partially integrated into the broader society might favor greater integration is a question largely left unaddressed.

Methodologically, meanwhile, the bank in practice remains divided between proponents of economic theory and those asserting the importance of qualitative social or cultural variables. In general terms, those in the former camp continue to implicitly employ assumptions regarding microeconomic behavior that require no disaggregation. Those in the latter camp, meanwhile, rely on group-based analyses that tend to assign uniform and static characteristics to ethnic group membership. This approach, too, overlooks the variation in response by the same group to differing project contexts, as well as the important ways in which individuals within groups can vary in their responses to proposed projects.

The salience of ethnic heterogeneity is highly variable. Could further refinements that make displacement policy and practice more attuned to individual incentives reliably deflate that salience? One lesson to be drawn from the World Bank experience is that if the people to be displaced evaluate the change in their welfare in collective and relative terms, they are more likely to produce significant contingent costs of maladaptation or resistance. That lesson corresponds with the lesson found in analyses of ethnic conflict management: to diminish the likelihood that the salience of ethnicity will increase, policy makers should encourage interethnic ties and discourage intra-ethnic ones (Horowitz 1985; Young 1976).[12]

The lesson, by itself, does not provide reliable alternatives to existing resettlement practices. Nor does it free policy makers either from the integrationist pressures arising from resource-hungry populations or from the political need to be responsive to influential constituencies. Assuming, however, that projects will continue to exploit the resource frontier, both the World Bank and its borrowers may prefer to minimize social debilitation among area residents, and to avoid forms of social disruption that may convert technically feasible projects into costly political or economic failures.

Though the evidence remains suggestive and episodic, expanding the range of individual resettlement options and further broadening opportunities for participation in resettlement planning may simultaneously enlarge the sphere of voluntary behavior and reduce the likelihood of collective ethnic response. Giving people more of what they want would be one beneficial consequence; dispersing patterns of want more broadly across all of the people potentially affected may well be another.

NOTES

1. By the 1990s, ten such safeguard policies had been adopted. Seven involve environmental concerns. The three social policies involve involuntary resettlement, cultural property, and indigenous peoples. This chapter focuses on application of the involuntary resettlement policy, emphasizing projects involving indigenous peoples, but does not separately review application of the indigenous peoples policy. This is because the resettlement policy has been more forcefully applied in a wider range of applications, giving more variation in results. With some noteworthy exceptions, the indigenous peoples policy has not been forcefully applied. For a comparison of the two in policy and practice, see Gibson 1993.

2. The growth in estimates of displacement also reflects broader recognition of displacement-related impacts. The terms *displacement* and *resettlement* typically encompass all persons affected by any loss of land or other assets, as well as those otherwise losing some or all of their income streams, regardless of whether they are physically forced to relocate.

3. The UN Commission on Human Rights adopted a resolution (1993/77) proposing that "forced eviction" be banned. See also resolution 1990/17 and appendix II (E/CN.4/sub.2/1991/47) of the UN Sub-commission on Prevention of Discrimination and Protection of Minorities, for a view that migration into indigenous peoples' lands without their consent violates their human rights.

4. The first policy statement, Operational Manual Statement 2.33 of February 1980, was revised as Operations Policy Note 10.08 of October 1986 and Operational Directive 4.30 of June 1990. Another conversion was pending as of early 2000.

5. Though this chapter focuses on projects in frontier areas, World Bank insistence that displaced illegal squatters are entitled to benefits also has been a major source of controversy in urban projects.

6. Furnivall (1956) saw colonial institutionalization of law and commerce as transforming Burmese communities into "a crowd of individuals."

7. A World Bank study (1994, 5/20–22) noted that as many as 30 percent of 123 Asian projects were delayed on average for more than two years because of land acquisition and resettlement problems. The study reported that the delays "were the dominant reason why some projects perform less well than anticipated."

8. The basic argument here is that the project context is dynamic and often perceptional, meaning that the placement of projects in such a table would shift with time and perhaps with the perception of the observer.

9. Like project documents, World Bank research usually does not include consideration of ethnic composition. In a study of rural development projects, however, Kottak (1991, 443) found projects to be less successful when project plans "ignored established socioeconomic and cultural patterns" in affected areas. Moreover, 59 percent of project problems identified in the study were said to result from ignoring or insufficiently analyzing socioeconomic conditions.

10. There is regional ethnic diversity in Java, which often becomes politically salient. But episodes of displacement often are localized, with resettlement occurring among co-ethnics, or involve transmigration to other islands, as discussed later in this chapter.

11. By contrast, a settlement scheme in the Gal Oya region, not supported by the World Bank, enjoys a reputation as a model for participatory development. Despite heightened ethnic unrest throughout the country, Tamils and Sinhalese at Gal Oya share water reliably, shelter each other from attack, and exhibit other forms of cooperation (see chap. 5 in this volume; Uphoff 1992).

12. But if the salience of ethnicity is already high, as may be the case where memories of official discrimination or violent conflict are fresh, polarization may reinforce demands for ethnic-based entitlements.

REFERENCES

Anderson, Benedict. 1983. *Imagined Communities: Reflections on the Origins and Spread of Nationalism.* London: Verso.
Arrow, Kenneth. 1983. *Social Choice and Justice.* Cambridge: Harvard University Press.
Barth, Fredrik. 1969. *Ethnic Groups and Boundaries: The Social Organization of Culture Difference.* Boston: Little, Brown.
Bates, Robert. 1983. "Modernization, Ethnic Competition, and the Rationality of

Politics in Contemporary Africa." In *States vs. Ethnic Claims: African Policy Dilemmas,* ed. Donald Rothchild and Victor Olorunsola. Boulder: Westview.

Behura, N. K., and P. K. Nayak. 1993. "Involuntary Displacement and the Changing Frontier of Kinship: A Study of Resettlement in Orissa." In *Anthropological Approaches to Involuntary Resettlement: Policy, Practice, and Theory,* ed. Michael C. Cernea and Scott E. Guggenheim. Boulder: Westview.

Boeke, J. H. 1942. *The Structure of Netherlands Indian Economy.* New York: Institute of Pacific Relations.

Cernea, Michael M. 1990. "Poverty Risks from Population Displacement in Water Resources Development." Discussion Paper, Harvard Institute for International Development, Cambridge.

———. 1991. "Involuntary Resettlement: Social Research, Policy, and Planning." In *Putting People First: Sociological Variables in Rural Development,* ed. Michael M. Cernea, 2d ed. New York: Oxford University Press.

———. 1993. "Anthropological and Sociological Research for Policy Development on Population Resettlement." In *Anthropological Approaches to Involuntary Resettlement: Policy, Practice, and Theory,* ed. Michael M. Cernea and Scott E. Guggenheim. Boulder: Westview.

Chambers, Robert, ed. 1970. *The Volta Resettlement Experience.* London: Pall Mall.

Colson, Elizabeth. 1971. *The Social Consequences of Resettlement: The Impact of the Kariba Resettlement Upon the Gwembe Tonga.* Manchester, U.K.: Manchester University Press.

Connor, Walker. 1969. "Myths of Hemispheric, Continental, Regional, and State Unity." *Political Science Quarterly* 84, no. 4.

———. 1972. "Nation-Building or Nation-Destroying?" *World Politics* 24, no. 3.

———. 1991. "From Tribe to Nation?" *History of European Ideas* 13, no. 1–2.

Furnivall, J. S. 1956. *Colonial Policy and Practice: A Comparative Study of Burma and Netherlands India.* New York: New York University Press.

Geertz, Clifford. 1963. "The Integrative Revolution: Primordial Sentiments and Civil Politics in the New States." In *Old Societies and New States,* ed. Clifford Geertz. New York: Free Press.

Gibson, Daniel R. 1993. "The Politics of Involuntary Resettlement: World Bank–Supported Projects in Asia." Ph.D. diss., Duke University.

Guggenheim, Scott E., and Michael M. Cernea. 1993. "Anthropological Approaches to Involuntary Resettlement: Policy, Practice, and Theory." In *Anthropological Approaches to Involuntary Resettlement: Policy, Practice, and Theory,* ed. Michael M. Cernea and Scott E. Guggenheim. Boulder: Westview.

Hannum, Hurst. 1990. *Autonomy, Sovereignty, and Self-Determination: The Accommodation of Conflicting Rights.* Philadelphia: University of Pennsylvania Press.

Heilbroner, Robert L. 1962. *The Making of Economic Society.* Englewood Cliffs: Prentice-Hall.

Horowitz, Donald L. 1985. *Ethnic Groups in Conflict.* Berkeley: University of California Press.

Huntington, Samuel P. 1968. *Political Order in Changing Societies.* New Haven: Yale University Press.

Kottak, Conrad. 1991. "When People Don't Come First: Some Sociological Lessons from Completed Projects." In *Putting People First: Sociological Variables in Rural Development,* ed. Michael Cernea, 2d ed. New York: Oxford University Press.

Levy, Brian. n.d. "Foreign Aid in the Making of Economic Policy in Sri Lanka, 1977–1983." Unpublished paper sponsored by the World Bank Research Department, Washington, DC.

Migdal, Joel S. 1988. *Strong Societies and Weak States: State-Society Relations and State Capabilities in the Third World.* Princeton: Princeton University Press.

Morse, Bradford and Thomas R. Berger. 1992. *Sardar Sarovar: The Report of the Independent Review.* Ottawa: Resource Futures International.

Mosley, Paul, Jane Harrigan, and John Toye. 1991. *Aid and Power: The World Bank and Policy-Based Lending.* London: Routledge.

Newman, Saul. 1991. "Does Modernization Breed Ethnic Political Conflict?" *World Politics* 43, no. 3.

Oliver-Smith, Anthony. 1991. "Involuntary Resettlement, Resistance, and Political Empowerment." *Journal of Refugee Studies* 4, no. 2.

———. 1994. "Resistance to Resettlement: The Formation and Evolution of Movements." In *Research in Social Movements, Conflicts, and Change.* Greenwich, CT: JAI Press.

Olson, Mancur. 1963. "Rapid Growth as a Destabilizing Force." *Journal of Economic History* 23, no. 4.

Rothschild, Joseph. 1981. *Ethnopolitics: A Conceptual Framework.* New York: Columbia University Press.

Sawant, Prakash R. 1985. *River Dam Construction and Resettlement of Affected Villages.* New Delhi: Inter-India.

Scudder, Thayer. 1973. "The Human Ecology of Big Projects: River Basin Development and Resettlement." In *Annual Review of Anthropology,* ed. Bernard J. Siegel. Palo Alto: Annual Reviews.

———. 1983. "The Relocation Component in Connection with the Sardar Sarovar (Narmada) Project." World Bank consultant's report.

———. 1990. "Victims of Development Revisited: The Political Costs of River Basin Development." *Development Anthropology Network: Bulletin of the Institute for Development Anthropology* 8:1.

———. 1991. "A Sociological Framework for the Analysis of New Land Settlements." In *Putting People First: Sociological Variables in Rural Development,* ed. Michael Cernea, 2d ed. New York: Oxford University Press.

———. 1992. "Constraints to the Development of Settler Incomes and Production-Oriented Participatory Organizations in Large-Scale Government-Sponsored Projects: The Mahaweli Case." Paper presented at the Symposium on

Irrigation and Society in the Context of Mahaweli, Sri Lanka, at Monte Verita, Ticino, Switzerland, August.

Smith, M. G. 1965. *The Plural Society in the British West Indies.* Berkeley: University of California Press.

Tambiah, S. J. 1986. *Sri Lanka: Ethnic Fratricide and the Dismantling of Democracy.* Chicago: University of Chicago Press.

Uphoff, Norman. 1992. *Learning from Gal Oya: Possibilities for Participatory Development and Post-Newtonian Social Science.* Ithaca: Cornell University Press.

Van Arkadie, Brian. 1990. "The Role of Institutions in Development." In *Proceedings of the World Bank Annual Conference on Development Economics, 1989.* Washington, DC: World Bank.

―――. 1988. *Indonesia: The Transmigration Program in Perspective.* Washington, DC: World Bank.

―――. 1993a. *Early Experience with Involuntary Resettlement: Impact Evaluation on India Maharashtra Irrigation II Project.* Washington, DC: World Bank Operations Evaluation Department.

―――. 1993b. *Early Experience with Involuntary Resettlement: Impact Evaluation on Thailand Khao Laem Hydroelectric.* Washington, DC: World Bank Operations Evaluation Department.

―――. 1993c. *Early Experience with Involuntary Resettlement: Overview.* Washington, DC: World Bank Operations Evaluation Department.

―――. 1994. *Resettlement and Development: The Bankwide Review of Projects Involving Involuntary Resettlement, 1986–1993.* Washington, DC: World Bank Environment Department.

Young, Crawford. 1976. *The Politics of Cultural Pluralism.* Madison: University of Wisconsin Press.

CHAPTER 3

USAID and Ethnic Conflict: An Epiphany?

Heather S. McHugh

This chapter examines the approach of the United States Agency for International Development (USAID) to ethnic conflict—whether it addresses ethnic conflict in its policies, programs, or projects; why it is interested in ethnic conflict; and how it approaches ethnic conflict and ethnicity.[1] As an independent agency within the U.S. foreign policy establishment, USAID is both actively involved in and greatly affected by the current heated debate on the formulation of post–Cold War foreign policy in the United States. Therefore, the first section of this chapter attempts to address some of the foreign policy themes that are emerging from the post–Cold War foreign policy debate and shaping USAID's response to ethnic conflict. A policy of "selective involvement" seems to best capture U.S. foreign policy today. In the second section of this chapter, both internal and external motivations for USAID's engagement in ethnic conflict are examined. In the third section, USAID's past experiences with ethnic conflict are briefly described. In the fourth section, the way in which USAID is now attempting to deal with ethnic conflict is detailed.

What Are U.S. Foreign Policy Objectives?

Since the end of the Cold War, borderless problems, such as civil, religious, and ethnic conflict, seem to have emerged with a vengeance as the predominant form of conflict in the world. Issues that were long buried under the tense stability of the Cold War have resurfaced—including separatism, the reconfiguration of state borders, war-crimes tribunals, and even genocide. The intensity of the problems has generated among donors a new terminology, including such phrases as "complex disaster," "early warning systems," "preventive development,"[2] and "failed states." The problems have even begun to push the international community into operating with different methodologies and theories—to dust off and revisit old methodologies and theories, such as containment, public safety programs, and spillover effects. A 1994 report in the *Chicago Tribune* read:

> This turmoil caused by civil conflict could disrupt export markets, encourage terrorism and other extremism, fuel regional arms races, and trigger refugee crises. "We no longer have the singular threat of communism," said Brian Atwood, a former Clinton administration top foreign aid official and administrator of USAID, "we're now dealing with the threat of chaos." (Atlas 1994, 1)

Without the anchor of political and economic realities and theories of the Cold War, recent U.S. foreign policy has been contradictory. Warren Christopher, while U.S. secretary of state, stated that the primary foreign policy task of the United States is "heading off the surfacing of long-suppressed ethnic and religious conflict" around the world (as quoted in Jenkins 1993). However, the White House has focused its foreign policy on a strategy of "enlargement of the world's free community of market democracies," and such economic issues as the North American Free Trade Agreement (NAFTA) and the General Agreement on Tariffs and Trade (GATT) comprise the main pillar of the Clinton doctrine (Nacht 1995, 194).

Alexander Nacht, of the Center for Strategic and International Studies, reviewed recent academic foreign policy literature and suggested that five schools of thought represent the major diagnoses of world politics in the post–Cold War era (ibid., 197–201).

- The "end of history" school, advanced by Francis Fukuyama, is based on the thesis that liberal democracy is the endpoint of ideological evolution and the final form of government; thus, U.S. foreign policy should focus on the spread of democratic ideals.
- The "clash of civilizations" school, advanced by Samuel Huntington, is based on the concept that the fault lines of international conflict will be based on culture divisions; thus, U.S. foreign policy should concentrate on containing the challenge of Confucian and Islamic culture to the predominant Western liberal tradition.
- The "balance of power" school, founded by Hans Morgenthau and practiced by Henry Kissinger, is based on the concept that five (or six) power centers will dominate world politics in the years ahead; thus, U.S. foreign policy should focus on ensuring that no single power, or combination of powers, threatens U.S. vital interests.
- The "primacy of economics" school, advanced by Charles Johnson, is based on the concept that increased attention to economic competition will define the future course of world politics.

- The "humanitarianism and global trends" school, put forward by Jessica Mathews and Robert Kaplan, stresses humanitarian and global trends that "transcend national borders" and blur "the dividing line between foreign and domestic policy" (Mathews 1989, 162); accordingly, U.S. foreign policy should be based not only on national interests but also on global issues, such as population growth, renewable-resource decline, and environmental interdependence.

Individually, none of these five schools comprehensively captures the rationale for U.S. policy. Instead, it appears that each of the five have contributed at times to the rationale for engagement. U.S. foreign policy seems to be based more on James Schlesinger's concept that the U.S. needs to "husband its strength and to choose with care those policy objectives that reflect interests sufficiently weighty that they can garner the public support to sustain them in the long run" (Nacht 1995, 204). This concept of selective involvement effectively captures the power of the media in determining where U.S. interests are at stake (e.g., as concerns Somalia), the power of U.S.-based ethnic or racial organizations in determining U.S. policies (e.g., the policy in South Africa), the power of economic concerns (e.g., those involving Iraq), and the power of U.S. geopolitical concerns (e.g., those involving Haiti).

This last point suggests that the major problem with Schlesinger's concept of selective involvement is that public opinion is fickle and events often change faster than a response can be articulated. Thus, at times U.S. foreign policy may seem capricious, slow, and vague while it fumbles for an appropriate response in time to be relevant. Clough (1994, 2) suggests that the answer to this debate over the direction of U.S. foreign policy is that "the American people are in the process of reclaiming foreign policy from the 'Wise Men' who have so assiduously guarded it for the past 50 years." It becomes obvious, then, that the failure to compellingly articulate a new direction for U.S. foreign policy will continue to constrain USAID's ability to react coherently to ethnic conflict. The concept of selective involvement, however, may allow USAID to act and react to ethnic conflict until there is a more comprehensive (or possibly restrictive) foreign policy.

USAID's Interest in Ethnic Conflict

USAID continues its attempts to cope with these new world realities, even as U.S. foreign policy and the international community fail to articulate a definite strategy relevant to ethnic conflict. Indeed, frustration seems to fill the halls of USAID's sister agency, the State Department, as well as the CIA— where "coping with ambiguous ethnic struggles just isn't as exhilarating as leading a global crusade against a Soviet menace" (McManus 1995, 23).

Despite the lack of clear articulation of an ethnic conflict policy, two recent events may serve to further focus USAID's attention on ethnic conflict. First, in 1995 the USAID administrator was designated as the president's special coordinator for international disaster assistance. With this designation, the president has directed all executive departments and agencies (including the Defense Department) to treat the special coordinator as the focal point for interagency deliberations on international disaster assistance for natural and complex disasters. Second, the National Security Council (NSC) asked then Administrator Atwood, in his capacity as special coordinator, to chair an interagency review of U.S. and international capabilities to respond to humanitarian emergencies. Presidential Review Directive number 50 (PRD-50) made a number of recommendations to the NSC on the capacity of U.S. government agencies to respond quickly to these situations. Ethnic conflict and ethnicity are specifically mentioned in the sections of PRD-50 that deal with prevention, early warning of crisis, and nongovernmental organizations (NGOs). Both of these events might indicate that the White House perceives USAID as a key player in matters of international security and, possibly, that USAID is the natural U.S. entity to deal with ethnic conflict in crisis countries.

External Forces Driving USAID's Interest in Ethnic Conflict

Events in Bosnia (and, to some extent, the other Central European countries), Kosovo, Angola, Mozambique, Ethiopia/Eritrea, Indonesia, Liberia, Somalia, and the Greater Horn of Africa[3] have focused USAID attention on ethnic conflict. Indeed, according to former Administrator Atwood (1994a): "these failed states threaten our nation. They cost us too much. They create diseases that impact on us. They destabilize other nations. They stymie economic growth and they deny us economic opportunity in the largest new marketplace—the developing world."

Both natural and man-made disasters (which include ethnic conflict) have escalated in number and complexity during the past several years. In 1998 an estimated 418 million people were affected by humanitarian crises of which man-made disasters accounted for 26 percent. According to the Interdisciplinary Research Program on Causes of Human Rights Violations (PIOOM) researchers at the University of Leiden, The Netherlands, between mid-1997 and 1998, there were

- 16 high-intensity conflicts (where there were more than 1,000 deaths due to armed conflict);
- 70 low-intensity conflicts (where there were between 100 and 1,000 deaths due to armed conflict);
- 114 violent political crises (where there were fewer than 100 deaths due to armed conflict);
- and 26 countries with peacekeeping operations (both UN and other). (PIOOM 1999)

In past years, USAID had determined that approximately 50 countries experience some sort of major conflict in any given (post-1990) year. Now, using PIOOM's trend analysis and other early warning systems, the agency finds that the forecasts are grim. Not only are pre-conflict situations, active conflicts (including ethnic conflict), and armed conflicts escalating in the post–Cold War era, but interstate conflicts are also on the rise. Analysis of trends indicate that:

- More than 100 "political tension situations" could develop into crisis;
- Active intrastate conflicts are increasing, leading to state collapse in countries such as the former Yugoslavia or near-state failure in countries such as Angola, Colombia, Cambodia, Haiti, Lebanon, Liberia, Mozambique, Sierra Loene, Somalia, Sudan and Congo-Zaire;
- In 1995 there were 101 armed conflicts; 135 in 1996; 161 in 1997; and 200 in 1998;
- Interstate conflicts are likely to escalate in the near future, including: Nagorno-Karabakh; Burma-Thailand; China (Spratly Islands); China-Taiwan; Venezuela-Colombia; East Timor; Ecuador-Peru; Eritrea-Yemen; Ethiopia-Eritrea; Ethiopia-Somalia; Ethiopia-Sudan; Kashmir; West Bank/Gaza; Israel-Syria; Japan-China; Latvia-Russia; Western Sahara; Nigeria-Cameroon; Nigeria-Chad; Poland-Belarus; Northern Uganda; Russia-Azerbaijan; Russia-Georgia; Russia-Chechnya; Saudi Arabia-Yemen; Serbia-Montenegro; Sudan-Egypt; Syria-Turkey; Turkey-Greece; and Cyprus. Many of these conflicts include countries of strategic and national interest to the U.S. government.

Other U.S. government agencies, including the State Department, have directed USAID efforts in areas characterized by ethnic conflict. In some cases, embassies focus USAID involvement in the field, quietly directing funding toward the areas most sensitive and vulnerable to ethnic conflict. In other cases, the embassy may set the entire tone of U.S. government assistance. Because ethnic conflict is likely to be a regional phenomena, at the same time U.S. embassies in neighboring countries might have different ideas of which ethnic group needs assistance. Since 1994, embassies in Rwanda and the Democratic Republic of the Congo targeted different and warring ethnic groups for assistance, causing confusion and frustration among NGO partners operating near national borders.[4]

In some ways, academic theory has contributed to USAID's interest in ethnicity. Some experts have suggested that the application of the political economy perspective to the development process can underscore groupings of ethnic communities.[5] Indeed, it seems that more USAID staff members are adhering to the methodology of political economy than in the past. Others have suggested that as USAID began to rely more on anthropologists in the mid-1970s and early 1980s to perform social soundness analysis or assessments, it began to focus more on ethnicity and ethnic communities. More recently, articles and books by Robert Kaplan, John Stremlau, Peter Sollis, Jessica Mathews, Ted Gurr, Alan Tonelson, and others have generated lively debate within the agency. One reporter has noted:

> Overpopulation, environmental decay, ethnic tensions and economic stagnation are an explosive mix in many countries in the developing world, leading them to 'either fragment or become more authoritarian,' contends Thomas Homer-Dixon of the University of Toronto, a leading researcher on the link between environmental scarcities and violent conflict. His research has impressed [Vice President] Gore, who has discussed it many times with President Clinton, White House officials say.
>
> Along with Homer-Dixon's work, the administration's thinking about underlying environmental and social factors has been influenced by journalist Robert Kaplan's cover story in February's *The Atlantic*. The article, "The Coming Anarchy," presented a compelling picture of spreading chaos growing out of poverty, disease, environmental damage, and tribalism. Not only did Clinton read the article but, in an unusual move, asked for an assessment from the National Security Council staff, CIA, State Department, and Pentagon. They endorsed many of Kaplan's concerns but faulted him for ignoring some positive trends, such as expanding democracy in this hemisphere. (Atlas 1994, 2)

Some longtime observers of USAID suggest that the agency responds more to popular culture represented by the media than to academic literature. In the period starting with northern Iraq in 1991 and continuing with Somalia, Bosnia-Herzegovina, Rwanda, and Kosovo, observers have quipped that Ted Turner and his Cable News Network (CNN), rather than the U.S. president, are in charge (Weiss 1994, 151). Weiss (ibid., 152) has argued, "As well as dramatizing needs, publicizing human rights abuse, stimulating action, and generating resources, the media have distorted the kinds of assistance provided, skewed the allocations of resources and personnel among geographical areas, ignored the role of local humanitarians, and focused international attention on the perceived bungling of various agencies." Policy makers within the agency, however, have noted that USAID's current interest in ethnic conflict was initiated by the agency's efforts to deal with the crisis in the Greater Horn of Africa—before the media really began to focus on ethnic conflict.[6]

It is not unusual for U.S. foreign policy to be shaped with an eye toward politically potent, domestically based ethnic, racial, or religious groups—as the "American political system is peculiarly susceptible to ethnically based pressures" (Gedda 1995).[7] For example, Gedda argues, "American Jews have weighed in on Middle East policy for years,[8] and lately Arab Americans are being heard from more than before" (ibid.). In the 1980s, African Americans largely succeeded in laying claim to U.S. policy toward Africa, especially toward South Africa (Clough 1994, 4). Later, the Congressional Black Caucus helped Clinton shape U.S. policy toward Haiti (Gedda 1995) and Nigeria. Indeed, as Haupt has noted (1994, 12), "Poland also has that most valuable entity for an ethnic group that wishes to affect U.S. foreign policy, a vocal American diaspora." And some experts suggest that Greek Americans have often successfully headed off a U.S. tilt toward Turkey and that Cuban exiles in south Florida exert a strong influence over U.S.-Cuba policy.

USAID is not exempt from pressure by U.S.-based ethnic organizations. In particular, there is growing pressure on USAID to use the ethnic-diaspora communities in the U.S. who have by now "accumulated the experience, the know-how, the personnel and the projects needed and wanted" by ethnic communities in USAID-assisted countries ("Get on the Right Track" 1994, 6). Indeed, Serge Duss, associate director of World Vision, and other NGO leaders have criticized USAID programs for not using American ethnic organizations for the implementation of democracy and economic programs—stating that U.S. ethnic organizations are the most qualified for this task ("Helsinki Commission Examines Aid" 1995, 1–2). Therefore, the more localized foreign policy becomes, the more likely it is that domestic organizations with ethnic ties to the developing world will influence the debate and place new demands on USAID, especially as more African Americans, Hispanics, and Asians are elected to local, state, and national political offices (Clough 1994, 5).

Internal Forces Driving USAID's Interest in Ethnic Conflict

One of the major concerns of USAID is the increasing amount of resources being diverted from development programs toward humanitarian assistance. The costs of ethnic conflict are incalculable, but the Joint International Program on Conflict Resolution and Ethnicity (INCORE)[9] has estimated that the financial cost of a "low-level" conflict, such as that in Northern Ireland, reached around $9 billion between 1969 and 1982. In 1993 alone, according to UN and USAID estimates, expenditures on emergency relief worldwide totaled more than $6 billion. Of this amount, international donors contributed $4.5 billion, of which the U.S. government's share was $1.5 billion. As evidence of the upwardly creeping costs of ethnic conflict, $1 billion was spent on just one disaster in Rwanda between April 1994 and August 1995 (Kumar 1995, 1–4). More recently, the U.S. government alone has committed $38.5 million to the crisis in Kosovo since March 1998. These escalating costs of humanitarian assistance do not necessarily include other costs associated with ethnic conflict, such as post-conflict development assistance focused on reconstruction and rehabilitation (e.g., repairing, demining, demobilization, and more).

For example, of the 100 million land mines placed in the world (100 million more are stockpiled), 18 to 30 million are estimated to be deployed in Africa in 12 mine-impacted countries. Of those 12 countries, Angola has 9 million mines, Mozambique has 1–2 million, Somalia has 1 million, and the Western Sahara has 1–2 million. Ethiopia/Eritrea and Sudan are likewise considered to suffer severely (ICRC 1994, 60–68). Land mines have a severe impact on economic and social structures. In Angola thousands of hectares of agricultural land in the fertile Mavinga Valley are largely abandoned owing to the widespread use of mines (ibid.).

In the case of Rwanda, the $500 million that the U.S. government committed to help refugees was more than double the entire amount of development aid that the United States has given that nation in the three decades since its independence (Atlas 1994, 2). This "development diversion" has meant that greater amounts of USAID's resources have been diverted from development activities toward humanitarian assistance programs focused on dealing with the consequences of ethnic conflict. In fact, as recently as November 1995, Administrator Atwood notified the rest of the agency that crisis prevention was a goal of the agency and that there is a direct link between "development indicators and the vulnerability of nations to implode and collapse" (Atwood 1995, 3). Lois Richards testified (1994):

> In Sudan, an ethnic war between Northern Sudanese and the South has lasted for over a decade and cost tens of thousands of lives. The United States has spent $731 million since 1983, mostly for emergency feeding programs, to save hundreds of thousands of people from starvation. There seems to be no solution in sight to this cycle of conflict, though the country is nearing exhaustion of its resources.

This effort has motivated USAID to take an increasingly active role in formulating foreign policy options to deal with ethnic conflict and has galvanized an increasing amount of internal debate. At the same time, USAID has not been able to link the need for development and costs of violent conflict to the domestic priorities of U.S. citizens.

The implications and implementation of USAID policy decisions have gradually focused the agency's attention on ethnicity and ethnic conflict. At the policy level, USAID staff members discuss ethnic issues with other donors, the White House, the Congress, and others. USAID's recently released "Strategies for Sustainable Development" (1994) articulates the Clinton administration's strong view that development is driven by stabilizing population growth, fostering broad-based economic growth, helping democracy to take root, protecting the environment, and effectively responding to both natural and human-made disasters. Carol Lancaster testified (1994a): "These strategies are propelled by the notion that we must involve traditionally disenfranchised groups in the developing world, groups such as women, rural agricultural producers, ethnic and religious minorities, and the poorest of poor, in the social and economic decision-making of their nations if real progress is to be attained."

Likewise, USAID's focus on participation, as both a crosscutting issue and a policy, reinforces the concept that development efforts—including project design, implementation, and evaluation—should include the potential beneficiaries (and other interested parties) of that effort. USAID, however, needs to make choices about what level of participation is appropriate or possible. USAID must decide if it can be responsible for expanding participation at all levels in a wide range of development decisions (and risk including competing or even combating ethnic groups) or if it should limit costs, complexity, and unpredictability by dealing with just a few groups and/or leaders (and risk creating the perception that the agency is taking sides) (McHugh 1995b, 9).

At the field and bureau levels, USAID staff members have become aware that ethnic conflict constrains the agency's ability to effectively engage in many development activities.[10] Likewise, other staff members are extremely concerned about identifying and dealing with the root causes of ethnic conflict.[11] For instance, many development experts mention that democratization itself can stimulate ethnic conflict. Indeed, a 1993 report on Kenya from the United Nations Development Program stated baldly that the "principal causes of the violence in the past two years are directly and unequivocally related to the ongoing process of democratization" (Richburg 1994, A1). A recent analysis of the relationship between democratization and ethnic conflict (McHugh 1995a, 15) has shown that as participation in the democratic process increases,

- demands on the system also increase, which can overwhelm the issues and views of ethnically nondominant groups (e.g., as more citizens turn toward the legal system for redress, the courts become overburdened and unable to respond to demand);
- the number of contending views also increases (e.g., as each ethnic group forms its own political party or associations and begins to advocate for its members' interests, this trend can overwhelm politicians and promote what some analysts call *demosclerosis,* or the inability of the system to promote many interests as participation in the democratic process increases); and
- entrenched elites become concerned about losing control over their traditional spheres of influence and respond by undermining the democratic process itself (e.g., as political parties expand, the government may respond by gerrymandering district lines to maintain the dominant ethnic group's majority representation).

Thus, within USAID there is considerable awareness that democratic development itself plays an important—if short-term—role in opening the door to ethnic strife.[12]

Where people sit within USAID (e.g., in the field or in Washington, in central bureaus or in the regional bureau) seems to determine whether they believe that the agency is responding to either internal or external signals to deal with ethnic conflict. It is apparent, however, that USAID has begun to take on ethnic conflict as a discrete issue, although the debate about how to deal with ethnicity and ethnic conflict is still raging.[13] The continued lack of consensus on U.S. foreign policy objectives may have serious implications on where USAID directs its assistance.

How Has USAID Dealt with Ethnic Conflict in the Past?

In the 1960s and early 1970s, USAID's experience with ethnic communities around the world eventually generated a reluctance to engage in activities associated with U.S. "national interests" on the part of some agency staff members (Elliott n.d., 4). In particular, USAID's experience in Vietnam, Cambodia, and Laos highlights the problem of interventions focused in part on ethnic conflict—USAID had to become involved in the domestic politics of these countries to seek political solutions to ethnic conflicts.

USAID was heavily engaged in these countries, so much so that at one time more than 25 percent of the USAID staff was located in Vietnam. After the war, the agency tended to recruit staff from the "antiwar" movement who tended to shy away from highly politicized USAID development programs.[14] Indeed, between 1975 and 1985 those agency staff members who ended up serving in such locations as Afghanistan, Mozambique, and Central America (to name just a few places) were considered to be stigmatized by these assignments.[15]

At the same time, foreign aid bills became the foci for legislative battles over the content and conduct of development programs. In particular, Congress wanted to make sure that USAID did not become involved in any more "Vietnams" (or "Chiles") and thus prohibited the agency from providing any assistance to foreign militaries, including police training. The new legislation also mandated decentralization of USAID staff located in Washington as well as an emphasis on direct in-field implementation of projects through private contractors. As a consequence, the implementing orders issued by USAID "effectively called for programs which transferred resources directly from the U.S. to the 'poorest of the poor' or the 'rural poor'" in developing countries—a substantial change from the agency's earlier emphasis on production-related training and experience (Elliott n.d., 3). The result of these legislative changes within the agency was to reduce USAID's involvement in "high-level" foreign policy operations, where development programs could be construed to be related to ethnic conflict.

The new agency programs, called the New Directions (or New Mandate) programs,[16] attempted to create equity by focusing on six selected areas: participation of the poor, rural poor beneficiaries, urban poor beneficiaries, nutrition, women beneficiaries, and specific sectoral norms (agriculture, health and population, and education). The Congressional Research Service (1981, 400) reported that the "New Directions programs involve[d] efforts to by-pass, to a greater or lesser extent, existing political and social structures by a foreign government agency to deliver services

directly to the least productive group in the recipient society." The programs were often structured by the USAID field staff in terms of rural
communities and equity issues, and in that sense they often dealt with ethnic groups.[17] Thus, field staff often directly dealt with issues related to ethnicity, despite the tenor of policy guidance from the agency's Washington
headquarters.

However, an emphasis on equity did not mean that the agency
focused on managing the specific concerns and issues of ethnic and other
marginalized groups. Rather, it seems that any programs that focused on
ethnicity in any capacity were more interested in integrating marginalized
ethnic communities into the "modern" world and attempting to reduce the
salience of ethnic identity.

Likewise, the indigenous peoples movement started influencing some
USAID staff members by the late 1970s, and according to some staff
members it was a full-blown movement within USAID by the mid-
1980s—but not at the policy level.[18] Indeed, at the policy level within the
agency in the 1980s, there was a de-emphasis of social analysis and social
equity and therefore a concomitant de-emphasis of ethnicity. Some
USAID officials have stated that during this period, the field could not
actively promote ethnic issues but had to concentrate on economic growth
issues.[19] Indeed, USAID emphasized economic growth because of the
belief that a growing economy was the best way to solve development
problems, but the agency later found that social and political problems
continued nevertheless. For example, in the Dominican Republic, many
Haitian sugarcane workers may have been put out of work because of
USAID funded agricultural diversity programs. In general, because
agency staff members were not allowed to treat ethnicity as an expressed
issue, no social safety nets were created (or even allowed to be discussed)
to deal with the possible development impact of economic programs on
ethnic groups.[20]

As Cohen notes in chapter 4 in this book, aid agencies seem to be split
internally over whether or how to deal with ethnicity. At USAID a dis-
connection exists between the operational realities field missions face in
developing countries and the political realities USAID's Washington staff
face in the U.S. capital. Indeed, if any USAID-Washington policy or program had any impact on ethnic communities, it was indirect—the result of
the fact that many ethnic groups are part of the poor/rural population.
USAID field missions, however, seem to have learned to hide project
objectives targeted toward ethnic communities and toward reducing ethnic tensions, under the rubric of whatever policy guidance was in fashion
in Washington at the time.

Despite efforts to distance USAID policy makers from ethnicity and ethnic conflict, over the years USAID's Washington bureaus have funded approximately 15 studies of ethnic issues, most actively in the early 1980s. USAID also funded 128 studies dealing with issues related to "indigenous populations" and 77 studies related to "tribes." USAID has consistently struggled with terminology for certain groups. Such terms as *ethnic, racial, tribal,* and *indigenous* are used sometimes interchangeably and sometimes distinctly. In the "USAID Thesaurus of Keywords Used to Index Documents" included in the USAID project information databases, ethnic groups are related to linguistic groups, minority groups, racial groups, religious groups, and tribal groups, whereas indigenous groups are related to aboriginal groups, foreign groups, and regional populations (USAID 1991a, 194, 245). These documents and descriptions of project activities are keyed into the system by individuals, so relevant classifications are extremely subjective.

The studies focusing on ethnicity include

- in Latin America, a study of four ethnic groups in Brazil (Kayayan 1973); education policy toward speakers of indigenous languages in Peru (Grant 1974); ethnicity and social class formation in Bolivia (Painter 1985); a study of ethnic minorities in Belize (Wilk and Chapin 1988); and reproductive health in six ethnic groups in Mexico (Cabral et al. 1998);
- in Africa, a study of social and economic variables, including ethnicity in Ghana (Kpedekpo 1975); a look at the multiethnic factor in Namibia (Shack 1977); cultural traditions and coping strategies in the Sahel (Riesman 1979); ethnicity and agriculture in Upper Volta (Saunders 1980); a study of the Bamileke ethnic group and economic growth in Cameroon (McFerson 1983); land tenure and nationalism in Mauritania (Park et al. 1991); a study of the role of religious institutions in Kenya (Kwamboka 1994); an Africa regional study of the effect of ethnicity on leadership succession (Bienen, Londregan, and van de Walle 1994); cross-border trade and ethnic groups in West Africa (McCorkle et al. 1995); a series of evaluations of international emergency assistance to Rwanda (Eriksson et al. 1996; Sellstrom et al. 1996; Adelman et al. 1996; and Borton et al. 1996); a look at ethnicity, gender and fertility in Nigeria (USAID/Africa Bureau 1996); and a study of civil conflicts in Northern Uganda (Gersony 1997);
- in Eastern Europe and the Newly Independent States, a study of emergency shelter which focused on the potential for ethnic hostilities (Cuny et al. 1992); community peace building in Bosnia and Croatia (Guest 1997); ethnic tension and conflict in Macedonia

(Blumhagen 1998); and a study of reconciliation possibilities in Bosnia and Croatia (Augenbraun et al. 1999);

- in the Middle East, a study of scientific cooperation and peace building (Kumar and Rosenthal 1998);
- in Asia, a study of tribal people in Thailand (Hanks et al. 1964); an analysis of interethnic assimilation and population change in Singapore (Lee 1973); ethnicity and fertility in Malaysia (DaVanzo and Haaga 1981); ethnicity in Hawaii[21] (Wright and Gardner 1983); private sector projects in Sri Lanka (Garms 1987); ethnicity and agriculture in Indonesia (Colfer, Newton, and Herman 1989); and a look at internally displaced people in Sri Lanka (Baron 1994); and
- at the Multi-Regional level, a study of ethnic socioeconomic redistribution in Sri Lanka, Malaysia, and Trinidad and Tobago (Grove and West 1978); a social analysis of the impact of development on ethnic minorities in Iran, Afghanistan, the Sudan, and Brazil, (Maybury-Lewis et al. 1980); the link between democratization and ethnic conflict (Peterson and Sayari 1992); a worldwide study of ethnicity and voting districts (Ordeshook and Shvetsova 1993); an examination of ethnicity throughout the world (Crosby and White, 1995); conflict in the Greater Horn of Africa (USAID/Africa Bureau 1996); an evaluation of post–civil war reconstruction which includes an examination of ethnic conflict (Kumar 1997); another evaluation of post–civil war reconstruction with a focus on elections (Kumar 1998); and a look at social reconciliation in postwar societies (Kumar 1999).

In addition, USAID has funded two examinations of ethnic conflict, including a worldwide study of ethnic conflict in developing countries (Horowitz 1981) and a study of lessons learned in ethnic conflict resolution (McHugh 1995a). Project experience, directly targeted toward ethnic groups, is difficult to document. The project documentation does not always articulate ethnic concerns, although the project designers, managers, and evaluators may have been well aware of underlying ethnic concerns in the field. A search of the USAID project database has identified 319 discrete projects that deal with ethnicity as either the direct or indirect focus of development activities.

How Is USAID Attempting to Deal with Ethnic Conflict Now?

One of the major problems in analyzing USAID's intervention criteria for ethnic conflict is the problem of defining what constitutes an ethnic

TABLE 1. USAID Project Experience with Ethnicity

Project Number	Country/Region	Status*	Ethnic Focus
2680360	Lebanon	A	relief and redevelopment programs for communities with more than one ethnic or sectarian group
3060204	Afghanistan	A	rehabilitation and repair of locations selected on the basis of various factors, including ethnicity
3830101	Sri Lanka	A	focused on the orphaned victims of ethnic conflict
3910488	Pakistan	I	a quota system for acceptance into the agriculture university
3980280	Near East, regional	A	increasing the access of ethnic groups to judicial and political processes
4100006	East Asia, regional	P	the provision of health care to Burmese ethnic refugees
4100008	East Asia, regional	?	focused on the cross-border transmission of HIV/AIDs among ethnic and highland minorities
4920419	Philippines	I	the provision of health care to ethnic minorities
4920470	Philippines	I	the provision of health care to ethnic minorities
5110460	Bolivia	I	leadership training for selected members of thirteen minority ethnic groups in the Amazon River basin
5110638	Bolivia	?	landholding rights of major ethnic groups
5200304	Guatemala	I	a research program focused on addressing ethnic factors affecting the social promotion of the population in the Altiplano area
5040105	Guyana	?	amelioration of ethnic tensions
6740000	South Africa	?	ethnicity
6980422	Africa, regional	C	assistance to Somali ethnic groups in Djibouti
6980541	Africa, regional	A	access of ethnic groups to political and judicial processes
6980541 (15)	Africa, regional (subproject)	A	human rights violations against the ethnic Somali group of northeastern Kenya
6980662	Africa, regional	I	health mass media campaign adapted to ethnic groups
7300335	Vietnam	C	ethnic minorities
9683008	Zaire	?	emergency assistance for displaced persons from the ethnic conflict in Zaire
9684005	Rwanda	C	emergency assistance to the victims of ethnic conflict

*A = active; C = completed, closed; I = incomplete; P = planned; and ? = status unknown conflict. Most of the literature on ethnic conflict focuses on Sri Lanka, Iraq, Ethiopia, Uganda, Burundi, Rwanda, Cyprus, Bangladesh, Sudan, India, Nigeria, and the Congo (Zaire). Other experts add to that list Haiti, Somalia, Mexico, Guatemala, Somalia, Ecuador, Peru, Bosnia, the former Soviet republics, the Philippines, and more.

One way USAID has dealt with this issue of the diversity of opinion on what constitutes an ethnic conflict is by dealing with ethnicity under the rubrics of "civil conflict" and "complex emergencies." As identified at a recent workshop sponsored by USAID, complex emergencies[22] are "forms of human-made emergencies in which the cause of the emergencies as well as the assistance to the afflicted are bound by intense levels of political considerations" (USAID 1995d). Thus, the reasoning seems to be, because of its political nature ethnic conflict can constitute one of the components of a complex emergency.

Humanitarian Assistance Policy Level

Because ethnic conflict has been so closely identified with much of USAID's disaster assistance programs, the agency's Bureau for Humanitarian Response (BHR) has begun to address ethnic conflict directly. In particular, BHR is attempting to identify the root causes of conflict; the differences between providing humanitarian assistance during a natural disaster and providing it during a complex disaster; reconstruction, rehabilitation, rebuilding, and redevelopment issues after a complex emergency is over; effective prevention techniques; early warning indicators; and more. Most importantly, BHR has identified a gap between short-term disaster assistance programs and longer-term development aid. To fill that gap, the Clinton administration created the Office of Transition Initiatives (OTI), which is intended to allow the agency to respond more rapidly to opportunities to initiate recovery from complex emergencies:

> This initiative will: provide mechanisms to rapidly assess the political and economic issues associated with transition from emergency relief; will implement on-the-ground programs that answer short-term needs; will begin the process of institutional and political recovery; and, will ensure a coordinated U.S. Government and international donor response. (Richards 1994)

Examples of specific activities that might be financed under the initiative include

- peace and security initiatives, such as initial demobilization and reintegration of ex-combatants, surveys and removal of land mines

(in cooperation with the Defense Department), and support to international tribunals or local commissions examining war crimes;
- political initiatives, such as community development and political decentralization programs that encourage political participation at the local level, support for alternative and indigenous media and public information campaigns, human rights support, conflict resolution and mediation training, and leadership development for elected, appointed, and future officials; and
- technical assistance to new governments, both at the national and local levels.

OTI has already tested new approaches, made some progress, and learned some harsh lessons through its programs in Haiti, Kosovo, Nigeria, Rwanda, Bosnia, Angola, Sierra Leone, Guatemala, Croatia, Liberia, East Timor, Indonesia, and elsewhere. However, it continues to struggle with many issues: When does the transition from humanitarian assistance to development assistance begin? What are the indicators for when the transition ends? How will USAID make or manage the transition from humanitarian assistance to development assistance in countries where it has no presence? How can the agency work more effectively with other bilateral donors and the UN system, particularly in areas where national foreign policies are different? One of the strengths of OTI is that it continues to work very closely with USAID's democracy and governance staff in other bureaus. This coordination allows the agency to begin to operationally integrate its humanitarian and development assistance activities.

Other offices with BHR (in particular the Office of Foreign Disaster Assistance) deal directly with the consequences of violent ethnic conflict. The strategic goal of the bureau is to save lives and mitigate suffering. The largest percentage of OFDA's assistance goes to relief and rehabilitation project grants managed by NGOs. Relief efforts can include airlifting relief supplies to affected populations in remote locations, managing primary health care and supplementary feeding centers for refugees, and providing shelter materials to disaster evacuees and displaced persons. Rehabilitation efforts typically focus on immunizing dislocated populations against disease, providing seeds and tools to farmers, and rehabilitating water systems.

But humanitarian assistance has been complicated by the political sensitivities that surround crisis caused by ethnic conflict.

Complex emergencies require sensitivity in the provision of humanitarian assistance. This type of emergency brings with it a host of new issues: attacks on humanitarian convoys, targeting of relief workers, and the denial of access to affected populations, to name just a few. If not done correctly, aid can exacerbate the humanitarian situation, rather than provide assistance. *Relief organizations must appear apolitical and ensure that their actions do not contribute to violent tensions in societies* [emphasis added]. Providing assistance to civilian populations can often be perceived by warring factions as supporting their opponents. Certain kinds of assistance, especially food, are vulnerable to manipulation when warring forces and armies gain control of supplies provided for humanitarian assistance, either by imposing levies on assistance operations or by stealing commodities. (OFDA 1996, 11)

OFDA's response is to try to "appear" to be apolitical when providing assistance to the victims of ethnic conflicts and civil war. However, such a principled position may be impossible to operationalize in the field. For example, when an ethnically identified group wins the war, or seizes control over the central government, or maintains control over centralized authority, donors and relief organizations face a serious quandary: the increasingly ethnic salience of humanitarian assistance. In particular, since donors are "programmed" to work through host governments, they are then perceived to support the ethnic group that controls central authority while relief organizations, which typically partner with NGOs and international relief organizations that target refugee and displaced populations directly, are seen as supporting the ethnic identity of those not in power. Moreover, if U.S. foreign policy doesn't initially recognize the new government, or if it is suspicious of the new government, it may choose to support NGOs rather than the central authority, increasing perceptions that it is biased against the ethnic identity of the new government.

This sort of problem arose in Rwanda after the genocide, where the international relief community was initially suspicious of the possible guilt or motives of the new government of reconciliation and began to work through NGOs. This caused the new Rwandan government to feel that they were being prejudged by the international community and found guilty. Frustration and anger grew as the international community funded NGOs while the new government lacked the desks, chairs, typewriters, computers, phones, even paper clips they needed in order to govern while NGOs were fully staffed, had functioning offices, and paid higher salaries to the few experienced and capable local staff available.

To complicate matters, many relief organizations did apparently bias their assistance toward particular ethnic groups. Other relief organizations tried to maintain neutrality in a very difficult and politically and ethnically charged situation. Eventually, the Rwandan government threw out most of the international NGOs (including the United Nations' human rights team), and still seems to resent many bilateral donors.

It is nearly impossible for the international community to respond to complex emergencies and violent conflict that have ethnic overtones in any way that is perceived to be neutral or apolitical. Therefore, how donors deal with ethnic issues related to humanitarian crisis is even more important than dealing with development programs but it is also the least likely area where donors will develop policies for how to deal with ethnicity.

Overlap between Development Assistance and Humanitarian Assistance

The link to development programs becomes a critical issue when the humanitarian crisis includes ethnic conflict. Donors are often remembered for their perceived biases during the relief phase of international assistance and might find it impossible to develop "neutral" development programs. Likewise, many development experts are naive about the humanitarian phases of international assistance and believe that they are starting out carte blanche. In Rwanda many people believe that the U.S. government favors the Tutsi government. In the Democratic Republic of the Congo, where the U.S. government was alone in providing nontraditional humanitarian assistance and initiating development assistance, the perception grew that the United States initially favored the former rebel leader, now president, Laurent Kabila's regime. When Rwanda invaded the Congo, U.S. foreign policy toward each country was in conflict, which continues to have implications for relief efforts focused on the various ethnic communities in these countries. And in the Balkans, the U.S. government's foreign policy was hijacked by diplomats' biases toward different ethnic groups which eventually led to a "flawed" diplomatic response (see *Yugoslavia: Death of a Nation* by Laura Silber and Allan Little for a terrific account of what happened during the war).

Even as it becomes more obvious that there is significant overlap between humanitarian assistance and development assistance (especially where ethnic conflict is an issue), the level of understanding within USAID is not yet notable. Rather, programs and activities are still frequently implemented as though in a vacuum, based more on budgetary "pipelines" directed from Washington, DC than on field realities. It is also apparent however, that the agency is becoming increasingly sensitized to ethnic conflict—sometimes at its own expense as staff are directly impacted by conflict—as field situations sober the agency's programs.

Development Assistance Policy Level

Will the new interest in ethnic conflict be consistent within USAID, or will it soon disappear as yet another new concern diverts the agency's attention? The answer depends on the extent to which issues related to ethnic conflict become institutionalized, as a problem area, within the agency. Some USAID officials have stated that ethnic concerns should be part of the agency's overall policy guidance to the field on how development projects should be designed, implemented, and evaluated.[23] Others have expressed doubt that this would lead to effective programs to deal with ethnic conflict. Some policy analysts are hesitant to ascribe every conflict to ethnic root causes, so there is little desire to develop embracing policy guidance on ethnic conflict. Even if there were agreement within the agency on the need for such guidance on ethnic conflict, it is doubtful that including ethnic concerns in policy would be rapidly institutionalized.

Prevention

USAID has made great strides, however, to incorporate conflict prevention into its mission. Indeed, prevention is so intuitively attractive that, in the aftermath of Somalia, the Balkans, and Rwanda, USAID and the Department of State each launched efforts, with the help of the intelligence community, to forecast similar complex disasters. "In spite of the difficulties in moving beyond rhetoric, the political and economic costs of outside intervention in civil wars so dwarf those of forestalling them that prevention is emerging as the diplomatic issue of the late 1990's" (Weiss 1994, 155).

Recent policy guidance issued by USAID on prevention follows on the heels of a commitment by the Clinton administration to seek to reduce regional conflicts by finding ways "to address the root causes of conflict both multilaterally and bilaterally, using development assistance and support to democracy" (USAID n.d. [1999], 2).

> The Agency remains committed to develop more preventive country, and/or regional strategies that address the root causes of deadly conflict and economic and political crisis where these theaten USAID strategic objectives or broader U.S. national interests. Our goal is to improve the use of development assistance to mitigate and to the extent possible prevent potential economic and political crisis. (ibid.)

Nowhere in the otherwise commendable policy document is there any mention of ethnicity or ethnic conflict. Unfortunately, this seems consistent with the belief among some USAID staff that the agency has only a superficial interest in ethnicity.[24] There are a number of hypotheses that may explain this attitude: 1) that development staff are more comfortable dealing with ethnic conflict as a subset of conflict; or 2) that ethnicity is a politically sensitive issue, and most development staff would rather not deal with politics. The possible result of this curious failure to address ethnicity directly is that USAID will not be able to reformulate its interventions to respond to ethnic conflict in an effective and participatory manner. Instead, there may be a temporary tendency to tweak existing sustainable development programs and approaches toward a focus on conflict, while attempting to remain apolitical.

Nevertheless, the agency's conflict prevention policy has made some positive changes in the way it addresses conflict. An informal conflict prevention contact group meets regularly to bring together representatives throughout the agency who are interested in and committed to dealing with conflict. During discussions of regional strategies and country programs, ethnic conflict is addressed and seems to be one of the key concerns of the group. And some USAID country mission plans now include conflict prevention, many in countries where ethnic conflicts abound (e.g. Senegal, Georgia, Nepal, and Tanzania). Indeed, it seems that the agency's Africa Bureau, in particular, has recently adopted an unwritten policy to deal more robustly with conflict.[25]

Another effort of USAID has been to work closely with the Central Intelligence Agency, the State Department, and the Defense Department to determine indicators for "failed states" and how the U.S. government will respond to early warning of state failure. One of the preliminary consequences of this integrated approach to prevention and early warning has been increased understanding that the timeline for response is different for each U.S. government branch. For instance, an adequate lead time for a warning of potential violence and disaster for the State Department is generally between 6 months and a year. USAID is inherently more concerned, with a lead time of "five to fifteen years"[26] to design and implement development programs that may have relevant impacts in the future.

The thinking at USAID seems to be that since the impact of development projects and programs takes such a long time before results (either positive or negative) are seen, development projects have to be created or adjusted early in the process for prevention to be effective. A number of assumptions are apparent in this thinking: that development assistance, by either a single donor or all donors together, has a real impact on developing societies; that the causes of ethnic conflict can be determined early enough so that projects can attempt to address these causes; that development can have an unintended negative impact on ethnic conflict; and that the cause of conflict remains fairly stable throughout a period of time.

A specific regional preventive response to existing ethnic, political, and food-related crises has been the U.S. interagency Greater Horn of Africa Initiative (GHAI). In 1994, President Clinton sent a delegation, led by USAID, to discuss appropriate short-, medium-, and long-term responses to the situations in "affected" countries with host governments and key donors. This delegation recognized that there is strong economic and political interdependence in the Horn—ethnic conflict in one nation has the potential to destabilize its neighbors; food shortfalls in one nation may cut off traditional cross-border trading practices in another. "Therefore," noted one participant, "the delegation determined that it was not enough to meet the needs of one country but rather to look at development of the entire region" (Hicks 1994).

Furthermore, the delegation found that meeting urgent humanitarian needs in the region was not enough: "In order for the region to attain food security and stability, donors, host countries, and the NGO community need to look beyond relief to recovery and development assistance" to deal with the root causes of conflict (ibid.).[27] The delegation recommended that

- in the medium term, assistance is needed to help African nations overcome the effects of war and famine and begin the transition from crisis to development by creating democratic institutions that are capable of responding to the needs of their people;
- in the long term, the causes of insecurity require a strategic focus on sustainable development in the region to help governments increase agricultural yields, decrease population growth, and promote stable democratic institutions.

The GHAI attempts to work with other donors, recipient governments, and NGOs to develop a strategy for linking humanitarian assistance and development activities. The focus of the initiative is prevention, early warning, and response. For example, the 1994 delegation reported: "relief feeding should be done in ways to keep recipients productive on the land instead of building dependency in feeding camps; at the same time, long-term development programs must address the recurring food insecurity to prevent food crises" (ibid.).

One issue that remains unresolved is that when USAID begins to target opportunities for preventing ethnic conflict, it might conclude that development activities are called for in a nonpresence country. Indeed, some USAID staff have begun to chafe at the limitation of only being able to offer the full range of program options to countries characterized by sustainable development criteria, which often is felt to restrict USAID's ability to act appropriately.[28]

An example of this agency-created paradox of funding activities in nonpresence countries has occurred in Sudan, where ethnic tensions have been reduced to civil war. Because until recently Sudan was not considered to be a sustainable development country,[29] USAID has not been able to provide any development assistance programs. It has, however, continued to provide "short-term" emergency assistance throughout the 1980s and 1990s to populations in the south. This assistance has included funding of many projects that would normally be funded by development assistance programs (e.g., strengthening local productive capacity—seeds, tools, fishing equipment). Additionally, many USAID staff members are concerned about similar "corruption" of humanitarian assistance in northern Iraq, where the building of schools has generated questions about the definitions of rehabilitation and development. Recently, USAID policies and initiatives have suggested that the agency may be able to provide "limited" support for "modest" development assistance programs to nonpresence countries by channeling such assistance through local and international NGOs (USAID 1995b, 8). Whether this limited opening will allow for effective strategies for the prevention of ethnic conflict may become more apparent in the future.

Democracy and Governance Programs

A recent USAID survey of the theory and practice of the resolution of ethnic conflict found that most prescriptions for such resolution could be framed in terms of traditional development project activities (see McHugh 1995a). Two concepts can be deduced from this: first, since development activities can unintentionally contribute to ethnic conflict, better-designed and better-implemented development activities will at least be a partial solution to reducing, mitigating, or preventing ethnic conflict; second, development can be deliberately targeted toward preventing ethnic conflict in the first place by supporting the process of institutionalizing peaceful change within society. The latter concept has recently been coined as *preventive development* by the United Nations and is rapidly gaining adherence. The idea seems to be (at least in theory) that effective institutions, such as legal systems, constitutions, and schools, will provide outlets where ethnic communities can express their concerns and will provide systems to address those stated concerns.

An examination of academic, USAID, and other donor documents found that activities with significant effects on ethnic groups and ethnic conflict roughly correlated with traditional development project activities. Thus, economic growth, health, population and nutrition, environment, and education programs were found to have significant effects on ethnic groups and ethnic conflict—although democracy and governance programs proved to be the most meaningful. Within the program area of democracy and governance, the study found that relevant development activities fell into six major categories: (1) legal systems reform efforts; (2) political, civil, and human rights concerns; (3) electoral systems programs; (4) decentralization; (5) regional arrangements; and (6) media. Within each of these categories, the study proposed particular strategies for addressing ethnic conflict.

The findings from the aforementioned study are focused mostly on project and program activities; the relevance of USAID's democracy and governance policy options to ethnic conflict and ethnicity is less obvious. Indeed, USAID is currently in the process of developing guidance for the design, implementation, management, and evaluation of democracy and governance activities. The democracy and governance section of USAID's general policy paper, "Strategies for Sustainable Development," does not address ethnicity or ethnic conflict (or any obvious proxy terms) anywhere in its somewhat vague contents.

USAID democracy officers have been developing separate policy guidance papers—focused on different democracy and governance program areas, including elections, rule of law, civil society, and governance. These papers were reviewed for clues to whether USAID sees ethnic conflict and ethnicity as a key component of democracy activities and, if so, how USAID policies attempt to deal with ethnicity.

Guidance on Rule-of-Law Programs

The official USAID policy guidance paper on rule of law (ROL) notes that this program is a key element in the agency's overall approach to sustainable development and that it is critical to its overall democratization strategy (USAID 1995c, 1). This very brief paper does not, however, discuss ethnicity, marginal groups, or conflict—although it does suggest that further discussion and policy decisions by USAID senior staff are still needed (ibid., 2).

A 1994 global evaluation of ROL programs conducted by USAID—the foundation for the policy guidance paper—does address this issue. In the evaluation, the authors found that ethnic groups are most affected by ROL programs focused on access creation (Blair and Hansen 1994, 36). Indeed, they found that minority, ethnic, or racial groups are particularly vulnerable to their rights being transgressed by government agencies or third parties without legal rectification (ibid.). The evaluation report suggests strategies to increase access by ethnic groups, including using public defenders, support for traditional legal-aid efforts, legal literacy, nurturing paralegal networks, assisting legal-advocacy NGOs, and alternative dispute resolution mechanisms (ibid., 36–37).

Guidance on Alternative Dispute Resolution

In 1998, the agency completed a comprehensive guide for practitioners on alternative dispute resolution (ADR) (see Brown et al. 1998). In the document, minority and ethnic issues are addressed throughout. The authors find that ADR programs are more effective than courts for addressing ethnic conflicts when the formal courts are discredited or ineffective (ibid., 11). The reasoning seems to be that specialized issue-specific ADR systems can be more effective when dealing with minority issues and that ADR systems offer more attractive outcomes than do the courts. Moreover, the guidance recommends using ADR programs to reduce tension and prevent conflict in a community when moderate ethnic conflict is focused around particular issues (ibid., 19). The authors have found that "evidence for managing conflict and tension around discrete policy issues, such as education policies (Foundation on Inter-Ethnic Relations) and land reform (Philippines Department of Environment and Natural Resources) is positive" (ibid.).

Guidance on Electoral Systems Programs

USAID's Center for Democracy and Governance has produced a paper on electoral assistance. Although this document has not been sanctioned as official agency policy guidance, it has become the de facto electoral assistance guide for the agency. In the paper, significant attention is devoted to "political conflict" and "social cleavages" within societies. Cleavages, based on religion, ethnicity, race, language, nationality, class, caste, or geographic region, are said to beget conflict and marginalization (Hirschmann and Mendelson n.d., 8–9). Therefore, the guide suggests, elections will not be effective if there are deep social cleavages and if ethnic groups are excluded from participation (ibid., 5).

The election guide further notes that some governments prohibit political parties from basing their programs on ethnic origin, religious affiliation, common linguistic group or region, and more. Other governments have literacy requirements that exclude certain categories of people from voting. Although the guide warns that violence or irredentist movements are possible when even small ethnic or regional groups are left out of the election process, it suggests that in "particular circumstances, these are understandable exclusions, but they do set a potentially dangerous precedent" (ibid., 12, 46).

The guide advises that in times of transition it "may be problematic" to press for the effective inclusion of ethnic groups during the first election, but "as one moves to second and third elections, and so to the consolidation and broadening of democracy, the policy dialogue that accompanies democratic assistance should give attention to the fuller inclusion of the poor, religious minorities, etc." (ibid., 9).

Guidance on Civil Society

Policy guidance in the area of civil society is being developed now, and two draft reports have been circulated within USAID. One key document suggests that special consideration will be given to democratic concepts and ideas coming from minority and regional groups in more remote provincial areas and to the promotion of the rights and participation of minority groups (Vermillion 1995). The other draft report, "Constituencies for Reform" (Hansen 1995), describes donor support for civil society in Kenya, Thailand, Chile, Bangladesh, and El Salvador. However, the report never mentions ethnic groups' participation in or exclusion from civil society, even when discussing Kenya.[30]

Guidance on Governance

Specific USAID policy guidance in the area of governance has not yet been developed. However, the agency has initiated a global evaluation of democratic decentralization, and most probably policy guidance will evolve from this evaluation's eventual findings. The concept paper developed for this evaluation contains valuable indications on where future agency guidance may be directed and includes sections relevant to projects focused on ethnic conflict.[31] For example, in the section on the benefits of decentralization, the concept paper discusses two strategies: decentralization projects have the potential to indirectly empower marginal and ethnic groups who find little or no political voice at the national level; and decentralization can directly reduce ethnic conflict (Blair 1995, iii).

The concept paper suggests that ethnic groups that are denied political participation at national levels may more easily establish a significant political influence at the local level—where it is "simpler for everyone to get involved . . . for political matters are more understandable, [. . . and where] minorities are more likely to enjoy a critical mass in small areas" (ibid., 10). The author of the concept paper further notes that decentralization can be an effective method of reducing ethnic conflict by "allowing geographically based groups to dominate in their own regions in return for accepting only a share of power at the national level" (ibid., 11). Actual policy guidance focused on decentralization will further refine these strategies and possibly propose other areas relevant to ethnic conflict.

Guidance on Media

A recent document on the role of the media in democracy suggests a policy approach for media activities that directly focuses on ethnicity. The Global Bureau's Democracy and Governance Center's media strategy document notes that in "some societies an antagonistic relationship between media and government represents a vital and healthy element of fully functioning democracies" (Hudock, 5). However, it warns that in certain country situations where ethnic conflict exists, such a confrontational, "tension-ridden relationship may not be appropriate," and the role of the press should be to "disseminate information as a way of mediating between the state and all facets of civil society" (ibid.). The rest of the document examines the issue of minority access to news and employment within media outlets and includes ethnic identity as a proposed assessment tool.

Crosscutting Policy or Program Issues

USAID and NGOs. For a variety of reasons, USAID is examining the potential for increased utilization of NGOs for project design, implementation, and funding. It is believed that NGOs have certain advantages over traditional development vehicles. For example, many believe that NGOs can have a more flexible response to complex emergencies and are less constrained by sensitivities to sovereignty and protocol (Stremlau 1995, 8–10).

In response, in March 1995 Vice President Gore announced USAID's New Partnership Initiative (NPI) at the World Summit for Social Development, held in Copenhagen. The overarching purpose of NPI is to "abandon our old model for combating poverty" based on government-to-government foreign assistance by channeling 40 percent of aid funds through NGOs (Gore 1995, 18). Thus, NPI seems to echo the concerns expressed in the 1973 New Directions program, where USAID focused on bypassing foreign governments in the delivery of foreign assistance.[32]

Although the focus of NPI will be to increase the role of NGOs, religious, ethnic, or cultural organizations will be excluded from participation with NPI unless "the purpose of the work which USAID supports is clearly developmental" (USAID 1995b, section 1, 3, 5). Other than this prohibition, NPI does not directly deal with ethnicity, ethnic issues, or communities where ethnic cleavages exist. Indirectly, NPI suggests that ethnic concerns can be dealt with through an emphasis on participation, a recognition of the diversity of conditions in the developing world, and a focus on capacity building at the local level.

Coordination of activity is important: NGOs must work together rather than pursue projects in relative isolation from each other, and they should consult with USAID during project planning and implementation stages (Saunders 1993, 25–26). The State Department Secretary's Open Forum Working Group on Conflict Resolution, Civil Society, and Democracy seeks to coordinate information and activities of various U.S. agencies (including USAID) and NGOs working in these development areas. Other interagency groups and forums that are mandated to include NGOs in activities, decision-making processes, and project design—such as the GHAI—either exist or are being instituted.

Starting such a process of working with NGOs does not require huge expenditures or direct involvement by foreign governments. Concerning Eastern Europe, where states are not at risk from outside aggression but goals of irredentism linger, the Project on Ethnic Relations based in Princeton, New Jersey, seeks to reduce tensions between the government of Romania and leaders of the Hungarian minority and to promote efforts to counter violence against the Romany (gypsy) populations throughout the region. Similarly, a USAID-funded project in Macedonia is attempting to reduce tensions between the Macedonian and Albanian populations in ethnically diverse areas by focusing attention on problem solving in schools and on parent-teacher associations.[33] This experiment of grassroots efforts to lower barriers to accommodation among groups may provide practical lessons for other international NGOs that try to reduce the risk of factional conflict elsewhere (Stremlau 1995, 8).

USAID has experienced some difficulty with NGOs, particularly religion-based NGOs, that provide humanitarian assistance to ethnic communities. In Rwanda, in particular, Catholic Church leaders and organizations are having problems participating effectively in the reconciliation process because of contention surrounding the church's role in the genocide (Kumar et al. 1995, 38).[34]

Likewise, international NGOs face the challenge that in situations of ethnic conflict their assistance to any domestic or refugee group may not be considered neutral (ibid., 46). As Anderson reports: "Sometimes NGOs align themselves with one sub-group in a society out of solidarity in a 'just' cause espoused by that group. This support may add to inter-societal tensions and contribute to the will of the side with whom the NGO is aligned to continue fighting rather than negotiate" (Anderson 1995, 4). In Rwanda, for example, many NGOs refused or showed reluctance to officially register with the government of Rwanda, thereby creating tension between themselves and the government (ibid., 63). This has furthered the impression by many Rwandans that international NGOs are concerned about the legitimacy of a government dominated by an ethnic minority and that certain NGOs have already judged the new government of Rwanda and found it guilty of participating in further human rights abuses.

USAID is aware of the potential for tension between NGOs and ethnic communities. The agency is also aware that NGOs are often effective providers of assistance during ethnic conflict and are often effective in helping to prevent ethnic conflict from erupting into violence. Commitment to NPI processes means that USAID will have to find a workable balance between support for NGO programs and institutional independence, while at the same time ensuring that NGOs do not indirectly contribute toward continuing ethnic conflict and that NGOs are not perceived to be biased against any particular ethnic community.

Structural Adjustment Programs. An examination of USAID's involvement with structural adjustment programs (SAPs) and macrolevel economic or political reform efforts reveals that USAID has articulated relatively little discrete concern with ethnicity and ethnic conflict in these programs. This could be an indication that when there is "tension between achieving objectives of economic efficiency and protecting the welfare of particular socioeconomic groups" (Hood, McGuire, and Starr 1988, 5), the socioeconomic groups are of secondary concern. It could also be an indication of USAID's relatively small investment in SAPs.

Analysts have suggested that there should be a special focus by the World Bank and the International Monetary Fund (IMF), other donors, and NGOs to attempt to reach those peoples—including ethnic groups—who suffer during these transition periods. Thus, some of USAID's privatization efforts have been directed toward specific ethnic concerns. For example, in several Asian countries where sensitivity to ethnic groups exists, a certain percentage of shares of privatized firms are set aside for particular ethnic and minority groups (Lancaster 1994b).

In addition to focusing social safety nets on ethnic groups that may be worst hit by the economic transition period, USAID should be aware of the potential impact SAPs may have on ethnic groups. For example, some host governments may be distributing resources according to allocations based on ethnic considerations, which could exacerbate or initiate ethnic conflict (Kingsbury 1994, 55).

The implementation of SAPs could be conducted in such a way that ethnic conflict is minimized. For example, ethnic leaders and organizations could be involved in the discussion and negotiation process from the start of the World Bank and IMF programs. Likewise, the World Bank and the IMF should be involved in postconflict peace negotiations if there is likely to be any sort of macrolevel economic or political reform. Accordingly, the potent combination of SAPs, because of their "pauperizing impact," and general resistance to the state, because of its increasing neglect of its basic democratic responsibilities toward its citizens, will contribute to increasing ethnic tensions (Adekanye 1995).

Conclusion

This review of USAID's past and present policies, programs, and projects reveals that the agency does indeed address ethnicity and ethnic conflict— although the level of focus seems to depend on where agency staff members are located. USAID staff members in the field have been directly addressing ethnicity and ethnic conflict and will continue to do so, with or without Washington support. But until the end of the Cold War, USAID staff members in Washington have dealt with these issues marginally at best.[35] Now, however, both the role that ethnic conflict can play in dismantling the benefits of development activities and the costs—in human, financial, and other terms—of humanitarian crisis based on ethnic violence and conflict have captured the attention of many USAID Washington staff members and policy makers. Nevertheless, USAID's Washington headquarters seems unsure of how to proceed and appears overwhelmed by the realities of dealing with the consequences of ethnic conflict without any coherent foreign policy guidance and with changing domestic and international pressures.

   Thus, development assistance, like world economics, is increasingly a seamless process of continuous interactions between domestic and international actors, as traditional distinctions between foreign and domestic affairs lose salience in the formulation and implementation of national policy (Stremlau 1995, 15). As the influence of ethnic, religious, and other grassroots organizations on U.S. foreign policy grows, the "wall separating foreign affairs from domestic influences has come crumbling down" (Mills 1994). USAID will face increasing pressures from domestic organizations, lobbying groups, and ethnic groups as it seeks to define its role in the U.S. foreign policy agenda. For example, some U.S.-based ethnic groups count as a victory the recently enacted Foreign Assistance Appropriations Act, which includes a provision that directs USAID to "report . . . on steps being taken to include individuals and organizations with language or regional expertise in the provision of assistance to the new independent states of the former Soviet Union." This provision has been translated by many ethnic organizations to mean that the U.S. Congress "wants USAID to involve Central and East European American ethnic communities in the delivery of assistance to that region" ("Get on the Right Track" 1994, 1–2). As USAID seeks to involve the nongovernmental sector in more of its development activities, as with NPI, this relationship with ethnically-based NGOs will be complicated when ethnic conflict and ethnicity command the development situation.

In addition to being concerned that ethnic conflict is increasingly diverting resources away from development activities and toward humanitarian crisis, USAID is also increasingly aware that development itself can trigger ethnic conflict. Development can cause change, and change can trigger conflict. The need, then, is for USAID to assist developing countries in institutionalizing the peaceful process of change. It seems that both the White House and USAID have begun to respond to this need by beginning to position the agency to take the lead in preventing ethnic conflict in developing countries and to be a key player in U.S. security matters.

If U.S. foreign policy goals and objectives remain vague, unarticulated, and subject to domestic influences, USAID may be stuck in a reactive role, unable to respond to ethnic conflict and other development problems in a coherent and comprehensive manner, and therefore unable to produce clearly defined results. USAID, then, must articulate its own goals, objectives, and methodologies—an extremely risky, perhaps impossible, venture. The fundamental necessity is that USAID should function as the long-term development assistance arm of the U.S. government, laying a solid economic and political base for the future, and not simply as a reactive, short-term diplomatic policy arm. As Atwood has reported (1994b, 1):

> The U.S. will continue to need the tools of traditional diplomacy: a strong military, an enhanced early warning and intelligence capacity, and a capable foreign service. But to protect our national interests in a changing world, we will also need [development] programs to address population growth, enhance food production, stop environmental degradation, create broad-based economic growth, and strengthen democratic institutions. These are investments in prevention. Given the mounting costs of chaos, they are economical indeed.

As USAID becomes viewed as an agency fulfilling political (and even security) needs of U.S. foreign policy in an increasingly interdependent world and is less viewed as an "economic" agency, the agency could find itself with more room to maneuver in response to ethnic conflict.

But has USAID really experienced an epiphany regarding ethnic conflict? or is the agency's approach more superficial and transitory? The answer seems mixed. USAID—at many levels—has an interest in ethnic conflict, but there is relatively little clarity about how to deal with the issue. At the moment, USAID staff is divided between those members who believe that ethnic conflicts are unique and separate from other types of conflict and those who believe that ethnic conflicts are a subset of conflict in general. The distinctions are important and have large implications for how donor organizations go about the business of development assistance, how they conceptualize conflict prevention, and how they strategize postconflict reconstruction and rehabilitation. At the moment, the best that can be said for USAID is that it employs a strategy of selective engagement with respect to ethnic conflicts. This reflects the larger pattern of U.S. foreign policy in general and highlights the lack of consensus within USAID that would allow the agency to develop concomitant policy guidance.

NOTES

The views presented herein are those of the author and should not be interpreted as reflecting those of USAID or the Academy for Educational Development.

1. As part of the process of writing this chapter, career and appointed USAID officials were interviewed off the record. The offices within USAID that these officials represent include the Policy Bureau, the Bureau for Humanitarian Response, the regional bureaus, field missions, and the office of the USAID administrator. An extensive literature search, including USAID and academic sources, was conducted as well.

2. This means not, as it might seem, that donors are trying to prevent development but rather that donors are attempting to cast development in terms of preventing conflict and crisis.

3. USAID includes in its definition of the Greater Horn region the countries of Rwanda, Burundi, Kenya, Djibouti, Ethiopia, Eritrea, Uganda, Sudan, and Tanzania.

4. From conversations with USAID officials. Additionally, some State Department officials have mentioned that USAID is taking the lead in the search for policy, program, and project options to deal with ethnic conflict.

5. From conversations with USAID officials.

6. Ibid.

7. Indeed, a Japanese foreign ministry official had to deny claims by some political observers that Japan had offered foreign aid to Eastern Europe to assist the then U.S. president George Bush to win the favor of ethnic Slavs in the U.S. Midwest in anticipation of the presidential election in 1992 ("Japan Pledges 400 Million" 1992).

8. The influence of American ethnic communities on U.S. foreign policy was discussed at the Senate's questioning of then ambassador Strobe Talbott's nomination to deputy secretary of state. During the hearing, it was noted that Talbott's early writings on Israel suggested that he was concerned about the "disproportionate" influence the U.S. Jewish communities exerted over U.S. foreign policy

toward Israel and about the influence of other ethnic organizations on U.S. foreign policy. During the hearing, Talbott agreed that such attempts to influence U.S. policy are in effect "promoting American values abroad" ("Senate Committee OKs Talbott" 1994, 1).

9. INCORE is a joint program of the United Nations University and the University of Ulster and is located in Northern Ireland. The purpose of the program is to provide a systematic approach to the study of ethnic conflict and to encourage links between research, training, policy, practice, and theory.

10. From conversations with USAID officials.

11. Ibid.

12. Ibid.

13. Ibid.

14. Ibid.

15. Ibid.

16. The New Directions legislation was passed in 1973.

17. From conversations with USAID officials.

18. Ibid.

19. Ibid.

20. Ibid.

21. This study by the East-West Population Institute was funded by the agency's Bureau for Science and Technology and focused on immigration trends and on whether the various ethnic groups in Hawaii were moving toward social and economic parity.

22. Complex emergencies are also called political emergencies or complex disasters.

23. USAID defines policies as mechanisms that provide guidance on the way USAID approaches program activities (USAID 1995a, 1). Policy guidance attempts to assist the field missions in developing USAID strategic plans and specific sector programs (ibid.). Projects are a set of interrelated activities taking place in a specific location (in a country or region or, if funded by Washington, globally), focused on a specific development sector (e.g., environment), and implemented for a specific period of time. Programs are "the sum of the project, non-project and policy dialogue actions undertaken by an A.I.D. field mission in pursuit of a given strategic objective" (USAID 1991b, 2). The agency's reengineering effort—aimed at redesigning processes, jobs, structures, and controls to achieve dramatic performance improvements—is part of the president's initiative for reinventing government. With this effort, terminology used within the agency is changing.

24. From conversations with USAID officials.

25. From conversations with USAID officials.

26. From conversations with USAID officials.

27. USAID's appeal for prevention funds to deal with the "root causes" of conflict—poverty, overpopulation, and environmental degradation—seems to be strongly influenced by the "humanitarianism and global trends" school of foreign policy.

28. From conversations with USAID officials.

29. Sudan's status with USAID is due to the overthrow of a democratically elected government, failure to repay debts, and its alleged sponsorship of international terrorism.

30. See Cohen's chapter in this book (chap. 4) for a closer look at the politics of ethnicity (or tribalism) in Kenya.

31. See Blair, November 6, 1995. "Assessing Democratic Decentralization: A CDIE concept paper." Final Version, Center for Development Information and Evaluation. Washington, DC: USAID. The evaluation was completed in 1997.

32. As Brysk observes in her contribution to this book (chap. 8), all donors in the 1990s experienced the eclipsing of government as a development arena. USAID's NPI definitely exemplifies this trend. Furthermore, as Brysk warns, in situations where one ethnic group has captured the state, such a policy of ignoring the state could unintentionally contribute to furthering ethnic competition and tensions.

33. This project (1800016) is titled "Emergency Medical Supplies." Nothing in this title would indicate that this project is targeted at reducing ethnic conflict. Likewise, the title suggests that the project is focused solely on humanitarian assistance, rather than including components dealing with development concerns. This illustrates the difficulty in identifying and categorizing ethnic conflict activities.

34. It is interesting to note similar difficulties with NGOs in Lebanon.

35. From conversations with USAID officials.

REFERENCES

Adekanye, J. 'Bayo. 1995. "Structural Adjustment, Democratization, and Rising Ethnic Tensions in Africa." *Development and Change* 26, no. 2 (April): 355.

Adelman, Howard, Astri Suhrke, and Bruce Jones. 1996. "Early Warning and Conflict Management." Report #4, Multi-Donor Evaluation of Emergency Assistance to Rwanda, for the Development Assistance Committee of the OECD. International Response to Conflict and Genocide: Lessons from the Rwanda Experience. USAID's Center for Development Information and Evaluation, PNABY106. Washington, DC: U.S. Agency for International Development.

Anderson, Mary B. 1995. "Relationships between Humanitarian Assistance and Conflict and Remedial Steps that Might be Taken." Paper presented at the Symposium on Humanitarian Assistance and Conflict in Africa, sponsored by the U.S. Institute of Peace, Washington, DC, October 2.

Atlas, Terry. 1994. "U.S. Seeks Way to Forestall Global Chaos." *Chicago Tribune,* August 28, Perspective, 1–2.

Atwood, J. Brian. 1994a. "Remarks by J. Brian Atwood: Administrator, U.S. Agency for International Development." Keynote address to the 38th annual conference of Sister Cities International, Louisville, Kentucky, July 29.

———. 1994b. "Op Ed Letter: Suddenly, Chaos." *Washington Post,* July 31, C09.

————. 1995. "Message to USAID Employees from the Administrator." USAID/General Notice, ES, EXEMSG from the Administrator, November 7.

Augenbraun, Eliene, Karl Feld, et al. 1999. "Reconciling Ethnic Conflicts: A Case Study of Bosnia and Herzegovina and Croatia." Center for Development Information and Evaluation Study, PNACA920. Washington, DC: U.S. Agency for International Development.

Baron, Nancy. 1994. "Psycho-Social Needs Assessment: the Voice of Internally Displaced People in the Non-Conflict Area of Sri Lanka." USAID/Sri Lanka Supported Study, PNABT230. Washington, DC: U.S. Agency for International Development.

Bienen, Henry, John Londregan, and Nicholas van de Walle. 1994. "Ethnicity, Leadership Succession, and Economic Development in Africa." Institute for Policy Reform (Washington, DC). USAID Policy and Program Coordination Bureau Discussion Paper, PNABR522. Washington, DC: U.S. Agency for International Development.

Blair, Harry. 1995. "Assessing Democratic Decentralization: A CDIE Concept Paper." Center for Development Information and Evaluation. Washington, DC: U.S. Agency for International Development.

Blair, Harry, and Gary Hansen. 1994. "Weighing in on the Scales of Justice: Strategic Approaches for Donor-Supported Rule of Law Programs." Center for Development Information and Evaluation. USAID Program and Operations Assessment Report 7, PNAAX280. Washington, DC: U.S. Agency for International Development.

Blumhagan, Dan. 1998. "Clashing Symbols: the Status of Ethnic Tension and Conflict in Macedonia." Center for Development Information and Evaluation Supported Study, PDABQ456. Washington, DC: U.S. Agency for International Development.

Borton, John, Emery Brusset, and Alistair Hallam. 1996. "Humanitarian Aid and Effects." Report #3, Multi-Donor Evaluation of Emergency Assistance to Rwanda, for the Development Assistance Committee of the OECD. International Response to Conflict and Genocide: Lessons from the Rwanda Experience. USAID's Center for Development Information and Evaluation, PNABY107. Washington, DC: U.S. Agency for International Development.

Brown, Scott, Christine Cervenak, and David Fairman. 1998. "Alternative Dispute Resolution Practitioners Guide." Center for Democracy and Governance. USAID Technical Publication Series, PNACB895. Washington, DC: U.S. Agency for International Development.

Cabral, Javier, Francisco Huerta, and Angel Flores. 1998. "IEC [Information, Education and Communication] Need-detection Survey on Reproductive Health in Six Ethnic Groups in Mexico." USAID Supported Study, PNACF236. Washington, DC: U.S. Agency for International Development.

Clough, Michael. 1994. "Grass-roots Policymaking: Say Good-bye to the 'Wise Men.'" *Foreign Affairs* 73, no. 1 (January–February): 2–5.

Colfer, Carol J. Pierce, Barbara J. Newton, and Herman. 1989. "Ethnicity: An Important Consideration in Indonesian Agriculture." North Carolina State

University. USAID Bureau for Science and Technology Supported Study, PNABK474. Washington, DC: U.S. Agency for International Development.

Congressional Research Service, Foreign Affairs and National Defense Division. 1981. "The New Directions Mandate and the Agency for International Development." In *AID's Administrative and Management Problems in Providing Foreign Economic Assistance,* hearing before a subcommittee of the House Committee on Government Operations, 97th Congress, October 6, 1981. Washington, DC: U.S. Government Printing Office.

Crosby, Jane, and Cheryl While, eds. 1995. "Ethnicity: A Rich, Diverse World." National Association of Social Workers. USAID/Bureau for Humanitarian Response Supported Study, PNABZ017. Washington, DC: U.S. Agency for International Development.

Cuny, Frederick C., Pat Reed, and Mark Frohardt. 1992. "Development of a Shelter Strategy in the Newly Independent States." USAID/Newly Independent States Bureau Supported Study, PNABN005. Washington, DC: U.S. Agency for International Development.

DaVanzo, Julie, and John G. Haaga. 1981. "Anatomy of a Fertility Decline and Ethnic Differences in the Experience of Malaysian Women, 1950–1976." Rand Corp. (CA). USAID Policy and Program Coordination Bureau Supported Study, PNAAK672. Washington, DC: U.S. Agency for International Development.

Elliott, V. L. n.d. "The Evolution of AID's Problems." Africa Bureau, USAID. Washington, DC: U.S. Agency for International Development.

Eriksson, Eric, Howard Adelman, et al. "Steering Committee of the Joint Evaluation of Emergency Assistance to Rwanda." Report #1, Multi-Donor Evaluation of Emergency Assistance to Rwanda, for the Development Assistance Committee of the OECD. International Response to Conflict and Genocide: Lessons from the Rwanda Experience. USAID's Center for Development Information and Evaluation. PNABY104. Washington, DC: U.S. Agency for International Development.

Garms, David J. 1987. "Interagency Private Sector Briefing on Sri Lanka and AID Program Activities." USAID/Asia and Near East Bureau Supported Study, PDAAW899. Washington, DC: U.S. Agency for International Development.

Gedda, George. 1995. "While Brits Fume, Clinton Plays Irish Politics: An AP News Analysis." *AP Worldstream,* March 18.

Gersony, Robert. 1997. "Anguish of Northern Uganda: Results of a Field-based Assessment of the Civil Conflicts in Northern Uganda." USAID/Uganda Supported Study, PNAAC245. Washington, DC: U.S. Agency for International Development.

"Get on the Right Track." 1994. *Ukrainian Weekly* 52, no. 35 (August 28): 6.

Gore, Albert. 1995. Quote in an editorial in the *South China Morning Post,* March 13, 18.

Grant, S. R. 1974. "Peruvian Language Education Policy Toward Speakers of Indigenous Tongues." Florida State University. USAID Supported Study, PNAAC488. Washington, DC: U.S. Agency for International Development.

Grove, D. J., and Pat West. 1978. "Ethnic Socio-Economic Redistribution: Sri Lanka, Malaysia, Trinidad and Tobago, and Israel." Rice University. USAID Policy and Program Coordination Bureau Supported Study, PNAAF003. Washington, DC: U.S. Agency for International Development.

Guest, Ian. 1997. "Moving Beyond Ethnic Conflict: Community Peace Building in Bosnia and Eastern Slavonia (Croatia)." Center for Development Information and Evaluation Conference Paper, PNACD096. Washington, DC: U.S. Agency for International Development.

Hanks, L. M., J. R. Hanks, et al. 1964. "Report on Tribal Peoples in Chiengrai Province, North of the Maekok River." USAID Supported Study, PNAAE245. Washington, DC: U.S. Agency for International Development.

Hansen, Gary. 1995. "Constituencies for Reform: Strategic Approaches for Donor-Supported Civic Advocacy Programs." Center for Development Information and Evaluation. USAID Program and Operations Assessment Report 12. Washington, DC: U.S. Agency for International Development, December.

Haupt, Robert. 1994. "Hungary: NATO Warning Shot Falls Short." *Australian Financial Review,* December 7, 12.

"Helsinki Commission Examines Aid to Central/Eastern Europe and NIS." 1995. *Ukrainian Weekly* 53, no. 9 (February 26): 1–2.

Hicks, John F. 1994. "Prepared Statement of John F. Hicks, Assistant Administrator of the Bureau for Africa, U.S. Agency for International Development, before the Subcommittee on Africa, House Foreign Affairs Committee, U.S. House of Representatives." *Federal News Service,* July 27.

Hirschmann, David, and Johanna Mendelson. n.d. "Managing Democratic Electoral Assistance: A Practical Guide for USAID." Center for Democracy and Governance. Washington, DC: U.S. Agency for International Development.

Hood, Ron, Judith McGuire, and Martha Starr. 1988. "Socioeconomic Impact of Macroeconomic Adjustment." International Science and Technology Institute. USAID Policy and Program Coordination Bureau Supported Study, PNAAZ319. Washington, DC: U.S. Agency for International Development.

Horowitz, Donald L. 1981. "Ethnicity and Development: Policies to Deal with Ethnic Conflict in Developing Countries." U.S. Smithsonian Institution (Washington, DC). USAID Policy and Program Coordination Bureau Supported Study, PNAAQ298. Washington, DC: U.S. Agency for International Development.

Hudock, Ann. 1999. "The Role of Media in Democracy: A Strategic Approach." Center for Democracy and Governance, PNACE630. Washington, DC: U.S. Agency for International Development.

International Federation of Red Cross and Red Crescent Societies (ICRC). 1994. *World Disasters Report, 1994.* Dordrecht: M. Nijhoff.

"Japan Pledges 400 Million Dollars to Eastern Europe." 1992. *Japan Economic Newswire,* May 15.

Jenkins, Simon. 1993. "Armchair Strategists Keep Clear." *New York Times,* April 14, Features section.

Kayayan, H. K. 1973. "Socio-economic Comparison of Four Ethnic Groups in the State of Sao Paulo, Brazil." USAID Supported Study, PNAAA715. Washington, DC: U.S. Agency for International Development.

Kingsbury, David. 1994. "Programs for Mitigating Adverse Social Impacts during Adjustment: The AID experience." Center for Development Information and Evaluation Study, PNAAX275. Washington, DC: U.S. Agency for International Development.

Kpedekpo, G. M., F. W. Wurapa, D. W. Belcher, Alfred K. Neumann, and I. M. Lourie. 1975. "Analysis of Marital Status, Education, Ethnic, Religious, and Occupational Composition." University of Ghana, Medical School, Accra. USAID Africa Bureau Supported Study, PNAAH260. Washington, DC: U.S. Agency for International Development.

Kumar, Krishna. 1999. "Promoting Social Reconciliation in Post-Conflict Societies: Selected Lessons Learned from USAID's Experience." Center for Development Information and Evaluation Supported Study, PNACA928. Washington, DC: U.S. Agency for International Development.

Kumar, Krishna, ed. 1997. *Rebuilding Societies After Civil War: Critical Roles for International Assistance.* Center for Development Information and Evaluation Supported Study, PNABZ334. Lynne Reinner Publishers, Inc.

———. 1998. Post-Conflict Elections, Democratization, and International Assistance. Center for Development Information and Evaluation Supported Study, PNACC875. Lynne Reinner Publishers, Inc.

Kumar, Krishna, David Tardif-Douglin, Kim Maynard, Pater Manikas, Annette Sheckler, Kate Crawford, and Carolyn Knapp. 1995. "Rebuilding Post-War Rwanda: The Role of the International Community." Report by Team IV, Multi-Donor Evaluation of Emergency Assistance to Rwanda, for the Development Assistance Committee of the Organization for Economic Cooperation and Development. USAID's Center for Development Information and Evaluation. Washington, DC: U.S. Agency for International Development.

Kumar, Krishna, and Irving Rosenthal. 1998. "Scientific Cooperation and Peace Building: A Case Study of USAID's Middle East Regional Cooperation Program." Center for Development Information and Evaluation Supported Study, PNACA907. Washington, DC: U.S. Agency for International Development.

Kwamboka, Eileen. 1994. "Report to USAID: A Study on [of] the role of religious institution on [in] Kenya." USAID/Kenya Supported Study, PNACF179. Washington, DC: U.S. Agency for International Development.

Lancaster, Carol. 1994a. "Testimony March 2, Hon. Carol Lancaster, Deputy Administrator, USAID, House Agriculture/Foreign Agriculture and Hunger: U.S. Foreign Assistance Programs Review." *Federal Document Clearing House Congressional Testimony,* March 2.

———. 1994b. "Testimony May 12, 1994, Carol Lancaster, Deputy Administrator, United States Agency for International Development, House Small Business Privatization and Small Business." *Federal Document Clearing House Congressional Testimony,* May 12.

Lee, Che-Fu. 1973. "Demographic Analysis of Inter-Ethnic Assimilation and its

Implication for Population Change in Singapore." USAID Supported Study, PNABI085. Washington, DC: U.S. Agency for International Development.

Mathews, Jessica. 1989. "Redefining Security." *Foreign Affairs* 68, no. 2 (spring): 162.

Maybury-Lewis, David, et al. 1980. "Social Impact of Development on Ethnic Minorities." Cultural Survival, Inc. (MA). USAID Policy and Program Coordination Bureau Supported Study, PNAAH736. Washington, DC: U.S. Agency for International Development.

McCorkle, Constance, Charles Stathacos, and Jim Maxwell. 1995. "Cross-border Trade and Ethnic Groups in West Africa: Volume 1 and Volume 2." Abt Associates, Inc. USAID/Africa Bureau Supported Study, PNACE926. Washington, DC: U.S. Agency for International Development.

McFerson, Hazel M. 1983. "Private Sector: Ethnicity, Individual Initiative, and Economic Growth in an African Plural Society: The Bamileke of Cameroon." USAID/Center for Development Information and Evaluation, Special Evaluation, PNAAL016. Washington, DC: U.S. Agency for International Development.

McHugh, Heather S. 1995a. "Efforts in Ethnic Conflict Resolution: Preliminary Lessons Learned." Center for Development Information and Evaluation, Special Study, PNABU375. Washington, DC: U.S. Agency for International Development.

———. 1995b. "The Relationship between Democracy and Sustainability: A Disengaged Process." Center for Development Information and Evaluation, Special Study, Issue Paper 3, PNABW062. Washington, DC: U.S. Agency for International Development.

McManus, Doyle. 1995. "Clinton's Mad, Mad, Mad, Mad World: Is President Clinton's Foreign Policy a Contradictory Shambles—or Just an Inevitable Reaction to a New World Disorder?" *Los Angeles Times Magazine,* January 22, 14–23.

Mills, Stephan. 1994. "USA: Down-home Issues Driving Clinton's Foreign Relations." *Australian Financial Review,* January 27.

Nacht, Alexander. 1995. "U.S. Foreign Policy Strategies." *Washington Quarterly* 18, no. 3 (summer): 193–204.

Ordeshook, Peter C., and Olga V. Shvetsova. 1993. "Ethnic Heterogeneity, District Magnitude, and the Number of Parties." University of Maryland. USAID Bureau for Private Enterprise Supported Study, PNABP360. Washington, DC: U.S. Agency for International Development.

Painter, Michael. 1985. "Ethnicity and Social Class Formation in the Bolivian Lowlands." Clark University. USAID Bureau for Science and Technology Supported Study, PNAAW491. Washington, DC: U.S. Agency for International Development.

Park, Thomas K., Mamadou Baro, and Tidiane Ngaido. 1991. "Conflicts over Land and the Crisis of Nationalism in Mauritania." Land Tenure Center, Special Study for USAID, PNABH496. Madison, WI: University of Wisconsin-Madison.

Peterson, Lois E., and Sabri Sayari, eds. 1992. "Democratization and Ethnic Conflict: Summary of Two Meetings." USAID/Africa Bureau Supported

Conference, PNACA428. Washington, DC: U.S. Agency for International Development.

PIOOM (Interdisciplinary Research Programme on Root Causes of Human Rights Violations). 1999. "World Conflict and Human Rights Map 1998/1999." Leiden, Netherlands: Leiden University.

Richards, Lois. 1994. "Testimony April 19, 1994, Lois C. Richards, Acting Assistant Administrator, Bureau for Humanitarian Response, United States Agency for International Development, House Appropriations/Foreign Operations, FY 95 Foreign Operations Appropriations." *Federal Document Clearing House Congressional Testimony,* April 19.

Riesman, Paul. 1979. "Fulani in a Development Context: The Relevance of Cultural Traditions for Coping with Change and Crisis." USAID Supported Study, PNAAG856. Washington, DC: U.S. Agency for International Development.

Richburg, Keith B. 1994. "Kenya's Ethnic Conflict Drives Farmers Off Land." *Washington Post,* March 17, A1.

Saunders, Harold H. 1993. "Enlarging U.S. Policy toward 'Ethnic' Conflict: Rethinking Intervention." Paper presented at a symposium, "Ethnic Conflicts: Threat to Domestic and International Peace," sponsored by the National Defense University and the Joint Center for Political-Economic Studies, Washington, DC, November.

Saunders, Margaret O. 1980. "Agriculture in Upper Volta: The Institutional Framework, Local Ecology, Population, and Ethnic Groups in Upper Volta: The Mossi Farming System of Upper Volta." Purdue University. USAID Africa Bureau Supported Social Analysis, PNAAV278. Washington, DC: U.S. Agency for International Development.

Sellstrom, Tor, Lemart Wohlgemuth, et al. 1996. "Historical Perspective: Some Explanary Factors." Report #2, Multi-Donor Evaluation of Emergency Assistance to Rwanda, for the Development Assistance Committee of the OECD. Series Title: International Response to Conflict and Genocide: Lessons from the Rwanda Experience. USAID's Center for Development Information and Evaluation, PNABY105. Washington, DC: U.S. Agency for International Development.

"Senate Committee OKs Talbott." 1994. *Ukrainian Weekly* 52, no. 7 (February 13): 1.

Shack, W. A. 1977. "Namibia, Anticipation of Economic and Humanitarian Needs: the Multi-ethnic Factor in Namibia." African-American Scholars Council. USAID Supported Study. Washington, DC: U.S. Agency for International Development.

Silber, Laura, Allan Little, and the British Broadcasting Corporation. 1996. *Yugoslavia: Death of a Nation.* TV Books, Inc.

Stremlau, John. 1995. "Sovereignty at Bay." *Washington Quarterly* 18, no. 1 (winter): 8–27.

United States Agency for International Development (USAID). 1991a. "Keywords Used to Index Documents Included in the A.I.D. Development Information System." Center for Development Information and Evaluation, PNABJ677. Washington, DC: U.S. Agency for International Development, November.

————. 1994. "Strategies for Sustainable Development." Washington, DC: U.S. Agency for International Development.

————. 1995a. "Appendix A: Programs Included in the Annual Performance Report, 1995." Center for Development Information and Evaluation, Performance Measurement and Evaluation. Washington, DC: U.S. Agency for International Development.

————. 1995b. "Core Report of the New Partnership Initiative." Washington, DC: U.S. Agency for International Development.

————. 1995c. "Democracy and Governance Policy Paper #1: Policy and Implementation Options for Rule of Law in USAID." Bureau for Policy and Program Coordination. Washington, DC: U.S. Agency for International Development.

————. 1995d. "Glossary of Terms: USAID Humanitarian Assistance Workshop." USAID Humanitarian Assistance Workshop on Performance Measurement, cosponsored by the Bureau for Policy and Program Coordination and the Bureau for Humanitarian Response, Washington, DC, June 15–16, 1995. Washington, DC: U.S. Agency for International Development.

————. 1995e. "Guidelines for Strategic Plans." Washington, DC: U.S. Agency for International Development.

————. 1996a. "Ethnicity, Gender, and Fertility Preferences in Nigeria." Family Health International. USAID/Nigeria Supported Study, PNABY754. Washington, DC: U.S. Agency for International Development.

————. 1996b. "Multi-layered Conflict in the Greater Horn of Africa." USAID/Africa Bureau Supported Study, PNACC947, PNABY397, and PNACA995. Washington, DC: U.S. Agency for International Development.

————. 1996c. "OFDA Annual Report FY1995." Prepared by the Office of U.S. Foreign Disaster Assistance, Bureau for Humanitarian Response. Washington, D.C.: U.S. Agency for International Development.

————. N.d. [1999]. "The Administrator's Policy Restatement on Conflict: USAID/General Notice Information; Subject: Conflict Prevention Guidance for Strategic Planning." Prepared by the Policy and Program Coordination Bureau. Washington, DC: U.S. Agency for International Development.

Vermillion, Jim. 1995. "Civil Society in Mongolia." USAID Bureau for Policy and Program Coordination. Washington, DC: U.S. Agency for International Development.

Weiss, Thomas G. 1994. "The United Nations and Civil War." *Washington Quarterly,* 17, no. 4 (autumn): 151–55.

Wilk, Richard, and Mac Chapin. 1988. "Ethnic Minorities in Belize: Mopan, Kekchi, and Garifuna." Cultural Survival, Inc. (MA). USAID Bureau for Latin America and the Caribbean Supported Study, PNABI653. Washington, DC: U.S. Agency for International Development.

Wright, Paul, and Robert W. Gardner. 1983. "Ethnicity, Birthplace, and Achievement: The Changing Hawaii Mosaic." East-West Center (HI). USAID Bureau for Science and Technology Supported Study, PNAAN489. Washington, DC: U.S. Agency for International Development.

CHAPTER 4

Foreign Aid and Ethnic Interests in Kenya

John M. Cohen

Academics specializing in the design and implementation of foreign aid interventions have given little attention to ethnicity.[1] As a result, it should not be surprising that aid agency handbooks fail to be explicit about ethnic issues, for academic products have an important impact on their content. This neglect, however, does not mean that those involved in aid-funded interventions fail to pay close attention to ethnic relationships. In this regard, the objective of this chapter is to present a set of Kenyan case studies that illustrate the extent to which politicians, public sector officials, aid agency professionals, and expatriate technical assistance personnel consciously deal with ethnic issues over a wide range of projects, structural adjustment agreements, and aid conditionalities.

Background Profile on Ethnicity and Policy Making

In Kenya as in most sub-Saharan African countries, every government official's evaluation of both domestic-funded and aid agency–funded activities includes their specific effects on ethnic groups. In public speeches, press releases, and private interviews, officials and opposition leaders constantly talk about foreign aid in terms of ethnic areas and interests.[2] So, too, expatriate aid-related professionals working in Kenya constantly take ethnic interests into account, directly referring to the interests of specific ethnic leaders, groups, and areas. Among themselves and with Kenyan politicians and civil servants, such professionals typically discuss ethnic issues knowledgeably, frankly, and openly.

Kenya's estimated 25.7 million people are classified into approximately 40 ethnic groups.[3] Three groups, the Kikuyu, Luo, and Luyha, none of which is numerically dominant, make up an estimated 50 percent of the country's African population. Two smaller groups, the Kamba and Kalenjin, are each estimated to contain 10 percent of this population. In sum, five ethnic groups comprise approximately 70 percent of the African population.

Importantly, ethnic aggregation can be misleading, for there are crosscutting cleavages within groups and mutually self-serving relations between members of different groups.[4] First, a number of ethnic groups are in effect composite categories covering smaller distinct but related groups. For example, the currently dominant Kalenjins are made up of a number of smaller groups, one of which, the Tugen, is President Daniel arap Moi's ethnic group.

Second, a given ethnic group can be divided into factions. For example, the Kikuyu, the ethnic group of Kenya's first president, Jomo Kenyatta, has long been divided into two highly competitive region-based factions: the Kiambu Kikuyu and the Nyeri Kikuyu. This competition is expressly recognized in the rhetoric of politicians, formation of political groupings, reporting in the press, intergovernmental struggles for resources, and design and implementation of aid agency interventions.

Third, individuals belonging to an ethnic group not part of the national ruling coalition can and do become involved with that coalition's political party. Throughout Kenya's political history, individuals from all ethnic groups have voted for and worked with the dominant political party and the coalition that controls it. All ethnic constituencies elect members of Parliament (MPs) under the banner of the dominant party. But most MPs from ethnic groups not part of the coalition do not get ministerial appointments and have difficulty gaining access to government resources for their home areas. Further, civil servants in effect work for the dominant coalition as they implement its policies, projects, and programs. But being a public servant does not preclude one from (1) facilitating the transfer of government resources to one's home area or (2) using red tape and related strategies to stall or limit efforts by other ethnic groups to obtain government resources for their home areas.

In this regard, today's public sector is largely organized to generate the resources required by ethnic godfathers to stay in power, a variation on the common pattern of crony statism found in many sub-Saharan African countries.[5] The prevailing system relies heavily on the ability of ethnic leaders to control the distribution of projects, jobs, and rent niches required to support clientele networks and fragment ethnic opposition.[6]

From 1960 to 1965 the dominant ethnic coalition was led by President Kenyatta's Kikuyu, with the support of the Luo and the Kamba. After 1965 the Luo ceased to belong to the coalition and the Meru and Embu were added. Since 1978, political power has been held by President Moi's Kalenjin and a shifting coalition currently made up of the Masai and factions within the Kamba, coastal groups, the Luyha, and the Kisii. Because the

Kenyan political system and its patterns of competition are well described elsewhere,[7] only two points need to be highlighted here. First, Kenya is a republic based on a modified parliamentary model, with an elected president serving as both the head of state and the leader of government. The president controls a highly centralized governmental system that reinforces its decisions at the field level through top-down administrative deconcentration.[8] Second, for complex reasons grounded in Kenya's colonial history, the jurisdictional boundaries of local-level government units are largely coterminous with identifiable ethnic areas. Hence, most politicians represent jurisdictions dominated by one ethnic group, and the names of each of the country's more than 40 districts are closely linked by all Kenyans to specific ethnic groups.

Finally, it is methodologically difficult to determine the extent to which motives behind a decision are affected by personal, ethnic, or political interests. The emphasis of this chapter is on the knowledge and actions of aid agency professionals, not on proving the motive of ethnicity. Nevertheless, the case studies that follow are all drawn from projects I was involved in or observed at close hand. Ethnic identity is cited where I have concluded that ethnic interests were a dominant motive. Clearly ethnic identity alone does not establish motive. In this regard, it would not have been ethical to cite the government documents or comments of government officials that led me to decide that a particular decision was primarily affected more by ethnic interests.

Case Studies of Foreign Aid and Ethnic Interest

In the 1991/92 fiscal year, the Kenyan government received $873 million in official development assistance, which was provided by 15 multilateral and 17 bilateral aid agencies.[9] Of this assistance, 55.6 percent was provided through grants and 44.4 percent through loans. Together, aid agency resources comprised 73.6 percent of the total capital budget. The following seven case studies, drawn from a larger study,[10] seek to illustrate how this foreign aid affected and was affected by ethnic interests, competition, and conflict.

In the early 1990s an estimated 650 aid agency–funded and more than 2,000 domestic-funded projects were being carried out.[11] Case studies of four of these projects are presented here. The first focuses on long-term technical assistance projects that, among other objectives, provided short- and long-term external training for public sector economists and planners located in specifically targeted ministerial units. It demonstrates that the ethnic backgrounds of those selected for training were explicitly recognized and dealt with by government officials, expatriate training advisors, and aid agency professionals. The second case study centers on the failed efforts of the current government to obtain foreign aid funding for the construction of an international airport in Eldoret, a key urban area for President Moi's core coalition. This project demonstrates the salience of ethnic issues in aid agency evaluation of project location and objectives. The third case study reviews a series of foreign aid projects aimed at addressing the development of arid and semi-arid areas. What is important about these projects is the way the government and the aid agencies cooperated to ensure that all ethnic groups living in such areas received development assistance. The fourth case study describes two long-established rural development projects annually funding more than a thousand ongoing subprojects covering all districts and touching all ethnic groups. This case demonstrates how, in selecting subprojects, the funding agencies and their gatekeeping technical personnel implement systems designed to minimize the effects of ethnic interests on the distribution of the resources provided.

Several important support loans listed in the development budget were not projects. Rather, they were general or sector-specific soft loans tied to structural adjustment agreements, most of which were provided by the World Bank and the International Monetary Fund (IMF). In the early 1990s, the government was formally committed to complying with more than 150 conditions spelled out in these structural adjustment agreements.[12] These ranged from sweeping tasks, such as privatization of parastatals or civil service reform, to very specific tasks, such as keeping the budget deficit below 5 percent of the gross domestic product or introducing monthly expenditure reporting systems. The fifth case study focuses on the relationship between ethnicity and conditions requiring privatization of parastatals. It illustrates how members of the ruling coalition use parastatals to benefit members of their ethnic groups or opportunists from other groups whose support they need. It suggests that politicians and senior civil servants will hold back privatization to protect the advantages they gain from control of parastatals, and it reviews the types of strategies they follow to capture the benefits any sale of a parastatal might generate. How aid agencies acted in the face of such efforts demonstrates the careful attention given to ethnic issues by aid agency professionals.

The last two cases illustrate the relationship between ethnic interests and growing demands on the part of aid agencies that existing structural agreements be met and new reforms be carried out as a precondition to the transfer of further foreign aid. Frustrated by the government's rhetoric and slow implementation of the conditions of the structural adjustment agreements, as well as President Moi's drift toward autocratic politics, major foreign aid providers decided to reduce or suspend planned grant and loan flows to Kenya until the government complied with conditions in existing agreements and new aid conditionalities, such as democratization, freedom of the press, human rights, and prosecution of high-level corruption.

The first conditionalities were slapped on Kenya in November 1991.[13] This decision, taken in Paris at a formal meeting between the government and the aid agencies, was followed by subsequent meetings in the same venue. At one meeting, in November 1993, aid agencies awarded increased funding on the ground that some progress was being made in meeting important structural adjustment conditions.[14] But this compliance was to some extent illusory because ethnic interests hampered the effective implementation of government actions and the president was openly critical of both structural adjustment conditions and reinforcing conditionalities.[15] A subsequent meeting, held in July 1995, found the government insufficiently committed to the reforms[16] and threatened future substantial aid reductions and suspensions if more progress was not made on the agreements and conditionalities.[17]

By reviewing the effects of the aid conditionality requiring the government to reestablish multiparty democracy, the sixth case study demonstrates how aid agencies can threaten the interests of a ruling ethnic coalition and how such a coalition can cynically generate ethnic conflict in an attempt to demonstrate that an aid conditionality is wrongly conceived. The seventh study illustrates how ethnic competition has led to corruption on a massive scale. It shows how difficult it is for the ruling ethnic coalition to comply with the aid conditionality that those responsible for well-known, high-level government corruption be prosecuted.

Selection of Master's Degree Candidates in Capacity-Building Technical Assistance Projects

Between 1976 and 1994, the Harvard Institute for International Development (HIID) carried out four separate projects aimed at building the capacity of the Ministries of Finance (MOF), Planning and National Development (MPND), and Agriculture and Livestock Development (MALD).[18] These projects focused on training government economists and planners while providing expatriate "gap-filling" advisors who could support public sector functions while training was carried out.[19] Together these four projects funded Master's-level training for 108 junior officers and short-term overseas specialized training for more than 250 midcareer officers.[20]

Procedures for selecting trainees were affected by ethnic considerations at two levels. First, the list of officers selected for each training year was carefully balanced to limit any bias toward a particular ethnic group.

Discussions between the training advisor and division heads during the selection process was always direct and explicit. Among the ethnic-based selection patterns were (1) the postponement of training for an eligible officer when it would lead to selection of too many officers from a particular group and (2) the selection of an officer less qualified than other eligible officers because his or her group was underrepresented. Second, senior ministry officers responsible for approving those selected for training pressured the training advisor to make changes in the selection list to advance officers from their groups. They also established barriers to training candidates from the "wrong" groups. One tactic employed at the senior approval stages was to transfer such candidates out of the unit targeted for capacity-building training programs. Another tactic was to pressure the training advisor to add officers from the approving officer's ethnic group or to delete officers from groups the approving officer did not favor.

Senior officers did not give much concern to whether "the best and the brightest" were selected for training. Nor did they act to implement an official policy aimed at dealing with past imbalances, such as is the case in the United States with affirmative action or in Malaysia and India in regard to ethnic advancement policies. The focus of those deciding who was to receive training was on supporting members of specific ethnic groups. It was not on the need to ensure the quality of future economic policy analysts and development planners in government.

Aid agency project officers in Nairobi, as well as HIID advisors, were concerned about the number of officers trained to the Master's level who departed from government service. This concern with retention was justified because 52 (48.1 percent) of the 108 trained to the Master's level under the four projects had left the public sector by 1994.[21] Analysis of retention patterns reveals that ethnicity is one of the causes of departure of officers from the public sector positions they were trained to fill. First, some senior government officials openly discriminate against officers from particular ethnic groups. This discrimination takes the form of slow promotions, negative evaluations, meaningless assignments, transfers to undesirable jobs or field locations, and failure to approve personal requests. Such discrimination lowers the morale of the officer being discriminated against and is one of several factors likely to lead him or her to depart the public sector. Second, some senior ministry officials use their position to actively discriminate against officers who join ethnic-grounded parties that are in opposition to the government coalition or who are clients of ethnic godfathers such officials oppose.

The four training projects reviewed were funded by a number of aid agencies, including the United States Agency for International Development, the United Nations Development Program, the World Bank, the

Canadian International Development Agency (CIDA), the Swedish International Development Agency, the Germans, and the Dutch. The effects of ethnicity on selection, training, and retention of public sector personnel trained under these projects was openly discussed among aid agency professionals and technical assistance advisors. But the issues discussed are rarely put into memorandums and reports. Only people who participated in these meetings, such as myself, have the information required to present the effects of ethnic considerations on public sector capacity building.

Eldoret International Airport Project

Since the early 1990s, President Moi and the Kalenjin politicians who support him have argued for the construction of an international airport at Eldoret, a Rift Valley Province town located in the president's home area. Eldoret is not an economic center. Rather, it is the de facto capital of the ruling political coalition.

The projected cost of this airport is $96 million. Aside from the land purchase and construction rents the project would generate for the president and his fellow Kalenjins, having a larger airport would help break the dependence of the Kalenjin on Kenya's major international airport, which is located in Nairobi, the heartland of the Kikuyu. Opponents to the project argued that building the Eldoret airport would both strengthen the Kalenjin regional autonomy and waste scarce budgetary resources.[22]

Discussions between the government and the aid agencies approached for funding support have focused on the implications of the project for ethnic balance and greater Kalenjin autonomy. This has particularly been the case since 1992 when many in the president's coalition began to talk about *majimboism,* which is the Swahili term for a system of quasi-federal provinces having substantially devolved powers.[23] In the end, the aid agencies declined to provide funding for the project. The publicly stated reasons for this refusal were that there was little need for an airport of the size planned, that aid resources were limited, and that many other projects needing funding had greater economic and social priority. But the more persuasive reason was that any aid agency financing the project would play directly into Kalenjin-Kikuyu ethnic hostilities over *majimboism.*

Despite the absence of foreign aid, the government awarded a contract to a Canadian firm, which is currently involved in building the facility on a turnkey basis. Initial funding came from domestic budget resources, which were already quite limited, a fact that generated a great deal of criticism from opposition parties. Leaders of such parties, largely Kikuyu and Luo politicians, argued that the project was a white elephant that would lead to enormous waste of limited government resources; increase the country's indebtedness while denying essential recurrent expenditures for other decaying airports in Nairobi, Mombasa, and Kisumu; and not contribute to economic growth. In the face of this criticism, the president still tried to obtain funding from CIDA. But the Canadian high commissioner quickly declared, largely because she recognized the relationship between the project and ethnic interests and competition, that CIDA had no intention of providing funding, even though the contractor was a Canadian firm. With the inability of the government to find an aid agency to help fund this large project, it was substantially scaled back. The domestic press and politicians directly attribute this result to actions by aid agencies to scuttle the project.[24]

Arid and Semi-Arid Lands Projects

The Arid and Semi-Arid Lands (ASAL) program, launched in 1979, was a major government and aid agency initiative to induce development in arid, marginal districts of the country. Twenty-two districts, containing an estimated 30 percent of Kenya's population and over 80 percent of the country's total land area, fall into this category. The initiative sought to assist "disadvantaged" districts so they could catch up with more developed, agrarian parts of the country. All parties to the design of the ASAL initiative recognized that the "more developed and wealthier" districts were those of former President Kenyatta's core ethnic coalition and that the districts in need of support were home areas to the ethnic coalition that supported President Moi when he took power in 1978.[25]

The ASAL concept is attributed to a former permanent secretary of the MPND who was an intellectual force in the government and a Kamba.[26] So it was not by chance that the first ASAL project, the Machakos Integrated Development Project (MIDP), was located in the permanent secretary's home district. A biographer argues that the permanent secretary was a strong nationalist and antiethnicist who never pushed for a project for his home district. Further, he argues that the funding agency, the European Economic Community (EEC), went over this permanent secretary's head to the vice president to have the project placed in Machakos District. However, the biographer notes that once the permanent secretary's home district was selected, he did everything possible to make sure it was designed, financed, and promptly implemented.

But there is a deeper story. Kamba support was important to President Moi. Two critical Kamba politicians were Paul Ngei, a longtime MP and minister, and Mulu Mutisya, a powerful grassroots politician. They wanted the project for Machakos District. Their behind-the-scenes influence, supported by the president, put pressure on the EEC delegate and the vice president to select their home district for the first ASAL project.

During the design phase of MIDP, an aid agency conference led to the assignment of other arid districts to different aid agencies. This balkanization of the program received strong government support because the political coalition being built by President Moi came from ethnic groups in ASAL districts. By mid-1991 there were 11 aid agency–funded ASAL field projects covering 14 districts and funded by eight aid agencies.[27]

Throughout the buildup of ASAL activities, there was explicit discussion between the government and the aid agencies over the relationship between the president's emerging ethnic coalition and the rationale for selecting particular locations for projects. The districts receiving priority design and implementation advantages were those most closely connected to the president. For this reason, it was not by chance that the second, fourth, fifth, and sixth projects designed and funded were located in the home areas of the president and his most influential Rift Valley supporters. In sum, the history of the ASAL intervention demonstrates the extent to which aid agency professionals are attuned to the linkages between the ethnic coalition in power and the need for leaders in that coalition to bring large projects to their home areas.

The Rural Development Fund and the EEC-Micro Project

The Scandinavian-supported Rural Development Fund (RDF) and the European Community–funded Micro Project (EEC/MP) illustrate how government professionals and expatriate technical assistance advisors work to minimize the effects of ethnic interests on annual project allocations. They also illustrate the extent to which aid agencies will go to ensure that their assistance is equitably divided among ethnic-based districts and efficiently used to promote social and economic development.

The RDF is the only source of annual discretionary funding that is available to every district in Kenya.[28] Established in 1974, this project is used by district leaders to fund a wide variety of subprojects, such as water systems, cattle dips, farm-to-market roads, conservation investments, and income-generating enterprises. It is considered a "budget gap-filling" project that can fund priority subprojects that ministerial budgets cannot accommodate. Between 1974 and 1988 the RDF carried out 5,557 subprojects at a cost of more than $40 million. In 1990 the project was supporting about 1,200 subprojects.

The EEC/MP is similar to the RDF.[29] Both projects are managed by MPND officers and assisted by expatriate technical advisory teams. The significant difference between the two projects is that the RDF provides discretionary funds to all districts every financial year while the EEC/MP provides funds to only one-third of the districts every financial year. The other major differences are that while EEC/MP funds only one subproject in a district, funding levels for EEC/MP subprojects are much higher than those for RDF subprojects. Most EEC/MP subprojects involve infrastructure construction. One significant result of these differences is that MPND officers managing the EEC/MP are under much greater pressure from politicians in President Moi's coalition to make sure their district is selected, if possible more than once every three years. As with RDF subprojects, EEC/MP subprojects are supposed to be identified at the local level, recommended by the District Development Committee (DDC), and selected according to criteria applied by the MPND and advisors funded by the EEC.

The technical assistance personnel who assist the MPND officers managing the two projects perform a gatekeeping function.[30] Their major tasks are designing selection criteria, participating in selection processes, evaluating engineering designs, monitoring expenditures, and, wherever possible, using field visits to confirm certificates of completion. The openly acknowledged subtext of these duties is that advisors ensure that ethnic interests do not bias the selection process by district or by investment, that corruption is kept to a minimum, and that materials are not misappropriated by local godfathers and field officers.

RDF and EEC/MP projects have high political profile because they provide politicians with an opportunity to shepherd subprojects and so be seen to bring resources to their constituencies.[31] At times, politicians seek to obtain DDC approval for subprojects that do not meet technical appraisal criteria or have not originated at the grassroots. If they are important members of the president's ruling ethnic coalition, they often try to force subprojects on the MPND. Thus, the selection process becomes an uneasy compromise between "neutral" technical and overtly political-ethnic considerations. Gatekeeping advisors pay close attention to such competition. They are not reluctant to blow the whistle when they find ethnic politics or corruption leading to inefficient use of resources. Scandinavian and EEC aid agency staff members overseeing RDF and EEC/MP projects have made it clear to the gatekeeping advisors they fund that one of their principal objectives is to reduce ethnic bias both in the division of annual allocations among districts and in the selection of subprojects in particular districts.

Privatization of Parastatals

By 1992 the government had entered into several structural adjustment agreements with aid agencies that contained conditions requiring it to reduce the number of parastatals. To a large extent this was because these state-owned enterprises were inefficiently run, failed to earn profits, and required large subsidies from the Treasury.[32] Since the mid-1980s such subsidies have been a major contributor to the government's large budget deficits. It was clear to aid agency professionals, expatriate advisors, and members of the press that ethnic interests were a major reason for parastatal inefficiency and economic losses. For example, one of the major drains on limited budgetary resources was the poorly managed and heavily subsidized National Cereals and Produce Board, a parastatal that, despite aid agency pressure, the government protected because, among other things, it benefited politicians who had moved into large-scale grain production in Rift Valley Province.

Perhaps the major ethnic aspects of parastatal inefficiency was that senior positions went to former MPs and senior government officials who were members of the president's ruling coalition. The president used these appointments as rewards to shore up his ruling coalition and build Kalenjin wealth so that members of that ethnic group could hold their own with the Kikuyu, who had benefited greatly under President Kenyatta. He did so with little regard to their affect on his budget or the economy. Such appointments generally assisted the president to maintain political support. Indeed, they became more important in the 1990s as he sought to firm up his coalition.

Many of those appointed to head parastatals used their positions to pillage their organizations' resources. Their practices extended far beyond rewarding themselves with such costly benefits as high salaries, luxury cars, subsidized housing, and opportunities to create unnecessary jobs for their kinsmen. In the early 1990s, for example, one powerful minister secured the appointment of colleagues to parastatals controlled by his ministry. He then established a family-held private bank (nonbanking financial institution) and required his appointees to deposit the revenues of their parastatals in his bank. These deposits were used to finance the construction of an office building. When the minister was transferred to another ministry, the building was not finished. His bank lacked the funds to complete the building and was unable to return the deposits of the parastatals. Because the minister still had substantial influence, the para-*statals were not inclined to go after the assets of the failed bank.

As the processes of pressuring the government to comply with privatization conditions unfolded, aid agencies became increasingly direct about the link between foot-dragging and ethnic interests. Specific individuals and their linkages to President Moi were discussed. For example, angry attention focused on the head of the deficit-plagued post and telephone parastatal, who was forced by the aid agencies, much against his will, to stop construction of a 20-story skyscraper at the eighth floor, resulting in a substantial reduction in his construction-related kickbacks.

Aid agencies recognized the costs of granting cash cows as political rewards, so they began to take steps to stop the pillaging. Referring to the example given earlier, they pressured the government to prohibit the deposit of parastatal revenue in any bank other than the Central Bank and regulated the practices of the nonbank financial institutions that were being used to suck resources out of state-owned enterprises.

As pressure to get privatization moving built during the late 1980s and early 1990s, the government took another approach, one that used the sale of enterprises or stock in them to continue to benefit its ethnic-based coalition of supporters. Given the emergence of such priorities, aid agency staff members had serious misgivings about the government's privatization procedures.[33] One common practice is to sell undervalued shares to Kenyan businessmen who have influential politicians and senior government officials as silent partners. Another practice is to sell parastatals quietly without providing public information on the valuation of enterprises to be sold, pricing of stocks, or payments. An example of such practices is found in the 1994 sale of Kenya Cashew Nuts Limited, a state-owned enterprise located in Coast Province, a region dominated by smaller ethnic groups that have been loyal members of President Moi's coalition. Little information was provided by the government on the price of the sale or the purchasers. The current evidence suggests that the parastatal was bought for undervalued prices by a group of coastal cooperative officials, who then sold it at a markup to a Kenyan firm owned by Asian nationals. This information, if true, would be typical of the quick-profit business turnovers common to Kenya, a practice made famous during the early Kenyatta years when a number of Asian nationals were forced to sell their retail textile firms to African nationals, who then sold the firms back to the former Indian owners with 10 to 20 percent price markups.

Efforts of President Moi's government to ensure the sale of parastatal stocks to the benefit of the current political elite are at times highly visible. For example, in 1994 the Parliament, dominated by the Kenya African National Union (KANU), passed the Capital Markets Authority Amendment Bill. It gave the government control over elections or appointments to the private Nairobi Stock Exchange (NSE), as well as power to approve new stock brokerage firms seeking to operate on the increasingly lively NSE. To a large extent these steps were taken because the government perceived the NSE as being dominated by Kikuyus and Asian nationals fronting for Kikuyus. Throughout these efforts to control the stock exchange, aid agencies have been involved in pushing for its protection from government control or manipulation.

In particular they were concerned about the extent to which senior officials charged with implementing the divestitures were unaccountable to independent audit. Their concern increased when the government sought to undermine review of sales by the Office of the Controller or the auditor general.[34] In response to such practices, the aid agencies demanded greater transparency and accountability. Internal IMF and World Bank staff memorandums and public press statements focused closely on how President Moi's government used parastatals to provide political patronage to key ethnic godfathers central to the maintenance of his ruling coalition.[35] So World Bank professionals, with IMF support, drew up schedules for privatization and subjected the government's activities to stringent monitoring.[36] Kalenjin hard-liners opposed the move toward stepped-up privatization and urged the president to stop dealing with the World Bank and the IMF.[37] By 1994, influential presidential advisors and the moderate minister of finance, a Luhya, made the economic costs of such an action clear to the president, leading him to approve the World Bank's divestiture plan, including the sale of some parastatals once considered too strategic to sell.[38]

Aid agencies are well aware of the relationship between ethnicity and parastatal inefficiencies. As a result, they understand the ruling coalition's resistance to privatization and tendency toward opaque practices when sales are made. Thus, they considered ethnicity in drafting structural adjustment conditions related to the preparation of privatization targets and schedules, as well as in regard to the establishment of systems for monitoring privatization processes and results.

Democratization and Reinstitution of Multiparty Political Competition

Throughout the Kenyatta era, the power of the dominant party, KANU, declined in importance.[39] After gaining the presidency in 1978, Moi strengthened KANU so it would provide a foundation for his ruling coalition. In 1982 he succeeded in obtaining the passage of an amendment to the Constitution that established a de jure one-party state. His administration also adopted an intimidating new set of electoral procedures and reduced press freedoms. Shortly thereafter aid agencies imposed an aid condition requiring the government to (1) amend the Constitution to end the one-party state and allow a multiparty system to operate; (2) establish an impartial elections board, reinstate the secret ballot, redistrict where population shifts require it, and update voter registration roles; and (3) relax direct and indirect state censorship of the press.

To date, the government has amended the Constitution to allow a multiparty system to operate but has moved slowly on reforming the election process and barely tolerates a free press.[40] Because the opposition is fragmented, largely due to ethnic competition, KANU won the December 1992 elections with only 35 percent of the vote.[41] Explicit negotiations between the government and the aid agencies over these aid conditions, as well as the effects of their outcome on ethnic interests, competition, and conflict, have been widely acknowledged in press reports and academic studies.[42]

The march toward multiparty democracy touched off ethnic violence, particularly in the Kalenjin-Masai heartland of Rift Valley Province. There "opposition" to multiparty politics was used as an excuse by local politicians to drive an estimated 30,000 to 40,000 Kikuyu and Luo settlers off their land, killing approximately 1,000 people in the process. Both the domestic and the international press are full of detailed reports on the linkage between democratization conditionality and this ethnic violence.[43] To a large extent, much of this literature outlines how the Kalenjin and Masai used the threat of opposition parties operating in Rift Valley to mobilize gangs of young men to force migrants out of the province, allegedly with the assistance of the country's security forces. It also focuses on the efforts of the president to curb the formation and activities of opposition parties, frequently charging that such parties "thrive on tribalism . . . while jostling for leadership positions."[44] Currently the government is concerned with efforts by a famous white Kenyan citizen, Richard Leakey, to form a new party that consolidates opposition parties. He has been explicitly labeled as a racist by President Moi, and he and a number of supporters were recently roughed up, with the police looking on.[45] But rather than elaborate such conditionality-generated ethnic conflicts, this case study will focus on how the United States dealt with the relationships between the democratization conditionality and ethnic competition.

The major pressure on the aid agencies to impose the conditionality of democratization on the Kenyan government came from the United States. American ambassador Smith Hempstone, a Republican political appointee and former journalist for a conservative Texas newspaper, led the charge.[46] He was highly visible in the political arena. His close contacts with Kikuyu and Luo opposition leaders and his statements and arguments for multiparty politics were publicly criticized by the politicians in power.

Hempstone drew on USAID personnel in his efforts to tie progress on democratization to the receipt of foreign aid. He commandeered a well-known American political scientist who was working throughout eastern and southern Africa as an analyst for the aid agency's democracy and governance projects. This expert, Joel Barkan, was on leave from the University of Iowa to work on the larger project. The ambassador knew Barkan was particularly knowledgeable about Kenya. Using his influence, he obtained USAID's permission to have Barkan focus primarily on Kenya. In a series of internal memorandums, Barkan made the ethnic basis of the emerging opposition parties clear to Hempstone and greatly facilitated the ambassador's ability to understand the steps required to force President Moi's coalition to agree to carry out the democratization conditionality.

In 1994 USAID launched a $7 million project titled "Kenya Democracy and Governance Project." This project, which was agreed to by the government because of the pressure of conditionality, focused on strengthening Parliament, the auditor and controller general's offices, and civil society. Because the government showed little interest in the first two project components, only the third received any funding. In the words of the project document, civil society funds were to be used to sponsor conferences on "democracy in a multi-ethnic society," support local human rights groups in their efforts to track "state-sanctioned ethnic cleansing," and study "weaknesses in civil society," giving particular attention to the "Asian-African split" and "ethnic divisions among Africans."[47]

The ambassador who replaced Smith, Aurela E. Brazeal, was much less aggressive about democratization and human rights conditionalities. Her conciliatory approach, based on praising progress rather than demanding changes, was not effective. As a result, hard-liners in President Moi's coalition became more forceful in trying to stiffen government resistance to conditions in structural adjustment agreements and related aid conditionalities. But Smith's aggressive role has recently been taken over by the German and Japanese ambassadors and the Australian high commissioner.[48] So international pressure to promote democratization continues.

Clearly, these facts suggest an embassy and aid agency mission deeply involved in ethnic issues. Perhaps no other case study presented in this chapter illustrates how directly concerned aid agencies are with the effects of their resources on ethnic interests, competition, and conflict.

Prosecution of High-Level Corruption

Historians will someday note that tolerating (if not stimulating) corruption was central to President Kenyatta's strategy for building an African upper class that could hold its own with the large number of whites who were "staying on" after independence. He did this by appointing fellow Kikuyu and other ethnic supporters to positions in government that generated rents. Kenyatta tolerated "good corruption," which was based on reasonable kickbacks, investments of gains in economic enterprises, and limited transfers of new wealth to foreign banks. This strategy worked well. By the mid-1970s there were enough wealthy Kenyans with homes, farms, and firms equal to the holdings of the whites and enough African members of country clubs formerly exclusively white that a new Swahili term was coined: *wabenzi,* referring to "people of the Mercedes tribe."

Toward the end of his life, President Kenyatta was less attentive to governance, and corruption began to spread, especially as the bureaucracy swelled and new opportunities for dishonesty appeared. When Moi became president, he allowed corruption to accelerate, in large part to make sure his ethnic group and the groups supporting his efforts to consolidate power became wealthy enough to hold their own with the new Kikuyu elite Kenyatta had assisted. Under Moi there has been "bad corruption," with excessively large kickbacks, no limitation on greed, and rent earnings going into unproductive consumption or foreign accounts and real estate. By the early 1990s, corruption had become massive and widespread, threatening economic growth and ethnic stability.[49]

Aid agency officials have played a major role in documenting high-level corruption, most notably in regard to the Turkwell Dam, one of the largest projects ever carried out in the country. In 1986 the EEC offered to provide grant and soft loan funding to construct a hydroelectric project in Turkana District.[50] The project's estimated cost exceeded $400 million. Before the aid agreement was signed, French construction firms supported by French banks paid large bribes, estimated to be in the neighborhood of $25 to 30 million, to the president and a few of his closest Kalenjin colleagues. As a result, the EEC agreement was scrapped and the government contracted the project to French firms under hard loan financing. The EEC aid representative was so angered by this outcome that he wrote a memorandum documenting all aspects of the affair and sent it to the heads of aid agency missions in Nairobi. Shortly thereafter he left the country.

More high-level cases of corruption have appeared since the mid-1980s. The case that has attracted the most attention is that of the Kenyan firm Goldenberg International. Foremost among Goldenberg's scams is its claimed export of gold and diamonds, for which it received or has claimed in excess of $250 million to $470 million (depending on the documentation and exchange rates used) from the government's export compensation scheme.[51] The Goldenberg case aroused attention because Kenya produces only a small amount of gold and no diamonds; there was no record of the Swiss company to which the claimed exports were delivered; due to special treatment granted by the MOF, the export payment was made at 35 percent of claimed export value, which was 15 percent above the 20 percent legally authorized under the scheme; and Goldenberg could not demonstrate that it had remitted its alleged foreign exchange earnings, for which the compensation was claimed or paid.

The head of the company is an Asian national, Kamlish Pattni. Confidential documents prepared by aid agencies suggest that the key investors in Pattni's firm were relatives of the president (Kalenjin), the commissioner of customs (Kalenjin), and the governor of the Central Bank (Kalenjin). These documents further allege that the participants were facilitated in their efforts by side payments to the vice president and minister of finance (Kikuyu/Masai), the commissioner of mines (Luo), and two former permanent secretaries of the MOF—one a Kamba, who appears to have been deeply involved from the beginning, and the other his Kikuyu successor, who arrived after the extent of the fraud was already known in most circles. If these allegations are correct, they vividly demonstrate the brazenness of ethnic-based rent-seeking coalitions.

Throughout the early 1990s, this case was so widely reported in the domestic press that the aid agencies were forced to take action.[52] At the previously described November 1991 Paris meeting, key aid agencies demanded that corruption be rooted out by the government as an additional condition for the receipt of future aid flows. However, no public prosecution has followed this demand. Not until 1994 did the current minister of finance, using all the political resources available to him, manage to prevail over President Moi's inner circle to initiate criminal investigations into the case. The local press directly attributed these investigations to pressure from the IMF and a coalition of aid agencies.[53] The current expectation is that only Pattni and the Kikuyu permanent secretary will be charged, with Pattni, who is very useful to Kalenjin members of the president's inner circle, being let off easy.[54] Responding to the lack of progress on these cases, aid agencies withheld further funding at a special meeting of the Paris Club in August 1995.[55]

As noted in the RDF and EEC/MP case study, aid agencies fund gatekeeping advisors to minimize ethnic influence and bureaucratic corruption in their projects. Aid agencies have also introduced microcomputers and management information systems into ministries, in part to increase transparency as a means of reducing corruption. But addressing high-level corruption is a departure for them. The aid agencies appear to have recognized that continuation of the present state of corruption will undermine the entire structural adjustment package and mortgage future generations of Kenyan taxpayers. Hence the aid agencies are now holding the government's feet to the fire.[56] But the large-scale corruption they are after is so closely connected to the president and his Kalenjin-based coalition that they are unlikely to be successful in obtaining meaningful prosecution, restitution to the Treasury of stolen government funds, or a crack-down on corruption in the public sector.

Implications of Kenyan Cases

The Kenyan case studies demonstrate over a range of projects, structural adjustment agreements, and aid conditionalities that in Kenya aid agency staff members pay close attention to ethnic issues. If this pattern holds for other developing countries, which I believe is the case, academic studies aimed at assisting aid agency professionals to better understand relationships between foreign aid and ethnicity are not essential. Rather, what is needed are more comparative case studies of ethnicity-aid relationships that, on analysis, generate guidelines professionals can adopt in their efforts to limit the negative effects ethnicity can have on aid interventions and reduce the negative effects aid interventions can have on ethnic groups.

Unfortunately, it will not be easy to generate further case studies. To a large extent this is because such studies can only be written by academic nationals and expatriate field practitioners who are in close contact with government officials, aid agency professionals, and those affected by foreign aid interventions. The first group of potential researchers are often reluctant to carry out such studies. Social scientists from developing countries who write on the complexities of ethnic competition take political risks that many of their Western colleagues would find too high. The second group of professionals typically have little time to write case studies. Still, ways must be found to get both groups to provide comparative, detailed case studies on ethnicity-aid relationships. Only when more evidence is available will aid agencies be able to better design interventions that are sensitive to ethnic interests, competition, and conflict.

NOTES

1. The limited writing on this topic is focused on the effects of dams, irrigation systems, and resettlement schemes on ethnic groups. See, for example, Elizabeth Colson, *The Social Consequences of Resettlement: The Impact of the Kariba Resettlement Upon the Gwembe Tonga* (Manchester: Manchester University Press, 1971). The literature on project design, management, and evaluation is largely silent on this topic. For example, an influential statement on the design of rural development projects strongly argues for going beyond technical, economic, and financial feasibility to consider "socio-cultural feasibility" (Wayne Weiss, Albert

Waterson, and John Wilson, "The Design of Agricultural and Rural Development Projects," in *Planning Development Projects*, ed. Dennis A. Rondinelli [Strouds-burg: Dowden, Hutchinson, and Ross, 1977], 106–7). But in the accompanying description of such a feasibility study, no mention is made of ethnicity. This pattern is also found in such well-known texts as Dennis A. Rondinelli, *Development Projects as Policy Experiments: An Adaptive Approach to Development Administration* (London: Methuen, 1983); Louise G. White, *Implementing Policy Reforms in LDCs: A Strategy for Designing and Effecting Change* (Boulder: Lynne Reinner, 1990); and Derick W. Brinkerhoff, *Improving Development Program Performance: Guidelines for Managers* (Boulder: Lynne Reinner, 1991). When ethnicity is mentioned in texts, it is mentioned only tangentially. See, for example, Albert O. Hirschman, *Development Projects Observed* (Washington, DC: Brookings Institution, 1967), 46, 140–42, 146; Coralie Bryant and Louise G. White, *Managing Development in the Third World* (Boulder: Westview, 1982), 49, 257, 291.

2. For example, "Who Benefits from Aid? Opposition MPs Claim Their Tribes Are Neglected," *Weekly Review,* July 22, 1994, 17–23.

3. Irving Kaplan et al., *Area Handbook for Kenya* (Washington, DC: U.S. Government Printing Office, 1976), 85–104, 423–35.

4. For example, "Kenya's Clothes: Moi's Recent Illness Has Sparked Hustling among the Political Ambitious, with a New Contender on the Scene to Be Reckoned With," *Africa Confidential* 26, no. 11 (1995): 3–4.

5. Thomas M. Callaghy, "The State and the Development of Capitalism in Africa: Theoretical, Historical, and Comparative Reflections," in *The Precarious Balance: State and Society in Africa,* ed. Donald Rothchild and Naomi Chazan (Boulder: Lynne Reinner, 1988), 80–88; Richard Joseph, *Democracy and Prebendal Politics in Nigeria: The Rise and Fall of the Second Republic* (Cambridge: Cambridge University Press, 1987).

6. See, for example, "Bribery and Extortion: The Moi Way of Buying Support and Loyalty and Silencing Opposition Is a Perversion of Constitutional Government," *Finance,* November 15, 1992, 18–23. The press recently noted, "ministers with a strong local following among the Kamba, Kisii, Luyha and Coastal groups have indicated that they cannot guarantee a large pro-KANU turnout next time until they receive favors for these ethnic loyalties" ("Moi Goes Up-Country," *Africa Confidential* 36, no. 3 [1995]: 3).

7. David W. Throup, "The Construction and Deconstruction of the Kenyatta State," in *The Political Economy of Kenya,* ed. M. G. Schatsberg (Baltimore: Johns Hopkins University Press, 1989), 33–74; Joel D. Barkan, "The Rise and Fall of a Governance Realm in Kenya," in *Governance and Politics in Africa,* ed. Goran Hyden and Michael Bratton (Boulder: Lynne Rienner, 1991), 167–92; Jennifer A. Widner, *The Rise of a Party State in Kenya: From "Harambee!" to "Nyayo!"* (Berkeley: University of California Press, 1992).

8. John M. Cohen and Richard M. Hook, "Decentralized Planning in Kenya," *Public Administration and Development* 7, no. 1 (1987): 77–93; Joel D. Barkan and Michael Chege, "Decentralising the State: District Focus and Politics of Reallocation in Kenya," *Journal of Modern African Studies* 27, no. 3 (1989): 431–53.

9. Republic of Kenya, *Development Estimates for the Year 1991/92* (Nairobi: Government Printer, 1991), tables I–III.

10. John M. Cohen, *Ethnicity, Foreign Aid, and Economic Growth: A Case Study of Kenya*, Development Discussion Paper 520 (Cambridge: Harvard Institute for International Development, 1995).

11. Republic of Kenya, *Public Investment Programme* (Nairobi: Government Printer, 1991).

12. Republic of Kenya, Ministry of Finance, Budgetary Supplies Department, "The Status of Donor Conditionalities," internal memorandum, July 5, 1992.

13. Jane Perlez, "Citing Corruption in Kenya, Western Nations Cancel Aid," *New York Times*, October 21, 1991, 1.

14. "Kenya: A Difficult Courtship," *Africa Confidential* 24, no. 10 (1993): 4–6; "From Paris with Money: Donors Resume Aid to Kenya," *Weekly Review*, November 26, 1993, 21–29.

15. An example of the numerous press reports on this resistance is "Rejecting the Bitter Dose: Kenya Finds the Donor-Prescribed Economic Reforms a Bit Too Unpalatable," *Weekly Review*, March 26, 1993, 14–26.

16. For example, Suguta Marmar, "Will the Paris Club Players Be Duped Again? The Public Thinks Donors Are Losing a Major Battle of Wits," *Sunday Standard*, July 30, 1995, 10; Donatella Lorch, "Is Kenya Sliding Back toward Repression?" *New York Times*, October 1, 1995, 3; idem, "Kenya's Asphalt Jungle, with a Law to Match It," *New York Times*, October 5, 1995, 4.

17. See, for example, Chris McGreal, "Kenya Gets Human Rights Warning," *Guardian Weekly*, July 30, 1995, 4; "Aid for Kenya: Stop, Go," *Economist*, August 19, 1995, 37. Domestic press reports are illustrated by "Voices of Criticism: Many of Kenya's Donors Have Placed a High Premium on Political Reform," *Weekly Review*, May 26, 1995, 23, and "After Paris What? Kenya Should Brace Itself for Difficult Relations with Bilateral Donors," *Weekly Review*, July 28, 1995, 12–25.

18. John M. Cohen and Stephen B. Peterson, "HIID's Advisory and Training Experience in Kenya," in *Assisting Development in a Changing World: The Harvard Institute for International Development, 1980–1995*, ed. Dwight Perkins (Cambridge: Harvard Institute for International Development; Harvard University Press, 1997).

19. John M. Cohen, "Foreign Advisors and Capacity Building: The Case of Kenya," *Public Administration and Development* 12, no. 5 (1992): 496.

20. John M. Cohen and John R. Wheeler, "Training and Retention in African Public Sectors: Capacity Building Lessons in Kenya," in *Getting Good Government: Capacity Building in the Public Sector of Late Developing Countries*, ed. Merilee S. Grindle (Cambridge: Harvard University Press, 1996).

21. Ibid.

22. "Eldoret Airport: False Start for Controversial Project," *Weekly Review*, September 8, 1995, 15–16.

23. Kenya gained independence on December 12, 1963, under what was called the "Majimbo Constitution." It was based on extensive powers for local-level governments, the recognition of which resulted from British efforts to protect white

settlers and deal with ethnic distrust among Kenyan nationalist leaders who were members of competing tribes. See, for example, Cherry J. Gertzel, *Government and Politics in Kenya: A Nation Building Test* (Nairobi: East African Publishing House, 1965). Current debates on *majimboism* have had extensive press coverage, most recently in "Majimbo: Are They Bluffing?" *Weekly Review,* October 7, 1994, 4–13, and "Changing the Constitution," *Weekly Review,* January 6, 1995, 4–9. The president plays both sides of this issue, depending on his needs: see "On the Wrong Track: President Moi Rejects Tribal Clamor for Majimbo," *Weekly Review,* October 14, 1994, 4–9.

24. For example, "A Coincidence in Timing?: Donors Are Suspected to Be Behind This Week's Reform Decision," *Weekly Review,* September 8, 1995, 19; "Jitters over Eldoret Airport," *Weekly Review,* April 21, 1995, 20–22.

25. Government of Kenya, *Arid and Semi-Arid Lands Development in Kenya: The Framework for Implementation, Programme Planning, and Evaluation* (Nairobi: Ministry of Agriculture, 1979).

26. David Leonard, *African Successes: Four Public Managers of Kenyan Rural Development* (Berkeley: University of California Press, 1991), particularly 198–99.

27. ASAL projects, districts, and funding agencies are summarized in Steve Wiggins, "The Planning and Management of Integrated Rural Development in Dry Lands: Early Lessons from Kenya's Arid and Semi-Arid Lands Programs," *Public Administration and Development* 5, no. 2 (1985): 91–108.

28. C. Anonsen et al., "Kenya's Rural Development Fund: A Study of Its Socio-Economic Impact," consulting report prepared by Chr. Michelsen Institute (Bergen, 1985); "Kenya: The Rural Development Fund," appraisal report prepared by a Scandinavian mission to Kenya, Danida (Copenhagen, 1990).

29. Genevieve de Crombrugghe, "Report of an Evaluation of Micro-Projects in Kenya," consultant report, COTA (Brussels, 1985); Gratien L. Pognon, Sylvie Wabbes, and Edith Gasana, "Microprojects in Kenya," evaluation of European Development Fund (EDF) cofunded programs under Lome II Convention ([Brussels], 1988).

30. Cohen, "Foreign Advisors and Capacity Building," 497.

31. Joel D. Barkan, "Bringing Home the Pork: Legislative Behavior, Rural Development, and Rural Change in East Africa," in *Legislature and Development,* ed. Joel Smith and Lloyd Musolof (Durham: Duke University Press, 1978), 265–88.

32. Barbara Grosh, *Public Enterprise in Kenya: What Works, What Doesn't, and Why* (Boulder: Lynne Rienner, 1991).

33. "Skepticism over Privatization in Kenya," *Reuters,* June 12, 1994.

34. For example, "Kenya: The New Capitalism and Its Cronies," *Africa Confidential* 35, no. 24 (1994): 4–5; "Skepticism over Privatization in Kenya," *Reuters,* June 12, 1994.

35. For example, the Washington-based IMF official overseeing the shadow program, Hiroyuki Hino, openly criticized the slow pace of privatization and the lack of transparency and noted that loss of parastatal cash cows to the private sector would remove a major source of patronage from the president's resources ("Kenyan Official Hits Out at IMF on Privatization," *Reuters,* March 2, 1995).

36. "Kenya: A Very Private Affair," *Africa Confidential* 35, no. 10 (1995): 10–11.

37. "A Test of Political Will: Success of the Parastatal Sector Reform Will Depend on Strong Support from the Government," *Weekly Review*, May 27, 1994, 32–3.

38. "Kenya: A Very Private Affair"; "Kenya: After Multi-Party Politics, a One-Party Style," *Africa Confidential* 35, no. 14 (1994): 1–2.

39. Joel D. Barkan and John J. Okumu, "'Semi-Competitive' Elections, Clientelism, and Political Recruitment in a No-Party State: The Kenyan Experience," in *Elections without Choice*, ed. Guy Hermet et al. (New York: Wiley Interscience, 1978), 88–107; Joel D. Barkan and John J. Okumu, "Linkage without Parties: Legislators and Constituents in Kenya," in *Political Parties and Linkage: A Comparative Perspective*, ed. Kay Lawson (New Haven: Yale University Press, 1980), 289–324.

40. Frank Holmquist and Michael Ford, "Kenya: Slouching toward Democracy," *Africa Today* 39, 3 (1992): 97–111.

41. Joel D. Barkan, "Kenya: Lessons from a Flawed Election," *Journal of Democracy* 4, no. 3 (1993): 85–99; "Kenya: Adieu au Vieux I," *Africa Confidential* 35, no. 4 (1994); "After Multi-Party Politics, A One Party State," 1–21; "Moi Goes Up Country," 3–4.

42. For example, Frank Holmquist and Michael Ford, "Kenya: State and Civil Society in the First Year after the Election," *Africa Today* 41, no. 4 (1994): 5–25; International Republican Institute, *Kenya: Political Update* (Washington, DC: International Republican Institute, 1995).

43. For example, Human Rights Watch, *Divide and Rule: State-Sponsored Ethnic Violence in Kenya* (New York: Human Rights Watch, 1993); Makau wa Mutua, "Human Rights and State Despotism in Kenya: Institutional Problems," *Africa Today* 41, no. 4 (1994): 50–56. Typical of domestic press reports are "Moi's Tribe Goes on the Rampage," *Daily Telegraph*, May 1, 1992; "Kenya: Silent Slaughter," *Economist*, July 16, 1994, 39–40; "Mess in Maela: Officials Charged with Resettling Eviction Victims Engage in Profiteering," *Weekly Review*, January 13, 1995, 4–10; Holmquist and Ford, "Kenya: State and Civil Society," 11–14.

44. "Kenyan President Renews Attack on Leakey," *Reuters*, May 14, 1995.

45. "Taking the Plunge: Dr. Richard Leakey Is in the Line-Up of Muite's Party," *Weekly Review*, May 12, 1995, 4–9.

46. Widner, *Rise of a Party State in Kenya*, 174–75.

47. "Kenya Democracy and Governance Project (615–0266) (1994–97)" (Washington, DC: U.S. Agency for International Development, n.d.).

48. For example, "Poking His Nose Too Deep: Mutzelberg Is Accused of Meddling in Kenya's Internal Affairs," *Weekly Review*, July 21, 1995, 11–12; "Diplomacy and National Dignity," *Weekly Review*, August 4, 1995, 3, 10–11.

49. Martha Mbuggus, "Kenyans and the 'Chai Syndrome.'" *Nation*, December 18, 1991, 1. See also, Gichuru Njihia, "Inquiry Riveted by Tales of Corruption in High Places," *Nation*, August 11, 1991, 4; "Bribery and Extortion," *Finance*, November 13, 1992, 18–23; Liz Sly, "Caught in Corruption's Stranglehold," *Chicago Tribune*, November 19, 1995, 18–19.

50. Blane Harden, *Africa: Dispatches from a Fragile Continent* (Boston: Houghton Mifflin, 1991), 182–216.

51. "The Goldenberg Report: Irregular Payment of Export Compensation," *Finance,* April 30, 1995, 20–25. The $470 million comes from data in International Republican Institute, *Kenya: Political Update,* 5; "New Avenues for Corruption: Reforms Have Opened Opportunities for Creative Schemers," *Weekly Review,* January 6, 1995, 26–27.

52. For example, "Audit-General: A Sorry Litany of Funds Misuse," *Weekly Review,* June 22, 1990, 26–27; "Puzzling Questions over Gold Firm Deals," *Nation,* April 20, 1991, Business section, 1; Kjihia, "Inquiry Riveted by Tales of Corruption in High Places," 4; "Days of Corruption Over, Vows AG Wako," *Kenya Times,* April 11, 1991, 4; Peter Warutere, "Gold Exporting Firm Deals Raise Eyebrows," *Nation,* April 13, 1992, 1–2; "Uproar over Goldenberg," *Nation,* May 15, 1992, 1; "Millions Missing from Public Funds," *Standard,* July 16, 1992, 1, 11.

53. "Kamlesh Pattni Arrested," *Weekly Review,* March 25, 1994, 19–24; "Kenya Court Orders Six to Answer Fraud Charges," *Reuters,* December 10, 1994. "Pattni: The Billionaire Businessman Is in the Docks for the Fourth Time," *Weekly Review,* May 26, 1995, 18. Despite the indictment, an additional $40 million is claimed by Goldenberg International: see "Has the Grand March Turned into the Grand Farce?" *News Focus,* April 17–23, 1995, 16.

54. "A Close Shave: The Attorney-General Halts the Criminal Proceedings against V-P Saitoti," *Weekly Review,* March 17, 1995, 12–17; "Man on the Spot: Wamalwa Finds Himself under Pressure over the Goldenberg Affair," *Weekly Review,* April 7, 1995, 13–21; "The Big Losers: Twists and Turns of the Goldenberg Saga," *Weekly Review,* April 14, 1995, 4–9.

55. "Aid for Kenya: Stop, Go," 37; Greg Barrow, "Money Scandal Shakes Kenya," *Guardian Weekly,* October 15, 1995, 3.

56. Most recently, "Surprise Verdict: The IMF Pegs the Conclusion of ESAF to the Resolution of the Goldenberg Case," *Weekly Review,* September 15, 1995, 18–19.

CHAPTER 5

Ethnic Cooperation in Sri Lanka: Through the Keyhole of a USAID Project

Norman T. Uphoff

It is unlikely that there is any necessary or fixed relationship between foreign assistance and ethnic conflict (or cooperation). However, this does
not mean that there is no connection. External aid used in some ways can
be seen to exacerbate or stir up ethnic tensions, indirectly if not directly,
while aid used differently can have some moderating effects. The relationship is best understood as being loosely causal, not invariant, and unlikely
to be linear. This means that the ethnic effects of foreign assistance are
quite contingent and contextual, generally consistent with the dynamics
studied under the rubric of chaos theory (Gleick 1987) or complexity theory (Waldrop 1992; Cowan, Pines, and Meltzer 1994).

Most cases in the literature deal with situations where foreign aid has
contributed to ethnic difficulties, favoring or being used by one group vis-
à-vis another. This case documents and discusses a contrary situation,
where an externally aided project, funded by the United States Agency for
International Development (USAID) along with the government of Sri
Lanka, contributed to—or better said, elicited and reinforced—positive
relations between the Sinhalese and Tamil communities in Ampare District, where the project was located. The district is located on the other side
of the island from its capital city, Colombo, in the southeastern part of a
country that has been otherwise racked by conflict between violent elements of these two ethnic groups frequently since the early 1980s and periodically since the late 1950s, though not before.[1]

The Gal Oya irrigation scheme was the first major development project undertaken by the government of Sri Lanka (then Ceylon) after independence was granted in 1948. It was and still is the largest single irrigation
system in the country, serving over 50,000 hectares.[2] Since the scheme was
literally carved out of the jungle, with malaria and other diseases endemic,
with elephants and other wild animals presenting hazards, and with a

definite lack of amenities, it was not considered a desirable place to live when new lands were opened up.

The government in fact had difficulty getting households to move to the area at first. It was eventually able to settle the upstream areas (referred to as "the head" and "the middle") mostly with Sinhalese households that were brought in from the densely populated uplands and from the western and southern coastal regions of the country. Tamil households were relocated inland from the eastern coastal regions to populate the downstream areas (referred to as "the tail"). This meant that the usual problem of getting equitable water distribution between head-end and tail-end areas was made more complicated by having an ethnic division between these areas once the system began operation.[3]

For many reasons, the system never functioned very well, and by the late 1970s it was considered one of the most rundown irrigation schemes in the country. In 1979, USAID agreed to help the Sri Lankan government's Irrigation Department rehabilitate and improve water management in the portion known as the Left Bank subsystem, a 600-square-mile area where problems of water distribution and poverty were particularly acute. One reason for the problems was that the Left Bank command area had soils that were not well suited for growing paddy (flooded) rice, which all households in the area cultivated. Porous soils led to considerable seepage and conveyance losses in the canals (Government of Ceylon 1970).

Another reason for water shortage was that the yield from the catchment area had been greatly overestimated when the system was designed. The main reservoir had filled to capacity only twice in the first 30 years. Because the resident population of Gal Oya had increased considerably over three decades, the demand for water now greatly exceeded supply. Indeed, the lower third of the Left Bank area, settled mostly by Tamils, never got irrigation water during the long dry season, and the middle third got water only intermittently and unreliably. However, even in the top third of the system, where almost all households were Sinhalese, many areas at the ends of the distribution channels had inadequate or unreliable water supply due to the overall shortage and inefficient management of water.[4]

While it could be said that the "waste" of water by Sinhalese head-end farmers reduced the supply available to downstream Tamil farmers at the tail, there was no evident ethnic bias in the system's management. Most of the Irrigation Department engineers who managed the Gal Oya scheme were themselves Tamil, as a result of the generally better educational opportunities that this ethnic group had enjoyed for many generations.[5]

This chapter describes a situation of ethnic cooperation that has extended over the past 15 years despite deadly conflicts elsewhere in the country. The role of foreign aid in this is not simple to delineate or demonstrate. But some positive contribution was probably made through the donor-assisted project's introduction and support of community organizations in the Gal Oya area. These organizations were based on value premises of cooperation, participation, and equity to improve irrigation operational efficiency, so although they were not intended to mitigate or resolve ethnic conflict, I think they contributed to this result by creating local forums and leadership. Local organizations and representatives could mobilize constructive and conciliating orientations within communities, whereas elsewhere, in the absence of such social infrastructure, attitudes and acts based on group-based fear, aggression, or aggrandizement could more easily become dominant.

The water-user organizations in this case had the unanticipated effect of reinforcing cooperative and generous behavior generally and of strengthening community capacities to maintain unity, not just within the Sinhalese and Tamil communities, but between them. The suggestion of this chapter is that ethnic conflict can be muted and possibly even avoided by a structure of community organization and leadership that expresses constructive, positive-sum values. In situations of ethnic tension, whether this is heightened and inflamed or muted and sublimated depends very much on who speaks for the community.

Fortuitously, when the demons of ethnic strife reared their heads in Sri Lanka and threatened to enflame settlers in Gal Oya, who had been involved in grievous violence 25 years earlier, the USAID-funded Water Management Project had already begun promoting local organizations based on the very positive values of participation, equity, and efficiency. As I understand the social dynamics of what happened in the Left Bank of Gal Oya, it was not so much that this organizational effort changed people's minds and attitudes. Rather, it helped bring to the fore and entrusted with recognized leadership roles persons within the community who espoused and even championed positive values that already existed, however mutely, among local residents. This articulation and local support of cooperative, altruistic, and nonsectarian values directed community thinking and actions toward communal harmony, which was not a necessary but a possible outcome under the circumstances.

The positive role of foreign aid and of donor involvement in this situation was largely inadvertent, though USAID's good intentions provided a basis for its playing a reasonably benign role.[6] The USAID personnel whom I observed in Sri Lanka, from mission directors to project managers, generally wanted to avoid getting involved in politics, and this meant that they should not appear to favor one ethnic group over another. At higher diplomatic levels, I understood that U.S. representatives put some pressure on the Sri Lankan government to avoid ethnic discrimination. But the U.S. government was so committed to the Jayewardene regime, which was pursuing explicit free market policies to reverse the "socialist" policies of the preceding government, that such pressure was probably very mild. During the six years I interacted frequently with USAID personnel (1980–85), there was very little explicit discussion of or apparent attention to ethnic considerations, though there was quick and clear concern expressed for equal human rights whenever any question of ethnic favoritism or prejudice arose.

The Gal Oya Project Experience

After our first reconnaissance visit to Gal Oya in January 1980 to assess the situation, the Irrigation Department's senior deputy director for water management told us that if we could make progress there, we could make progress anywhere in Sri Lanka.[7] This was a nice way of saying that the Irrigation Department considered Gal Oya its most difficult—most broken-down, poorly managed—irrigation system in the country. Part of the perceived problem was that the people there were thought to be particularly conflict-prone and uncooperative. Few settlers had come fully voluntarily. Village headmen had often been told to send a certain number of households to Gal Oya to settle, and they took this opportunity to get rid of the most troublesome members of their communities. The government even gave some prisoners early release from jail on the condition that they would relocate to Gal Oya with their families.

When considering how to establish farmer organizations for improving irrigation performance, we looked to experience in the Philippines, where a good start had been made on establishing participatory water management by using young, specially trained organizers who lived in the rural areas among the farmers with whom they worked (Korten 1982; Korten and Siy 1988). So we decided to recruit Institutional Organizers and field them in the Left Bank communities as catalysts to help create farmer organizations.[8]

Our initial cadre consisted of 30 organizers, who, after two weeks of formal training through lectures and group exercises plus four weeks of field familiarization in Gal Oya, were posted into communities in a pilot area covering over 2,000 hectares. The top civil servant for the district, in his speech at the "graduation" ceremony for the organizers, cautioned them to have realistic expectations. He said they would find the work difficult, because the people were so quarrelsome and difficult. He suggested that bringing even 10 or 15 farmers in Gal Oya to work together would be a big achievement. What he did not say was that within the next four years, the organizers were supposed to get 10,000 to 15,000 farmers (nobody knew exactly how many farmers there were in the Left Bank) working together in effective, durable organizations. By such a reckoning, the odds were a thousand to one against success.

To make matters worse, when the organizers started their work in March 1981, they faced greater-than-usual water scarcity. The main reservoir was only one-quarter full at the start of the dry season for cultivation. The resident Cornell advisor suggested that maybe the water management effort should be delayed for a year, because if there were a crop failure (which was likely), it might be blamed at least in part on our program, and we would then have even more difficulty getting farmers to participate in the program subsequently. This was a reasonable surmise, since most social science predictions are that resource scarcity makes conflict more likely. The organizers, however, were already being asked by farmers what they could do to help counter the impending crisis, and they felt the program needed to make some good faith effort on farmers' behalf. A decision was made that we would proceed, but with organizers instructed never to make any decisions for farmers. The latter would have to make all decisions for themselves, since they were the persons who had to bear the consequences.

The organizing effort was started at the head of the system, which was almost all Sinhalese, because the engineers wanted to begin the work on physical rehabilitation there on grounds of technical efficiency. We accepted this "ethnically biased" schedule on the ground that there was little chance of augmenting the water supply for downstream (Tamil) farmers unless greater efficiency and reduction in water use could be achieved at the head through (Sinhalese) farmer cooperation and water-saving measures.[9]

To everyone's surprise, within six weeks, we found that 90 percent of the head-end farmers were undertaking some combination of (a) channel cleaning through voluntary group labor (some of the channels had not been cleared of silt, stones, and weeds for 5, 10, or even 20 years);[10] (b) rotation of water deliveries so that each farmer got an equitable share of the available water, usually sending water to the end of channels first (an act of unprecedented solidarity and trust since the Irrigation Department's water deliveries seldom kept to schedule and head-enders could get left "high and dry"); and (c) water saving, donating about one-sixth of the days of water to which head-end channels were entitled (according to the official schedule) to send water downstream to farmers more in need of water.[11]

Of special significance was the willingness of at least some Sinhalese farmers to save water for the benefit of Tamil tail-enders. On Gonagolla branch canal, one group of farmers agreed, all but one, to save one of each five days' allocation of water to send downstream to Sinawatte, a Tamil area. The farmer who objected to this generosity was persuaded to support the plan after a young farmer, Narangoda, who emerged as a strong and exemplary leader for the whole Left Bank, took him by bicycle down the long and bumpy canal road to see what conditions were like at the end. (Sinhalese seldom went into the Tamil area.) The dissenting individual came back quite moved by what he had seen, reporting that tail-end farmers did not have enough water even for drinking and bathing, let alone for growing a crop of rice. The Gonagolla farmers tried to save and donate two and even three days of their five days' water allotment once they became more conscious of how the drought was affecting others downstream. This act of generosity by Sinhalese farmers helped to gain support from the Irrigation Department's engineers, mostly Tamil, for our program of participatory irrigation management, which they initially balked at.

In August 1981, ethnic violence erupted in several towns in the project area and beyond, after fights between Sinhalese and Tamil youths broke out following a disputed volleyball game in the nearby district capital of Batticaloa. We were gratified to learn that half a dozen Sinhalese farmer-representatives, chosen by their peers under our program in the Gonagolla area, took it on themselves to go to the homes of two Tamil Irrigation Department staff members to make sure that no harm was done to them or to their property. Since these two officials had been openly criticized by farmers at a seasonal planning meeting held just five months before (Murray-Rust and Moore 1984, 55), this act of concern represented quite a turnaround in farmer-official relations. It helped to reverse negative attitudes that Tamil engineers had toward Sinhalese farmers, which was important for our program.[12]

In January 1982, there was danger of even more widespread ethnic violence. The Liberation Tigers of Tamil Eelam (LTTE), the most extreme of the separatist groups, had said it would declare (from the safety of London) a separate Tamil state in Sri Lanka. There were fears that this would spark the kind of strife that had torn the South Asian subcontinent apart in 1947 with the partition between India and Pakistan. The day before the announcement was threatened, farmer-representatives in the Gonagolla area went to Tamil fishermen on the reservoir nearby and said, apologetically, that they feared violence the next day. They suggested that the fishermen stay home that day and offered to guard the Tamils' boats and nets to make sure that no damage was done to them.

As it happened, the LTTE did not declare "Tamil Eelam," and the day passed without incident. But I found it almost as remarkable that farmers would be concerned about the safety of fishermen as that Sinhalese would take steps to protect Tamils. But these farmer-representatives, whom I got to know personally during my eight years of acquaintance with them, were remarkable people, very public-spirited and extremely conscientious in all senses of the word. They had been chosen by their fellow farmers to speak and act on behalf of the farming community, and they believed, though they had no formal legal authority, that they had the right, the obligation, and the social support to take initiative in ethnically reconciling ways.

During the period 1980–85, I was visiting Gal Oya every six months. I met with these farmer-representatives a few days after the threatened LTTE secession and learned about their actions. I asked them, point-blank, whether, under the current circumstances of ethnic tension, they thought that we could still have a single umbrella organization for the Left Bank farmers or that we should plan to have two. To give the farmers a legitimate reason for choosing the latter option, I added, "because of the language problem." The two languages, Sinhala and Tamil, are mutually unintelligible, so this contributes to division between the communities. Ratnayake, an elderly farmer-representative who spoke often for the group, answered me: "One is good," he said. I asked why, and he responded without hesitation in Sinhala, "There are no Sinhalese farmers and no Tamil farmers, only farmers." The representatives went on to describe how they sometimes exchanged cattle draft power, seeds, and labor with Tamil farmers downstream. As far as they were concerned, there was no reason for ethnic strife, and they were opposed to the violence that had broken out during 1981 (Uphoff 1992, 98–102).

During 1982–83, the project moved downstream to begin organizing farmers in the middle reaches of the system, starting to work in some Tamil communities. The most difficult area was M5. The lower 40 percent of this 1,000-hectare area that covered both Sinhalese and Tamil settlements had never gotten water during the dry season, and farmers challenged our organizers to help them improve water-use efficiency enough so that water could reach throughout the M5 command area. In 1982, the total water supply was even less than the year before, as the main reservoir was only 20 percent full at the start of the season. But with channel cleaning, rotational deliveries, and water saving through farmer cooperation encouraged by the organizers, water use was so efficient that almost all of the M5 area got a successful rice crop that year.

One of the most gratifying moments of my association with this program came in January 1983 when I visited channel M5.4.4. There 15 Tamil and 12 Sinhalese households were doing *shramadana* together (see n. 10) to restore the channel's effectiveness by desilting and recutting it (Uphoff 1992, 119–21). During the August 1981 ethnic disturbances, three Tamil households there had been driven out of the area when their homes were burned. Overall in the M5 area, the Tamil population had been reduced by

50 percent or more since 1981. Yet I found the 27 households getting water from M5.4.4 working diligently together to restore a channel that had not been properly maintained during most of the past 20 years, so that all could now get water. When I asked whether cooperation between the two groups would continue, the response was, "Why not?" Farmers felt that they had learned a sad but important lesson from the previous violence, which had not solved anyone's real problems of livelihood and living together.

After my visit to Sri Lanka in June 1983, I wrote in my trip report: "I was struck this time by how often people expressed concern with rising ethnic tensions. The increasing terrorism by separatists, and the many calls for retaliation and suppression, could boil over into widespread violence that would surely shake Gal Oya" (Uphoff 1992, 80). Tragically, four weeks after I wrote this, the impending violence did break out, apparently spurred and directed, if not instigated, by elements of the ruling party.[13] Happily, there was no violence in Gal Oya, though the three Tamil members of the group supervising the program—comprised of people from the Agrarian Research and Training Institute (ARTI) and Cornell University—were victimized in various ways in Colombo, where they lived. They suffered loss of property but fortunately escaped with their lives—in two instances, aided by Sinhalese friends.

In the fall of 1983, despite the worsened ethnic relations overall, ARTI deployed an initial group of young Tamils to start organizing work in the downstream areas, and in early 1984 a cadre of 30 Tamil organizers was recruited, trained, and posted to the lower parts of the Left Bank (Uphoff 1992, 143–45, 168–69). Good progress was made in these areas, but by the end of 1984, the organizing effort had to be suspended. It was reported to us that threats had been made against the organizers by the LTTE. The Tigers, as the LTTE guerrillas were called, had been assassinating Tamils who worked for the government since the late 1970s, calling them traitors to the secessionist cause. Within the ARTI program, we had been pleased with the many examples and demonstrations of solidarity and cooperation between our Sinhalese and Tamil organizers. But reluctantly we suspended the work in Tamil areas of the Left Bank because we did not want to risk anyone's life. If we could continue to improve water-use efficiency in the upstream areas, we knew this would be a benefit to Tamil communities downstream.

During 1985, the situation nationally became more grim, with 150 Sinhalese massacred by Tiger gunmen in the ancient capital city of Anuradhapura. Some of those killed were Buddhist nuns and pilgrims at one of the holiest shrines in the country in February. The Sri Lankan who coordinated the Gal Oya program from 1980 to 1983, C. M. Wijayaratna, told me that he was sure that the LTTE strategy, of trying to provoke a Sinhalese backlash against Tamils so that world sympathies would build for a separate Tamil state, would not succeed. He was right; there were no reprisals. However, there was a riot the next month between Tamils and Muslims in parts of Ampare and Batticaloa Districts, with as many as 30,000 persons displaced from their homes in March 1985. There was no violence in the Left Bank area.

During 1986, the situation continued with sporadic clashes in the country around Gal Oya, but without violence at least in the Left Bank area. This changed in May 1987, when the whole country was shocked by one of the most brutal acts in the protracted conflict. A busload of young Buddhist monks on pilgrimage, most of them novices between 12 and 16 years old, was hijacked about 10 miles north of Gonagolla. All 32 of the young travelers were taken into a nearby jungle and hacked with machetes or shot to death. The apparent intent of the LTTE was to provoke Sinhalese into retaliating with atrocities against their Tamil neighbors so that the Indian government might be pressured by its own Tamil population to intervene militarily and halt the Sri Lankan government's military campaign to wipe out guerilla enclaves in the north.[14]

I visited Gonagolla two weeks after this incident. Several Sinhalese farmer groups told me that they had an informal understanding with Tamil communities downstream: if the Tigers were making a raid upstream, Tamils would try to warn Sinhalese communities so that they could try to protect themselves; if the Sri Lankan army was moving downstream, Sinhalese would try to warn the Tamil communities so that they could get out of the way. Farmers were powerless to stop the warfare going on around them, but they could try to mitigate noncombatant casualties. When I met with about 50 farmers and their representatives in Gonagolla, I asked whether the Tamil engineer living among them was safe (i.e., living among Sinhalese). Narangoda, the local leader who had done so much to improve irrigation management and strengthen farmer organizations, said, "Yes, I regard him as my brother, and if someone comes to get him, they will have to get me first." Farmers all around nodded assent to these bold words.

Indeed, the area remained mostly peaceful despite what was going on to the north and east.[15] There were many Tiger clashes in downstream areas below where we were working during 1987 and 1988, but there was no ethnic violence within the Gal Oya project area until 1990, when small Sinhalese mobs killed several dozen Tamils in Ampare and Inginiyagala towns in June of that year. That incident did not involve farmers, however, and was apparently instigated by police who were seeking revenge for the LTTE's having killed as many as 600 policemen the night before. The

Tigers had broken a truce and attacked police stations up and down the east coast, capturing policemen who offered no resistance because they thought a cease-fire was still in effect between the government and LTTE forces.[16]

I was able to revisit the Gal Oya project area in March 1996, for the first time since 1989 (when I had to fly down in a Sri Lanka Air Force plane because road travel was not considered safe). It was sad to learn that after so many years of keeping communication open between the two communities, a "line" had become established within the project area, below which it was not considered safe for Sinhalese to go and above which Tamils seldom came. Tiger attacks on Sinhalese farming communities had left several dozen dead and had poisoned the atmosphere for cooperation between the two populations, though the farmers I was able to speak with still expressed hope for a return to peace and amicable relations.

Interpretation of the Project Experience

Despite very difficult circumstances, the farmer organizations in Gal Oya proved successful on the ground.[17] The skills and dedication of the organizers, the solidarity and good sense of farmers, and the cooperation and support of officials, plus some beneficial philosophical and structural features of program design, all led to a system of participatory management in Gal Oya that has continued to be effective long after outside assistance from ARTI and Cornell was withdrawn. More important, this system is now in place for all of the major irrigation schemes in the country as a matter of national policy.[18]

What can be learned from this experience about the amelioration and modification of ethnic conflict and about the role foreign assistance can play? The displays of intercommunal solidarity in Sri Lanka cannot be attributed to favorable religious values or cultural norms. The bloody recent history of violence within as well as between the Sinhalese and Tamil communities contradicts such an explanation (Bush 1994). Moreover, at least until 1981, the residents of Gal Oya were thought by outsiders to be among the most conflict- and violence-prone people in Sri Lanka, and there had been significant communal violence in Gal Oya in 1958. But this was not the case during the 1980s after the flare-up in August 1981 that drove out hundreds of Tamil families.

Community leadership seems to me the most important factor to be considered. A key issue affecting people's local behavior is always who speaks for the community. Will the community representatives express sentiments and purposes that are positive-sum and integrate people along ethnic and other lines? Or will they play on people's fears, ambitions, and greed, igniting zero-sum motivations that lead to negative-sum outcomes?

As I noted in the introduction to this chapter, under the Gal Oya project systematic efforts were made to bring forward community leadership that championed certain core values of fairness, participation, and collective action for the sake of more efficient and more equitable water management.[19] Self-management and collective self-reliance were promoted by both word and deed. This situation was the opposite of what all too often happens in foreign-aided projects. External assistance as frequently conceived has created not only dependency but also perverse incentives. Large amounts of money flowing are likely to attract the greedy and self-serving and to strengthen partisan, commercial, and bureaucratic forces, rather than encouraging community-minded, altruistic, grassroots elements.

In January 1985, the undersecretary of agriculture asked me how his ministry, which had responsibility for small-scale irrigation schemes, could learn from our experience in Gal Oya. (Our project had been implemented under the Ministry of Lands, which operated major irrigation schemes.) I said that the most important single factor was the kind of farmers who took up leadership positions; if the right kind emerged, many positive things were possible, but if a program got started with the wrong kind, it would never get the right kind.[20] Leaders who care for others and not just themselves are unlikely to come forward without some encouragement, or if they do, they are likely to be crowded out by aggressive or self-aggrandizing personalities, unless conditions are created to encourage and protect the more generous persons.

Once discouraged from taking leading roles, the more desirable kinds of people will not come forth because they have neither the temperament nor the incentive to fight for leadership. We had experience in Gal Oya of seeing a number of local leaders who had been domineering begin acting more democratically, playing more constructive, community-serving roles once they found themselves surrounded by fellow farmers expecting positive-sum kinds of outcomes to result from their cooperative activity. The previously self-serving leaders could only retain a prominent role in their communities if they got on board and supported the goals and values of our program.[21]

The farmer-representatives, eventually over 500 of them in the head and middle reaches of the Left Bank, were chosen by consensus and were unpaid. They had no formal legal authority, but they exercised great social authority. That the irrigation management program practically doubled the efficiency of water use in the area, helped farmers survive two water-short seasons, and raised rice yields 50 to 100 percent compared with before the project surely reinforced that authority. But also we could see that the cadre of leadership that emerged was very much a value-driven one.

Persons who would contribute so much of their time and even pay their own out-of-pocket expenses to improve community welfare were a very special cohort. But they were not as rare as one might expect. The program continues still to mobilize conscientious, service-oriented leadership through several "generations" of officers as responsibilities have been rotated every few years.[22] While not the poorest of the poor, these representatives have been for the most part average farmers in terms of income and landholding. They were certainly not the most prosperous ones. Selecting representatives from among small groups of 10 to 15 water users along the same field channel has meant that all persons chosen are well-known by their neighbors. Powerful local figures like merchants or school principals, even if they have their own farms, are almost ipso facto excluded from positions of leadership by this process. These are the persons most likely to be chosen if elections are held in a large group with a hundred members or more.

The strategy of organization developed and employed in Gal Oya followed certain structural and procedural principles that make it more probable that community-oriented persons will emerge into leadership roles (Uphoff 1992, 330–36). But also underwritten were normative principles and dynamics that helped to change the behavior of a community that was thought to be one of the most conflictual in the country, making it now one of the most cooperative, not just within ethnic boundaries but also between ethnic groups.

The basic proposition I would advance is that people's value orientations are not either-or but rather for the most part both-and. We are both selfish and generous, both cooperative and individualistic, not just one or the other. Which orientation will be most prominent and influential in a given situation depends very much on that situation, on what others are thinking and doing, not just on what the individual in question happens to believe.

We found that by creating public forums where the problems of the community, particularly with regard to irrigation, could be discussed, cooperative solutions were proposed by community members. The organizers seldom needed to take a very active role in discussions once they got the people used to meeting together, which was the organizers' main responsibility. I once asked an organizer why head-end farmers who had benefited previously from the anarchic system of water distribution, which enabled them to take more than their share of water when channels downstream were clogged up with silt and weeds, were now agreeing to help clean the channels and to accept a system of rotating water deliveries? The organizer responded, "It's hard to be selfish in public."

The public forums, which worked in a problem-solving mode, enlisted practically everyone in finding and then implementing solutions. Even persons who did not benefit much materially or directly participated in the process.[23] The overall balance of net benefits was not only positive-sum but Pareto-optimal in that head-enders' water-conserving efforts did not reduce crop yields. Reducing water "waste" meant that less water flowed out the lower end of their fields into drainage channels; more water flowed down the irrigation channel and remained available to tail-end farmers. Head-end farmers who cooperated in this new regime of water management had now some assurance that their downstream neighbors would be more cooperative in other activities, such as protecting fields against damage from stray cattle. Also, they did not have to get up at night to make sure no downstream farmers were stealing water from them. One of the principal benefits of the new system of water sharing, according to farmers, was they could sleep at night. They did not have to be up stealing water from others or protecting their flow.

What was developed in Gal Oya was a system of generous cooperation that paid material as well as psychic dividends. One might surmise that this attitude in irrigation matters carried over into ethnic relations. But my observation is that a common source of generous and cooperative attitudes, previously dormant and unexpressed, was tapped by a program of community organization that brought forward conscientious, constructive community leadership.

I will not present here the normative theory that in my view explains generous and cooperative behavior, as contrasted with selfish and individualistic behavior. This theory has been elaborated in Uphoff 1992 (336–52). I think that it has relevance to understanding ethnic relations and dynamics, but explicating this would require a chapter in itself.[24] My focus here is on the relationship between giving external assistance and the workings of ethnicity.

As I noted at the outset of this chapter, it is unlikely that there is any intrinsic relationship between the two that makes external aid either supportive of or adverse to ethnic harmony. For the most part, foreign donors have paid little attention to—or have been unwilling to invest seriously in—introducing or strengthening participatory, equitable local institutions of the sort that were established in Gal Oya. At the time the Gal Oya project was designed, ethnic conflict was just gaining momentum in Sri Lanka, so the design of the project was silent on Sinhalese-Tamil differences (or the government preferred to leave such issues unstated).

As it turned out, the farmer organizations brought into being through the organizers' efforts played some role—and maybe a critical role—in preventing the intrusion of ethnic conflict into the Gal Oya area. How great the role was cannot be measured. What this chapter can contribute to the broader literature on ethnic relations is a focus on the role of local leadership, which can dampen or enflame ethnic fears and aggression. During the early 1960s in the United States, when the civil rights movement was pressing to end racial discrimination in the South, it was quite clear that the most important factor determining whether or not there would be outbreaks of violence against civil rights workers was the perceived attitude of state and local elected officials, whether they would try to discourage violence or would "wink" at it.

Unfortunately, we see increasingly around the world a style and substance of leadership, at all levels, that tends, with its zero-sum logic, to exacerbate any inclinations that people may have to think in ethnic (we/they) terms. Even more unfortunately, we see increasingly that such a calculus leads to a negative-sum dynamic that reduces the well-being of all parties through competition, though some fare worse than others in this descent into conflict and often barbarism.

In Gal Oya we saw in action a logic of positive-sum cooperation, which had the effect of expanding well-being. Even the supply of water, which is often considered a prime example of a fixed-sum, limited resource, was increased due to its more efficient use and to reductions in water losses. Under such circumstances, it is easier for people to be generous toward others, including persons in other ethnic groups. But it was in fact people's willingness to act generously that in this case created an expansion of resources to meet a wider range of human needs. A zero-sum mentality would have preserved inequitable and water-losing practices.

At the microlevel, we saw the advantages of following consensus rules of decision making, rather than a system of majority rule. Electoral competition tends to create zero-sum situations, where winners take all. Transposing this to the macropolitical level is a daunting prospect, but it is worth considering. When gains are planned and achieved through a process of consensus decision making, explicit consideration is given to what others, not just one's self, can get from a particular course of action. This encourages thinking in joint, positive-sum ways that can be overlooked or lost in competitive or adversarial relationships.

It must be kept in mind, however, that the structural and procedural features of the organizational system that evolved (through farmers' ideas—we did not start with any a priori model of farmer organization) were permeated with a set of values, ideological and normative, that stressed the universality of human beings and needs. These values were apparent in the statement "There are no Sinhalese farmers and no Tamil farmers, only farmers," spoken to me by one farmer-representative. I am not sure how many residents of Gal Oya in 1981 believed this statement or believed it strongly. Farmers who had this conviction emerged as the spokespersons for the community through the process of forming farmer organizations.[25] This view became the dominant, legitimate opinion of the farming community in Gal Oya and the operating assumption for all or most people.

If competitive political processes bring forth the most extreme and divisive actors, as often happens, intragroup dynamics lead to antagonistic intergroup relationships (Bush 1994). In a comparison of ethnic relations in Sri Lanka and Malaysia, Horowitz (1991, 7, 17) notes that although there was more interethnic goodwill in the former before violence started in the 1950s, the non-Tamil parties have since then embraced strong Sinhalese chauvinist elements. Macrolevel politics in Sri Lanka, unfortunately, have had quite a different tone and trajectory than politics observed at the microlevel in Gal Oya. The challenge for foreign aid donors, policy makers, and community leaders is to find ways that moderating/reconciling leadership can obtain/maintain social legitimacy and political authority, at both levels.

This will require more sophisticated and explicit attention to ethnic factors than I saw in Sri Lanka. The good results reported here were made possible by the benign intentions of USAID, but that agency was lucky to get the involvement of ARTI and Cornell in project implementation, as both organizations were quite committed to equal ethnic opportunity. Most important was the idealism and heroism within the Gal Oya populace, which became visible once legitimated opportunities were provided for leadership that would bring out "the best" in the community.

In his conclusion, Horowitz observes from his study of ethnic politics generally that "small differences make big differences" (1991, 21). This is one of the main axioms of chaos theory (Gleick 1987). In a world where contingencies are more important than essences, it is hard to come up with deterministic explanations; only probabilistic predictions, not certain ones, can be made. Certain structural and normative relationships can indeed bias interactive processes in anticipated directions, making desired outcomes more likely. While structures and processes that bring forth nonsectarian local leadership cannot assure benign ethnic relations at the national level, they offer suggestions on how to encourage such outcomes, giving emphasis to certain normative orientations. The norms of cooperation and generosity can be promoted more actively than they have been in recent years, when individualism and self-interest have become the values that most governments and donor agencies, and many academics, have exalted. Reinforcing a normative climate in which these "contemporary" values of individualism and self-interest prevail will make more difficult the achievement of productive and harmonious ethnic relations. When donor agencies intervene in another country's internal social, political, and economic relationships, which inevitably happens with any externally assisted project, they have an obligation, similar to that of physicians, to do no harm. This is why considering the linkages between foreign aid and ethnic relations is important even if we cannot come up with firm predictions or infallible prescriptions.

In the Gal Oya case, it is important to point out that the assistance given for establishing farmer organizations was provided on a self-help basis. There was not a pot of resources for groups, ethnic or otherwise, to fight over in a winner-take-all manner. Genuine benefits for all participants could be created, but only by contributions of effort and resources from the intended beneficiaries themselves. This created a more sustainable flow of benefits and also one less likely to stimulate ethnic competition and conflict. Also, the aid was focused on creating institutional capacities rather than giving out concrete, individually allocatable benefits. Collective action is a public good in the sense that it is not divisible and is renewable with continuing inputs from participants, which contrasts with the divisible, nonrenewable benefits often furnished under donor auspices. This is fortuitous because strengthening institutional capacities for self-managed improvements is probably the most beneficial kind of foreign assistance that can be provided.

The question arises whether there was any advantage to undertaking such a form of local institutional development with foreign assistance—whether it might have been accomplished as well, or better, with only national or indigenous resources. One can certainly recognize that the latter option is preferable if possible. But these institutional changes had not occurred over the previous 30 years, so an a priori case can be made that something about external aid was important, if not required, for the transformations that occurred.

The Irrigation Department most probably would not have permitted experimentation with farmer organization for improving system management if this had not been part of a donor-assisted project—though the costs of this "software" component were borne by the Irrigation Department, paid for out of its rupee budget as part of the Sri Lankan government's counterpart contribution.[26] The cost of the farmer organization component was between 5 and 10 percent of the total project cost, and we estimate that it accounted for about 50 percent of the benefits achieved.[27] Indeed, a conservative calculation of benefits and costs after two years of the program indicated already a benefit-cost ratio of about 1.5:1, or a 50 percent rate of return.[28] The Irrigation Department came to appreciate the advantages of farmer organization fairly quickly once the program started, but it would not have initiated this on its own.[29]

The role of myself and other Cornell faculty as advisors was probably also important, though noting this should not detract at all from the importance of the very creative and dedicated inputs of a large number of very capable Sri Lankans. Quite possibly, ARTI's director put forward, at least in the first years, his most talented staff to work on this project because he thought ARTI needed to perform well on a donor-assisted project. ARTI's staff and consultants are generous in the credit they give to their Cornell counterparts, who complemented their strengths in various ways. Foreign consultants are seen as more neutral, as not attached to any particular party or ethnic group. They have generally high status (especially as professors), which can be drawn on in many ways; and they can have access to decision makers at any and all levels and in any and all kinds of institutions. This freedom of access and such respect were generally withheld from our Sri Lankan counterparts. So the presence of foreign colleagues, even if intermittent, helped to gain attention and acceptance for the program.

Such access and opportunities can be misused, and clearly it was important that the effort be binational—indeed multinational, as we included Philippine colleagues in planning the program, drawing on their experience with similar efforts to introduce participatory management in their own country. In assessing what was necessary to achieve the kinds of social dynamics and transformations I have reported for Gal Oya, no either-or formulation can be sustained. As with so many things, a both-and conception is more powerful and correct (Uphoff 1992, 280–303). It seems fairly sure that neither our excellent Sri Lankan colleagues nor the foreign advisors could have established the social infrastructure in Gal Oya by themselves. The complementarity of their knowledge bases and skills plus their solidarity and mutual reinforcement were essential to the success of their joint enterprise.

This implies that foreign aid as an autonomous enterprise is bound to fail or be less successful than expected. However, if national and local actors are supported by external resources, financial and human, to advance developmental causes that they would like to achieve in any case, the prospects that outside aid will contribute to sustainable progress are greatly enhanced. If such actors want to promote ethnically harmonizing outcomes, it is possible that external assistance can have this result, provided that decision makers and personnel for the donor agency are willing to support such an effort and proceed in ethnically sensitive ways. Unfortunately, such a restricted set of conditions is not always satisfied in today's world.

Postscript

In September 1998, I revisited Gal Oya with my Sri Lankan colleague C. M. Wijayaratna. Continuing military action by the LTTE had created a zone controlled by the Tigers, which included an area that had previously been mixed Sinhalese-Tamil. We tried to meet one of the most dedicated farmer-representatives, an elderly gentleman who lives right on the border of this area. We found a voluntary work party cleaning out the channel behind the farmer's home in preparation for the next season, but we were saddened to learn that the group's head had been assassinated by the LTTE just two days before—practically where we were standing—because he had negotiated an agreement with the Tamil farmers who lived downstream, in Tiger territory, so that they could all share water during the coming season. During the previous eight cropping seasons, agricultural activities had been disrupted by the actions of combatants on either side.

One could see in this situation either a defeat of the principle of communal harmony that farmers had upheld for many years or a persistent reaffirmation of interethnic solidarity in the face of violent efforts to keep the communities apart. The benign dynamics reported in this chapter are certainly at a disadvantage when dealing with brute force, yet they are not necessarily repressed. The farmers with whom we spoke were still hopeful that they could cooperate with their downstream neighbors, but they would have to do so less openly.

NOTES

1. During the preceding 150 years of British colonial rule, according to Rogers (1987, 201)—indeed up to 1956—there were no recorded conflicts between Sinhalese and Tamils, even though there were quite a few clashes along other ethnic lines, such as Sinhalese-Muslim and Buddhist-Catholic. Starting after independence in 1948, Sinhalese nationalism was promoted by various intellectuals and politicians and by a militant faction of the Buddhist clergy. The first violent clashes between Sinhalese and Tamils occurred in 1957–58, with some of the worst violence occurring in Ampare District, as described in Vittachi 1958. Conflict erupted in connection with a Sinhalese-majority government's policy that made Sinhala the official national language, replacing English, which had been considered a neutral language between Sinhalese and Tamils, even though more of the latter were proficient in English because of schooling and occupational advantages that Tamils had during the colonial period. The 1981 census distribution of Sri Lankans by ethnic category was 74 percent Sinhalese, 18 percent Tamil, 7 percent Muslim, and 1 percent other. (The latter category included Eurasians, mostly Christian, who were referred to by the term *Burgers,* a term surviving from the

Dutch colonial period, which preceded that of the British.) Religious classifications were 69 percent Buddhist, 15 percent Hindu, 8 percent Muslim, and 8 percent Christian. Just as the Sinhalese population was traditionally considered divided between "low-country" and "up-country" groups, the Tamil population has been roughly divided into four groups, two "older" and two "newer," as discussed in n. 4.

2. The total area encompassed within the Mahaweli irrigation and hydropower project undertaken during the 1970s and 1980s, linking a number of command areas within a large river basin, is larger, but none of the irrigation systems within it is larger than Gal Oya. The Mahaweli project, planned by the government of J. R. Jayewardene and constructed with massive foreign assistance, over $2 billion, may have been motivated partly by ethnic considerations, which donors were oblivious to (Gillies 1992). Priority was reportedly given to settling a disproportionate number of Sinhalese households in mixed Tamil-Sinhalese areas in the northeast of the country to tip ethnic and political balances to favor the Sinhalese population (and the ruling United National Party [UNP]) rather than to developing the areas best suited for agriculture, according to Iriyagolle (1978), who had good enough ties with the UNP to have access to such information. I do not know enough about this foreign-aided scheme to write on it. I was, however, closely involved with implementation of the Gal Oya project from 1980 to 1986 and have followed events there since through friends.

3. A Tamil critique of Sri Lankan government irrigation development policy in the 1980s did not consider the Gal Oya scheme to have been objectionable on ethnic grounds. University Teachers for Human Rights, a nongovernmental organization based at the University of Jaffna, commented that the scheme did not displace existing farmers, as did some of the subsequent Mahaweli resettlements, and that "although bringing in Sinhalese colonists, [the Gal Oya scheme] benefited many Tamil and Muslim farmers who had fields in the area" (University Teachers for Human Rights 1993, 3).

4. When the rehabilitation project started, in 1980, about 80 percent of the gates that controlled water distribution were broken or inoperative (Murray-Rust 1983). For this and related reasons of poor management, the available water was used only half as efficiently as expected by the government's norms for issuing irrigation water (Food and Agriculture Organization 1975). However, these norms were seldom achieved anywhere in the country.

5. This statement refers to the "old" Tamil communities in the north of the country, around Jaffna, and to those living in Colombo, Kandy, and other urban areas in the southwest, who were prominent in the professions and commerce. These groups had come to the island 800 to 1,000 (or more) years earlier, when south Indian kings invaded and occupied the northern part of the country. The "newer" Tamil population, the so-called estate Tamils who worked on tea and rubber estates in the central highlands, were brought by the British from south India as unskilled, low-caste laborers during the nineteenth century to work on plantation crops. Like the Tamil farmers and fishermen living along the eastern coast, who constituted a fourth Tamil group, these "estate Tamils" were often as poor as,

and many were even poorer than, the majority of Sinhalese households in rural and urban areas.

6. One of the motivations for USAID getting involved with the Gal Oya project in the late 1970s was to avoid getting drawn into the huge and likely-to-be-politicized Mahaweli project. The USAID representative with whom I spoke in January 1978 believed that USAID could contribute more to Sri Lanka's agricultural and institutional development by helping improve the performance of existing irrigation systems through better water management "software" than by investing in the "hardware" of expensive and controversial facilities to expand irrigated area. This foresight was commendable, but USAID subsequently succumbed to the Jayewardene government's lobbying to join other donors in financing the Mahaweli project. USAID wisely continued to focus mostly on downstream development, though helping finance and develop System B of the Mahaweli scheme drew it into contentious ethnic issues.

7. "We" is a complicated pronoun in this case. The Agrarian Research and Training Institute (ARTI), which operated under the Ministry of Agriculture, was contracted by the Irrigation Department to implement the socioeconomic components of the Gal Oya project, including the introduction of farmer organizations. The Rural Development Committee at Cornell University, which already had a cooperative agreement with the USAID Office of Rural Development in Washington to help make USAID projects more participatory, was asked to assist ARTI in this endeavor. This action research was expected to produce learning that could be useful on a broader scale. The first-person plural pronoun used in this chapter refers to staff of both ARTI and Cornell.

8. At first, the concept of catalyst seemed too physical and abstract, but it correctly implied that these persons were expected to evoke potentials that already existed in the community, rather than to act as change agents (Lassen 1980). This philosophy was, we think, very important for the success that followed.

9. Although the population breakdown for Ampare District as a whole was 30 percent Sinhalese, 20 percent Tamil, and 50 percent Muslim, about 70 percent of the farmers cultivating in the Left Bank area were Sinhalese and about 30 percent were Tamil. In the rest of the Gal Oya system, where there were relatively more Tamil farmers and also many Muslim farmers, there was somewhat better water supply for reasons of hydrology and policy. (Greater and guaranteed water supply was issued to the Right Bank, where a state-owned sugar refinery was located, to grow enough sugar cane to supply the factory, though this crop needs less water than does paddy rice, the main crop in the Left Bank.)

10. There is a tradition called *shramadana* throughout much of South Asia whereby community labor can be mobilized on a voluntary basis to serve some public purpose (the word means "gift of labor"). But this institution was seldom observed in Gal Oya, because in a settlement scheme with households coming from all over the country, there was not sufficient community solidarity to activate this custom.

11. See Uphoff 1992 (71–72), which book gives details of the Gal Oya project experience from 1980 to 1990. A second edition, published by Intermediate Technology Publications in London, continues the account through 1996.

12. When I talked with them about this some months later, the farmer-representatives expressed their personal anguish about the burning of Tamil shops in Gonagolla town, feeling ashamed by what "a few rogues" had done. They were unable to stop it, but they could and did protect certain individuals. One setback for us resulting from this ethnically motivated violence was the loss to the project of the one senior engineer (Tamil) who had been most supportive of farmer participation. He suffered a back injury when he was beaten badly in the offices of the Irrigation Department in Ampare and had to be transferred out of the area. Our information was that he was attacked by certain Tamils whom he had fired for corrupt practices and who were getting revenge under the cover of ethnic disturbance. (I saw the same thing happen in Nigeria during the summer of 1966, which should keep us mindful that not all violence that occurs during ethnic clashes is ethnically motivated.)

13. This controversial statement is practically common knowledge in Sri Lanka (Obeyesekere 1984, 80–81; Tambiah 1986, 32). In July, after a group of soldiers killed in an LTTE ambush were buried in Colombo, anti-Tamil riots broke out, with lynching of Tamils and destruction of Tamil property. The violence appeared to have been orchestrated by one or more cabinet members and their government-controlled trade union allies. The police and army failed to provide protection to Tamils, and no curfew was decreed to stop the killing and destruction for several days. About 70,000 Tamils were given shelter in emergency camps in Colombo, and many more were protected in private homes, often Sinhalese. On the riots, see Dissanayaka 1984.

14. The politics and factions of Tamil separatist efforts in Sri Lanka are very complex. The most detailed and balanced analysis that I have found is by Gunaratna (1987). There have been more than 30 factions-cum-parties or movements over the years, but the LTTE have remained the most powerful and aggressive. Jayatilleka (1995, 87) says, "By 1990, the LTTE had killed more *Eelam* militants than had the Sri Lankan army." (His book offers an incisive analysis of the LTTE strategy and history as well as an excellent assessment of partisan, class, and ethnic factors fueling the Sri Lankan conflict.) By 1989, practically all of the separatist factions had dissociated themselves from the LTTE, and some were even cooperating with the Sri Lankan government militarily to defeat the Tigers, who had used force to try to eliminate many of their Tamil separatist rivals, even gunning down EPRLF (Eelam People's Revolutionary Liberation Front) leaders at a meeting in India.

At least up until 1986, by my reckoning from newspaper reports, the Tamil separatist groups were responsible for the deaths of more Tamils than of Sinhalese. The Sri Lankan government made a great political error by not counting and publicizing the number of Tamils who were being killed weekly, even daily, in the separatists' struggle to force the whole Tamil community to support their ambitions. Apparently Sinhalese politicians were blinded by their own ethnic prejudices and perceptions, themselves seeing the conflict much as LTTE had defined it, as an ethnic struggle rather than as a blatant attempt by a minority to seize political power and territory.

15. Senthinathan, the Tamil engineer in charge of irrigation in Ampare District,

who had provided both administrative and personal leadership during the Gal Oya project after 1981 to improve irrigation performance and encourage farmer participation, took me to his home in Batticaloa for lunch during the June 1987 visit. He drove me in his old Volkswagen "behind Tiger lines," so to speak, wanting to reciprocate for having been a visitor in my home a year before. My Sri Lankan friends told me that traveling with Senthi would be safe because of the high regard he enjoyed among all communities for his fairness and hard work, and they were right. Sinhalese farmers throughout the Left Bank respected him greatly, and he was able to carry out his department's operations in areas under LTTE de facto control. (Near Batticaloa, I saw a spot where the Tigers had recently ambushed and killed several dozen Tamil guerrillas from a rival separatist organization.)

16. The Left Bank of Gal Oya remained unaffected also by the terrorism of the Janatha Vimukhti Peramuna (JVP; People's Liberation Front) and by the government forces' counterterror, which racked most of the rest of Sri Lanka between 1987 and 1989. The JVP was an extremist Sinhalese movement that nearly toppled the Sri Lankan government in 1971 and regrouped after 1983. To rally support to overthrow the Jayawardene government, it xenophobically opposed the government's pact with India to bring in outside troops to quell Tamil secessionism. The JVP's aims and brutality resembled those of the Khmer Rouge in Cambodia and the Sendero Luminoso in Peru. Its viciousness was reciprocated by government-backed death squads that operated much like those in El Salvador and Guatemala. At the height of this Sinhalese-on-Sinhalese violence in 1989, there were as many as 1,000 deaths a week. When the JVP's leader was captured and most of its politburo eliminated in November of that year, in a shoot-out reminiscent of the way Che Guevara was killed, the JVP faded away. The number of lives lost during this violent three-year confrontation was probably more than 50,000 (*India Today,* March 31, 1991, 87), which is more than the number lost in the LTTE-inspired Sinhalese-Tamil violence. For detailed analyses of the JVP, see Gunaratna 1990 and Jayatilleka 1995, 85–107.

17. I have not discussed here some other difficulties that the program faced—bureaucratic, budgetary, political, and so forth. These are covered in Uphoff 1992.

18. See Wijayaratna and Uphoff 1997. The Gal Oya irrigation system is now jointly managed by farmer-representatives and officials, with the project management committee having a farmer majority and a farmer chairman. The farmer organizations have in the past decade developed cash reserves, assets, and business worth about $250,000 from their collection of fees, carrying out of contracts, and so forth, and they are able to undertake their own employment and income-generating projects. In the dry season of 1997, the water supply in the reservoir was at a 15-year low. After being told that they could not cultivate more than one-quarter of the Left Bank and that they should not grow rice because it required more water than other crops, the farmer organizations took it on themselves to distribute the scarce supply equitably over the whole area. Sinhalese farmers could easily have kept all of the water for themselves and left Tamils without any. But through careful management of the water supply, almost the entire Left Bank area was planted and there was a better than average harvest of rice (Uphoff and Wijayaratna 2000).

19. Though we valued and supported the function of leadership, our program explicitly decided not to encourage "leaders." We deliberately avoided using the term commonly employed by officials and others, *farmer-leaders (govi naike),* in favor of the designation *farmer-representatives (govi niyojete),* because the latter term connotes greater accountability to the farming community. Farmers understood and approved of this difference, though some of the self-styled "leaders" opposed our efforts, at least initially. Eventually *farmer-representatives* became the designation used throughout Sri Lankan irrigation schemes, including the Mahaweli systems.

20. See Uphoff 1992, 199, for an analogy that compares more and less desirable kinds of local leaders, respectively, to "rice plants" and "weeds," a metaphor that is particularly cogent in Sri Lanka but that can be meaningful elsewhere as well.

21. One, known as Kalumahattea, was "Mr. Big" in the Left Bank, controlling 40 acres when the average size for a farm holding was less than 2 acres. He had been president of the Village Council, chairman of the Cooperative Society, and campaign manager for the former member of Parliament, and he was the SLFP (Sri Lanka Freedom Party) party organizer in the area. After several months of trying to thwart and undermine the new farmer organizations failed, he was "converted" to the new system, stating publicly that "politics is cancer for water management." He later turned against the organizations and then returned to the fold. Another important politician-farmer who tried to block the organizations played a similar role, publicly apologizing after four months for his initial opposition. (He said jocularly that he had misunderstood the program, thinking that the organizers were just city boys come to watch the village girls bathing in the canals.) He was alternatively a stalwart and a foe of the democratically controlled organizations. This is noted to indicate that the public roles people play are situationally influenced, not just reflections of people's own values and ambitions.

22. Communities in Northern Ireland have continued to bring forward some courageous antisectarian leadership despite the personal hazards and costs and despite the absence of any cadre like our organizers (Bush 1994).

23. Such behavior is not unique to Sri Lanka. White and Runge (1994, 1995) have documented and analyzed watershed management behavior in Haiti, a country with even less reputation for civility and civic cooperation than Gal Oya had, where persons living outside watersheds nevertheless contributed considerable unpaid labor to constructing checkdams to stop soil erosion.

24. A paper for the Society for the Advancement of Socio-Economics (Uphoff 1994) lays out the basic concepts and principles I would suggest for carrying through such an analysis. It received the SASE Founder's Prize as the best paper at the society's 1994 international meeting in Paris.

25. Our organizing strategy explicitly reversed the usual approach taken by government agencies (and nongovernmental organizations) in the past. We decided to work first and organize second, letting the farmer groups proceed for 3, 6, 9, and even 12 months on an informal, ad hoc basis. Only when a group of farmers felt the need for more formal organization and representation did they proceed to select a farmer-representative. This could be characterized as a demand-induced rather

than a supply-side approach to forming local organization. The representatives chosen this way were often quite different ones than would have been elected at the outset. The persons who had distinguished themselves by showing public-serving leadership when there was no monetary reward or political power attached were the ones usually chosen to become the groups' representatives. If we had started with formal organization and elections, the officers would probably have been the wealthier and politically better-connected members, who were already well known and whom others were reluctant to challenge. With selection of representatives coming after a period of informal work, persons with leadership potential but no past prominence could be and were chosen, based on their performance and merit.

26. The cost of the Cornell consultants was paid for by USAID out of its dollar funds, first under a cooperative agreement with its Office of Rural Development in Washington and then from mission (project) funds. The rationale was that this experimentation was intended to have wider benefits than just Gal Oya or Sri Lanka if methods for promoting participatory development could be demonstrated and refined. This externality was indeed achieved, but USAID has shown almost zero interest since 1985 in learning from Gal Oya. This reflects the lack of institutional memory in a large bureaucracy with continuing personnel turnover and with the propensity to "reinvent wheels." USAID is once again, after the Reagan-Bush years, getting enthused about participatory development, but it has made no attempt to assess or build on the theoretical and practical advances achieved in Gal Oya under its auspices.

27. This has been confirmed by the quantitative analysis by Amarasinghe, Sakthivadivel, and Murray-Rust (1998).

28. A calculation in the Philippines of the return to such investment in "software" for participatory irrigation management found a similar rate of return, around 50 percent (de los Reyes and Jopillo 1986). Interestingly and unfortunately, a World Bank team designing a similar project for four major irrigation schemes in the north of Sri Lanka declined to include a farmer organization component similar to that in Gal Oya, considering this as "gold-plating" the project. Ironically, several years later, that project took four of our best institutional organizers to try to retrofit farmer organizations into those schemes. A USAID external evaluation team calculated an overall rate of return for the Gal Oya project of 47 percent (International Science and Technology Institute 1985), surely too high. A more conservative calculation by ARTI and Cornell put this figure somewhere between 16 and 24 percent, while a postproject analysis for the International Irrigation Management Institute (Aluwihare and Kikuchi 1991) put the rate of return at 14 to 24 percent. Thus, the project performed quite respectably in purely economic terms, apart from any contribution to ethnic harmony, with both kinds of benefit due, I would argue, mostly to the investment in participatory organizations.

29. The director of irrigation in the early 1980s, Mr. A. J. P. Ponrajah, was initially adamant that the Irrigation Department did not need farmer organizations, and he agreed (after the project had already begun and the organizers had been recruited) to give the program a two-year trial in a meeting with the USAID proj-

ect manager, Ken Lyvers, and myself in January 1981. His successor, K. D. P. Perera, told a seminar at the International Irrigation Management Institute in 1987 that, "frankly speaking," the program of farmer participation would not have been introduced without the USAID project. He had been senior deputy director for design and construction during the early 1980s and knew the thinking of the Irrigation Department at its highest levels. He said the same thing at a workshop of the Irrigation Management Division in 1989, which I also attended. Unfortunately there are no transcripts of either meeting.

REFERENCES

Amarasinghe, Upali, R. Sakthivadivel, and Hammond Murray-Rust. 1998. *Impact Assessment of the Rehabilitation Intervention in the Gal Oya Left Bank.* Research Report 18. Colombo: International Irrigation Management Institute.

Aluwihare, P. B., and Masao Kikuchi. 1991. *Irrigation Investment Trends in Sri Lanka: New Construction and Beyond.* Colombo: International Irrigation Management Institute.

Bush, Kenneth. 1994. "The Intra-group Dimensions of Ethnic Conflict in Sri Lanka and Northern Ireland." Ph.D. diss., Cornell University.

Cowan, George A., David Pines, and David Meltzer, eds. 1994. *Complexity: Metaphors, Models, and Reality.* Reading, MA: Addison-Wesley.

de los Reyes, Romana, and Sylvia Maria Jopillo. 1986. *An Evaluation of the Philippine Participatory Communal Irrigation Program.* Quezon City: Institute of Philippine Culture, Ateneo de Manila.

Dissanayaka, T. D. S. A. 1984. *The Agony of Sri Lanka: An In-Depth Account of the Racial Riots in 1983.* Colombo: Swastika.

Food and Agriculture Organization. 1975. *Water Management for Irrigated Agriculture (Gal Oya Irrigation Scheme), Sri Lanka: Project Findings and Recommendations.* Rome: Food and Agriculture Organization.

Gillies, David. 1992. Principled Intervention: Canadian Aid, Human Rights, and the Sri Lankan Conflict. In *Aid as Peacemaker: Canadian Development Assistance and Third World Conflict,* ed. Robert Miller, 51–70. Ottawa: Carleton University Press.

Gleick, James. 1987. *Chaos: Making a New Science.* New York: Viking.

Government of Ceylon. 1970. *Report of the Gal Oya Project Evaluation Committee.* Sessional Paper I-70. Colombo: Government Printer.

Gunaratna, Rohan. 1987. *War and Peace in Sri Lanka.* Colombo: Institute of Fundamental Studies.

———. 1990. *Sri Lanka—a Lost Revolution? The Inside Story of the JVP.* Colombo: Institute of Fundamental Studies.

Horowitz, Donald. 1991. *Incentives and Behavior in the Ethnic Politics of Sri Lanka and Malaysia.* Working Papers in Asian/Pacific Studies. Durham, NC: Duke University.

International Science and Technology Institute. 1985. *Final Evaluation of Sri Lanka Water Management Project (No. 383–0057)*. Washington: International Science and Technology Institute.

Iriyagolle, Gamini. 1978. *The Truth about Mahaweli*. Colombo: private publication.

———. 1985. *Tamil Claims to Land: Fact and Fiction*. Colombo: Institute of Public Affairs.

Jayatilleka, Dayan. 1995. *Sri Lanka: The Travails of a Democracy—Unfinished War and Protracted Crisis*. New Delhi: Vikas, with International Centre for Ethnic Studies.

Korten, Frances F. 1982. *Building National Capacity to Develop Water Users' Associations: Experience from the Philippines*. Staff Working Paper 528. Washington: World Bank.

Korten, Frances F., and Robert Y. Siy, Jr., eds. 1988. *Transforming a Bureaucracy: The Experience of the Philippine National Irrigation Administration*. West Hartford, CT: Kumarian.

Lassen, Cheryl. 1980. *Reaching the Assetless Poor: Projects and Strategies for Their Self-Reliant Development*. Ithaca: Rural Development Committee, Cornell University.

Murray-Rust, D. Hammond. 1983. "Irrigation and Water Management in Sri Lanka: An Evaluation of Technical and Policy Factors Affecting Operation of the Main Channel System." Ph.D. diss., Cornell University.

Murray-Rust, D. Hammond, and Mick Moore. 1984. *Formal and Informal Water Management Systems: Cultivation Meeting and Water Delivery in Two Sri Lankan Irrigation Systems*. Cornell Studies in Irrigation, no. 2. Ithaca: Irrigation Studies Group, Cornell University.

Obeyesekere, Gananath. 1984. "The Origins and Institutionalization of Political Violence." In *Sri Lanka in Crisis and Change*, ed. J. Manor, 153–74. New York: St. Martin's.

Rogers, John D. 1987. *Crime, Justice, and Society in Colonial Sri Lanka*. London: School of Oriental and African Studies, University of London.

Tambiah, S. J. 1986. *Sri Lanka: Ethnic Fratricide and the Dismantling of Democracy*. Chicago: University of Chicago Press.

University Teachers for Human Rights. 1993. "From Manal Aru to Weli Oya and the Spirit of July 1983." Special Report 5. University Teachers for Human Rights, University of Jaffna. Mimeographed.

Uphoff, Norman. 1992. *Learning from Gal Oya: Possibilities for Participatory Development and Post-Newtonian Social Science*. Ithaca: Cornell University Press.

———. 1994. "The Rehabilitation of Altruism and Cooperation: A Post-Newtonian Paradigm for Positive-Sum Behavior." Paper presented at the Sixth International Meeting of the Society for the Advancement of Socio-Economics, Paris, July 13–17.

Uphoff, Norman, and C. M. Wijayaratna. 2000. "Demonstrated Benefits from Social Capital: The Productivity of Farmer Organizations in Sri Lanka." *World Development 28*, no. 11.

Vittachi, Tarzi. 1958. *Emergency '58: The Story of the Ceylon Racial Riots.* London: Andre Deutsch.

Waldrop, M. Mitchell. 1992. *Complexity: The Emerging Science at the Edge of Order and Chaos.* New York: Simon and Schuster.

White, T. Anderson, and C. Ford Runge. 1994. "Collective Property and Collective Action: Lessons from Cooperative Watershed Management in Haiti." *Economic Development and Cultural Change* 43, no. 1:1–41.

———. 1995. "The Emergence and Evolution of Collective Action: Lessons from Watershed Management in Haiti." *World Development* 23, no. 10.

Wijayaratna, C. M., and Norman Uphoff. 1997. "Farmer Organizations in Gal Oya: Improving Irrigation Management in Sri Lanka." In *Reasons for Hope: Instructive Experiences in Rural Development,* ed. Norman Uphoff, Milton J. Esman, and Anirudh Krishna, 166–83. West Hartford, CT: Kumarian.

CHAPTER 6

Making Ethnic Conflict: The Civil War in Sri Lanka

Ronald J. Herring

The Puzzle: Descent into Civil War

Sri Lanka's internal strife has been among the most enduring, lethal, and puzzling of current domestic conflicts. This outcome is puzzling because of the absence of sustained ethnic conflict prior to the late 1970s and the remarkable developmental record of Sri Lanka as a model for provision of "basic human needs" within the context of a well-institutionalized democratic political system that allowed significant opportunities for participation and mediation. Mick Moore (1990, 347) reflects a widely shared view when he claims that among poor countries, Costa Rica and Sri Lanka "could once have been seen as staging posts on the road to a social democratic utopia."

This chapter concentrates on the period before and immediately after the pogroms against the minority Tamil community in 1983. In the July riots, at least 2,000 people were killed, and 18,000 homes and 5,000 shops were destroyed; property damage was estimated to be 300 million dollars.[1] With the pogroms, conflict escalated into a form we may usefully call ethnic, while recognizing the very real danger of essentializing ethnicity.[2] Many on both sides abhorred the political projects of those who employed appeals to ethnicity or race as grounds for mobilization and victimization. There were islands of peace and cooperation even in strife-torn areas, as Norman Uphoff's contribution to this volume illustrates. As in most "ethnic" conflicts, the stakes were multidimensional: they included material advantage, territoriality, cultural validation, and political power. Nevertheless, the conflagration did bring into play reciprocal stereotypes and political language of the sort we commonly associate with ethnicity.

The resultant structure of conflict engaged many more ordinary people, reaching beyond organized militants and state operatives. Prior to this phase, a radical youth movement of the Tamil minority in the Tamil-majority Jaffna area struggled against the organs of the state and Tamil collaborators—officials and political leaders—in pursuit of a Tamil homeland *(Eelam)*. This familiar conflict among the state, militants, and political moderates was ethnic only in the sense that the protagonists were of one minority and based their grievances largely on that status; their targets were of mixed ethnicity. The state in turn had shown itself willing to suppress militant opponents whatever their ethnicity, as illustrated in the violent repression of the 1971 insurgency of armed Sinhalese youth. Escalation from 1983 eventually reached a level of conflict approaching civil war, with international ramifications. Indian troops were introduced in 1987 as a peacekeeping force, though in the event they were more at war than guarding peace. Despite the eventual exit of the Indian army and numerous peace initiatives, a state of intermittent terror and armed conflict still characterizes Sri Lanka as this book goes to press, seventeen years after the pogroms.

It is neither possible nor desirable to recount here the history of ethnic relations in Sri Lanka (or its predecessor, Ceylon). Nevertheless, there is history; all explanations rooted in the recent past are conditioned by a more distant past. The historical development of collective identities under colonialism involved some familiar stereotyping of the minorities as economically privileged and complementary narratives of the majority as a victim of foreign and minority control of the economy. Sinhala nationalism grew up with a recognizable Sinhala ethnic identity. This conflation of dominant ethnicity and nation is linguistically embedded; *jatiya* means literally "group" or "kind" in Sinhala, but in ordinary use it refers to both the majority ethnic group and nation or nationality.[3] Despite the organization of collective identities and narratives of privilege and victimization, no organized conflict between Sinhala and Tamils emerged in the movement against colonial rule.

Formation after independence of a Federal Party by Tamil politicians in 1952 indicated by its very name early concern among minority Tamils for devolution in opposition to centralization. Yet there was no Tamil community politically; some Tamil politicians indeed had acquiesced in the disenfranchisement of Tamil plantation workers in 1948—class trumped ethnicity. Serious tensions between Sinhalese and Tamils first became manifest in response to linguistic policy following the 1956 elections, in which "Sinhala Only" was a major campaign plank of the winning party (Wriggins 1960; Vittachi 1958). This language strategy emerged not as an attack by the majority on the minority but as an electoral strategy for differentiating two political formations, both headed by elite Sinhala families. The Sri Lanka Freedom Party used Buddhist imagery and promotion of Sinhala language to construct a claim to rule that separated it from the highly Westernized United National Party (UNP). Tensions around the status of Tamil as a language simmered for decades, fueled by constitutional changes that were felt to have demoted Tamil further (Sri Lanka 1980d, 1–57). Episodes of conflict occurred in 1956, 1958, 1961, and 1977. Yet the tensions and stereotypes[4] that are characteristic of plural societies hardened and escalated after 1983 into something more akin to civil war than ethnic competition.

It is plausible to search for sources of this escalation in external development flows for two reasons. First, the link between mass protest and structural adjustment cross-nationally is strong (Walton and Ragin 1990); resultant insecurity and deprivation so frequently produce mass protest that the term *IMF riot* (in reference to the International Monetary Fund) appeared in the literature. The disruptive effects of externally funded economic change seem especially appropriate for investigation in Sri Lanka because the flows were so large relative to the size of the domestic economy and because the open economy was so radical a departure from previous national policy (Herring 1987). Moreover, ethnic scapegoating in times of economic trouble is not uncommon; in Sri Lanka, economic crisis in the 1930s resulted in blaming of foreign workers, specifically Malayalis (Jayawardene 1984, 133), though not in Sinhala-Tamil conflict. Second, there is timing. Contrary to some academic and much indigenous political discourse, Sinhala-Tamil conflict is neither primordial nor evident in the society's history. Ethnic peace and collaboration prevailed for centuries, broken briefly after the 1956 elections produced a victory for political forces promoting Sinhala as the official language. The emergence of significant organized conflict escalated incrementally after a regime promoting an open economy reliant on foreign aid won the elections of 1977 with strong support of the international development community.

Though there exists a pattern of mass turmoil in the wake of structural adjustment, Sri Lanka presents a dual anomaly. First, mass anger at deprivation from reduction of entitlements emerged early in comparative perspective. Decades before the emergence of food-related social upheavals connected to the worldwide spate of liberalization that began in the late 1970s, protests against food price increases in Ceylon were organized through a powerful general strike that toppled the government in 1953 (Herring 1994). Second, retrenchment of the welfare state after the elections of 1977 produced unexpected—perhaps even anomalous—quiescence in terms of political protest. Subsequently, political decay and civil turmoil reached unprecedented levels (Manor 1984), but not in the form of adjustment-driven protest so common elsewhere (Walton and Seddon 1994).

This chapter explores the ways in which civil war in Sri Lanka cannot be properly understood without attention to external developmental flows.

The position is complex. First, liberalization itself (in the classic sense of increasing allocative authority of markets and reducing political shelter from market forces) seems to have contributed to hostilities by providing both new anger and new targets of envy—a niche for scapegoating. But the effect was muted because the sticks often deployed to enforce compliance were mildly used. Second, the carrots themselves—relatively large flows in per capita terms and especially in relation to size of the economy—exacerbated ethnic tensions through their effects on patronage and ethnic territoriality. These factors are primarily economic. A second set of more indirect effects is political: the regime could not have survived so long without the carrots provided by international actors. Accompanying changes in regime form and practice closed off other avenues of redress, just as potential solutions, such as decentralization of the political system, became less tenable as envisioned futures. The liberalizing regime, sustained to an anomalous extent by international financial support, dominated a specifically political process that fueled escalation of ethnic conflict. Donors repeatedly expressed concern about human rights abuses but were unable to act in concert, continuing instead to support the regime at critical junctures.

Of special importance to this analysis is an underlying assumption of path dependency. There are critical junctures and identifiable tipping points in which relatively small changes alter the course of history. The numbers involved in the events immediately before and during the pogroms of 1983 were relatively small, yet those events set in train alterations of ethnic perceptions, tactics, and mobilization—with concomitant state responses—that proved irreversible. What might have remained a deadly but limited cat-and-mouse game between the state and militant youth in Jaffna instead engulfed the nation.[5]

"An Explosion of Aid": Sustaining the Open Economy

The public moral economy embedded in Sri Lanka's development strategy was profoundly altered by elections in 1977. Decades of expansion of the functional scope of government in the economy, accelerated by the 1970–77 leftist United Front government (Shastri 1986), resulted in the antithesis of neoliberal policy prescriptions: a tightly regulated, welfarist, and (ineffectually) closed economy (Herring 1987). The elections were largely a referendum on development strategy; champions of a liberalized open economy triumphed decisively (Warnapala 1979).

The elections were also about moral economy in another sense. The victorious UNP promised both prosperity and a *dharmistha* (righteous) society (Kemper 1990; Little 1994, 78ff.). Government intervention had left a legacy of corruption, favoritism, victimization, and decidedly unrighteous behavior; the new regime linked the issues of renewal of public life and social relations to economic advance. Simultaneous valorization of material accumulation and Buddhist culture presumably presaged some contradictions but was a dominant political strategy of President Jayewardene.

International development agencies had long been critical of Sri Lanka's "premature welfarism" (e.g., World Bank 1953). With the global paradigm shift to basic human needs in the early 1970s, however, Sri Lanka somewhat ironically became a positive rather than negative development model in the mid-1970s. The pre-1977 welfare state provided basic human needs at a level anomalous for so poor an economy. In terms of measures that count, such as life expectancy and infant mortality, Sri Lanka achieved levels closer to European social democracies than to subcontinental neighbors and wealthier countries in Latin America.[6] Despite inevitable failings (e.g., Pieris 1982; Marga Institute 1981), public programs contributed to the security and well-being of the poor quite remarkably in comparison with other low-income nations (Isenman 1980; Dreze and Sen 1989, 227–30 and passim).

The critique of Sri Lanka's development path from authoritative agencies abroad was that social consumption slowed investment and growth; protectionism and hostility to foreign capital retarded development. The UNP government that won the 1977 elections essentially agreed; market forces were to play a greater role in allocating resources, and integration with the world economy was to be pursued. The Central Bank termed the new strategy "a sweeping departure from a tightly controlled, inward-looking, welfare-oriented economic strategy to a more liberalized, outward-looking and growth-oriented one" (Central Bank of Ceylon 1978, 2).

This bold strategy contained inherent contradictions. For political reasons, employment creation was a central objective; unemployment of the United Front period—frequently reported as high as 25 percent—had fueled the electoral backlash that brought the UNP to power. Jobs were to be created through encouragement of domestic and foreign capital but more immediately through ambitious public works, such as the Accelerated Mahaweli Development Scheme, a project for bringing new tracts of irrigated land under cultivation while substantially increasing hydroelectric generating capacity (Sri Lanka 1979, 1980c). Massive expansion of public works implied neither laissez-faire doctrine nor state shrinking but did resonate with the established public culture of patronage politics. Moreover, attracting foreign investment necessitated large infrastructural expenditures. The political problem was how to raise resources for public investment and job creation while relieving the economy of public claims and intervention.

This contradiction was met with an explicit strategy of dependence on unprecedented levels of external funds. If capital were to be granted tax incentives to invest and yet infrastructural investment were to be increased when budget deficits were large and chronic, foreign flows were inevitable. Likewise, relaxing import controls could be expected to put pressure on the balance of payments, chronically in deficit. Covering these dual deficits presupposed generating support in the external development establishment.

A sharp devaluation of the rupee in November 1977 was followed by IMF approval for "the comprehensive program of economic reform"; approval concretely meant a standby arrangement of SDR 93 million (*IMF Survey* 6 [1977]: 23). With this endorsement, the finance minister visited groups of investors and officials of aid-giving nations and agencies. In the first full year of the new policies, official loan commitments more than doubled the 1977 level, in marked contrast to the experience of other developing nations after the onset of aid weariness. Net flows from all lenders increased from $48 million in 1977 to $175.9 million in 1979; loans carried a grant element of 64.8 percent (World Bank 1980b, I, 102, 191). Levels of foreign financing reached an annual level almost four times that of the 1970–77 leftist United Front period as a percentage of gross domestic product (GDP). Brian Levy (1989, 449) terms the result "an explosion of aid."

Foreign flows were large relative to the size of the economy and generous in terms of conditions. The finance minister claimed, "due to the confidence placed by the international community in our new economic policies, we have been able to obtain greater volume of foreign aid and foreign assistance *per capita* than perhaps any other third world country." The minister noted that more than a third of the assistance was in the form of outright grants, the balance as long-term loans "at minimal interest." He made direct connection to policy reform explicit: "Without the courageous and imaginative steps we took . . . nothing would have moved, nothing would have happened" (Sri Lanka 1980b, 2). International endorsement of the open economy was both clear and enthusiastic.

International flows facilitated a higher level of imports and, indirectly, exports (since the import component of intermediate goods was over 75 percent), but their effects extended beyond the balance of payments. Domestic capabilities of the government rested on levels of international trade. Taxes on international trade provided an increasing share of revenue after liberalization, reaching a high of 55 percent in 1979, far above the mean for Asian nations. Sri Lanka recorded the lowest ratio of revenue to expenditures in Asia for 1980–82 (IMF 1984, 24, 42). Two rupees were spent for every one raised internally. Without strong international support, current account deficits would have curtailed the level of trade and produced unmanageable fiscal dilemmas for the government. The foreign contribution to financing of the net cash budget deficit in 1976 was 32.5 percent; in 1980, 70.4 percent (Central Bank of Ceylon 1979, table 10.1). The Public Investment Programme of the Ministry of Finance and Planning for 1980–84 projected a strategy in which net external inflows would be greater than domestic sources, constituting 54 percent of total public investment over the five-year period (Sri Lanka 1980c).

Though Sri Lanka was proclaimed an IMF success story because of the relatively high growth rates after 1977, it would be wrong to count the experience as confirmation of the Washington consensus on development policy.[7] To some extent, higher growth rates represented simply the effect of a large influx of external resources into a very small economy, combined with initially favorable terms of trade and the short-term explosion of pent-up demand once restrictions on imports were relaxed. Nevertheless, the acceleration of economic activity in the early years roughly doubled the growth rate of the difficult period of hardship and stagnation preceding policy change (Herring 1987). Fortunes were made. The consumption culture shifted in a dramatic fashion, evident to even casual observation. But the claim for success of IMF conditionality is also strained because the new policy did not conform to neoliberal orthodoxy. Deficit spending increased, driven by an expanded public sector; public control of investable resources increased. Both dynamics were enabled by external official aid. In the first decade of liberalization, the state expanded as fast as the economy.

International acclaim and material support proved to be less unconditional than the government believed. After a 1980 budget deficit amounting to more than 26 percent of GDP, accompanied by a rate of inflation of at least 30 percent, the consortium of donors meeting in Paris in July pressured the government to cut current account and budget deficits and to raise more resources internally. Familiar disputes were repeated in meetings with the Aid Sri Lanka Consortium and the IMF in the summers of 1982 and 1983; belt-tightening was urged, the government cited domestic constraints and blamed external factors, and compromises were made.[8] What stands out is the anomalous leniency of international financial institutions; budget deficits of this magnitude often presage withdrawal of support, certainly from the IMF. As a result of leniency in this case, resort to the level of commercial borrowing that usually follows severe budgetary and current account deficits was avoided, leading to a manageable debt-service burden.[9]

Despite early discussion of Sri Lanka as an adjustment success story and a candidate for newly industrialized country status, the reality was a dependent welfare state operating at somewhat lower levels of coverage. Half the population remained on food stamps. This level of domestic welfarism could not have been maintained without foreign support. In exchange for this extraordinary treatment, the international community was more insistent about some things than others. In both political rhetoric and in practice, the open economy was dominant. The thrust of the new economic policy was more globalization than neoliberal orthodoxy.

State shrinking failed to materialize; expansion characterized more sectors of state activity than contraction. These conditions mitigated popular anger at the state itself. Massive inflows of project assistance probably increased the net rental opportunities of the bureaucracy. Public projects continued to be utilized for patronage and thus retained their political utility despite liberalization. After 1983, the ethnic war made extraordinary fiscal demands; the Ministry of Defense eventually claimed about three times the percentage of expenditures it did in 1978, but it would be wrong to attribute deficit expansion to conflict alone.[10]

Part of this story is familiar, part anomalous. Sri Lanka's experience suggests that international pressures for liberalization are not so monolithic or consistent as they are often portrayed (Girvan 1980; Dell 1984). The regime maintained a working relationship with the IMF despite budget deficits in excess of 10 and even 20 percent of GDP. Domestic political pressures restricted privatization or wholesale destruction of the welfare state. Indeed, the political sensitivity of safety nets was illustrated over time in the prominence of distributive populism in the successful UNP electoral campaigns of 1988 and 1989. Austerity typical of restructuring was moderated by extraordinary external enthusiasm and leniency, yet cuts in basic needs expenditure occurred. Though impossible to prove, it is almost certainly true that the latter would have been politically unsustainable without the former.

Projects, Patronage, and Ethnic Territoriality

Though the government cut some areas of public consumption, public expenditures in the aggregate expanded: political praxis triumphed over economic policy rhetoric. Capital and current transfers to public corporations, as well as revenue derived from the operation of government enterprises, rose steadily in the early years of liberalization (Herring 1987). Much of this expansion was driven by the strategy's reliance on attracting private foreign capital. The finance minister defended his government's ambitious public investment planning by arguing that it was to provide "the infrastructure facilities necessary to support private entrepreneurship" (*Ceylon Daily News* July 28, 1984). Foreign project loans and grants increased the size of the public sector, most significantly in the Accelerated Mahaweli Project in irrigation and power development. Total expenditures on public salaries and wages—one important measure of patronage—increased both in absolute terms and as a share of GDP, reaching 9.9 percent in 1985 (Central Bank of Ceylon 1985, table 1.41). While the share of public investment more than doubled as a percentage of GDP in the 1978–82 period compared to 1970–77 averages, international assistance (grants, loans) almost quadrupled as a percentage of GDP (IMF 1984, 42, 24).

Directing public expenditures away from consumption in favor of investment was largely successful. Public capital expenditures increased as a percentage of total public expenditure (Central Bank of Ceylon 1982, 250); gross domestic investment increased from an annual average share of GDP of 16 percent for the 1970–77 period to an annual average of 27.7 percent for the 1978–83 period.

Increased public investment increased budget deficits, which were perennial bones of contention between the government and donors. In 1979 a National Housing Development Authority was established to construct 100,000 living units (later expanded to a target of 1,000,000) either directly or through aided self-help programs. An Electoral Housing Program undertook direct construction of 155 houses per electorate. The World Bank and IMF opposed both the diversion of investment funds from capital formation and the interest subsidies to aided home builders. Nevertheless, the plan was attractive to USAID, which contributed heavily. Such projects are tailor-made for servicing regime patronage interests. Not only can significant boons be selectively allocated, but ruling politicians gain attractive opportunities for skimming operations.[11] James Brow (1990, 131 and passim) illustrates how state patronage in the form of new houses was used to both celebrate Sinhala nationalism—the "splendid civilization of the Anuradhapura kingdom"—and simultaneously reward local supporters of the UNP (which caused considerable anger in the village).

Patronage inevitably runs these risks; there will always be some feeling that others are getting more than their fair share. To the extent that the UNP as a political machine benefited primarily Sinhala supporters, large increases in patronage flows contributed to the sense that the government was not a national but an ethnic champion. Certainly the lion's share of boons appeared in Sinhala areas. For the year before the Colombo pogroms, for example, per capita capital expenditure in Jaffna was less than half the national average; foreign aid utilization for the years 1977–82 in Jaffna was zero (Committee for Rational Development 1984, 15). There was good reason for the Tamil community to doubt that their options and prospects would improve over time. Mick Moore (1990, 357) goes so far as to argue that the contradictions between World Bank principles of liberalization and the expansion of the public sector in Sri Lanka signaled that external development assistance had changed from support for policies to support for the "government per se." He concludes: "I suspect that the UNP has undermined the democratic political system and perpetuated its own rule partly from the elemental desire to remain in clover" (370–71).

Among the projects that contributed to the Tamil sense of subnational victimization, the Accelerated Mahaweli Project in irrigation and power development figures most prominently. In some ways it was the defining symbolic project of the Jayewardene regime. Gillies (1992, 54) wrote, "Inspired by engineering feats of an ancient kingdom and hailed as the world's largest foreign aid project, the Mahaweli scheme was to be a symbol of progress and national identity." The massive flow of funds into Mahaweli can usefully be viewed as carrots for policy change; certainly the government played symbolically on its success in attracting aid projects as evidence of international support for its economic philosophy and performance. The enormous project provided significant opportunities for both domestic and international patronage—ranging from lucrative public works contracts to subsidized irrigated land for farmers, as well as contracts for consulting, construction, and engineering firms of rich nations. Mahaweli displaced many smaller-scale projects and consumed a disproportionate share of public investment. Of the project aid committed between 1979 and 1981, 45 percent was earmarked for Mahaweli, and 49 percent of all resources targeted for public investment between 1982 and 1984 were planned for the project (Levy 1989, table 3).

The Mahaweli scheme was celebrated as a new initiative, but colonization schemes in the dry zone of Sri Lanka had a long history. Beginning in 1935, with large subsidies, colonial policy supported export of peasants from the decaying overcrowded Sinhalese areas of the island (where agrarian discontent was concentrated) to public lands.[12] The Mahaweli project continued that historical process with additional objectives of power and water development. The project assumed such symbolic importance in the UNP's development plans that a ministry was devoted to it.

The template for Mahaweli was itself the product of foreign assistance. The original scheme was drawn up by a joint U.S.-Sri Lankan team; the master plan was prepared by the United Nations Development Program/Food and Agriculture Organization in 1968 as a 30-year undertaking. In 1977 the UNP government began to publicize its plans to accelerate the program of 30 years into a 6-year period. This acceleration could not have been contemplated realistically without significant external aid.

In November 1977, after the UNP had been in power just a few months, a government delegation visited Washington, D.C., to request support for Mahaweli. The president of the World Bank, Robert McNamara, recited cautions about the dangers of so massive a project on an accelerated track. But as the process unfolded, the bank ended up following the bilateral donors, who were eager to commit to specific dam projects (Levy 1989, 452). The British, German, and Canadian governments signed on quickly; Germany made a commitment of $230 million, the largest ever for them at the time. The Netherlands and Sweden were supportive, as were the Japanese. The World Bank complained that governments were announcing commitment levels even before feasibility studies had been done.[13] Richer nations seemed to be in competition with each other to find high-visibility projects in Sri Lanka.

There are three elements in the argument that the Mahaweli project exacerbated ethnic tensions. First, the project symbolically and demographically exacerbated ethnic territoriality. The interethnic Committee for Rational Development (1984, 57–59) noted that Tamils believed that colonization schemes, especially in the East, had in the past changed the ethnic composition of areas in which Tamils were a majority. Patrick Peebles' (1990) data support this conclusion. Peebles finds that the percentage of Sinhalese in affected areas of the eastern dry zone increased from just over 19 percent in 1946 (two years before independence) to over 83 percent in 1976. Moreover, tensions surrounding large-scale encroachments on the Left Bank of Maduru Oya, in Batticaloa District, primarily by Sinhalese, presaged predictable conflict over settlement policy. The Committee for Rational Development concluded (1984, 60): "The country cannot afford the constant communal conflict which will result from a large influx of *ethnically motivated* colonists and settlers who come to the area with a confrontational attitude." They proposed settling the landless of a district first, before importing settlers.

As early as 1976, in the Vaddukodai Resolution, Tamils had charged that "a system of planned and state-aided colonization" was "calculated to make the Tamils a minority in their own homeland" (Little 1994, 83). The very notion of historic Tamil terrain was officially rejected; in the government's view, the placement of irrigation and power projects reflected technical and economic considerations and took place largely in areas where the Tamils did not want to settle anyway. Symbolically, colonization programs reinforced the idea of nation, specifically hinting at the resurrection of the glorious hydraulic civilization of the golden age of the Sinhalese Buddhist kings, an age prior to and destroyed by medieval Tamil invasions in the official narrative. From a Sinhala perspective, recolonization should by right benefit the community that historically built the hydraulic civilization and that was sometimes displaced by dam building. The very idea of a Tamil homeland—or Eelam, in its stronger incarnation—was disputed by a government focused on the economic development of the whole nation and symbolically interested in a narrative of ancient glory of irrigated kingdoms. The government's position on Mahaweli was that development in Tamil areas would be an "integrative force" and that project selection was based on "economic considerations" premised on the need to "increase as rapidly as possible Sri Lanka's power generating capacity"[14]—capacity that was seen as crucial for attracting foreign investment and stimulating domestic capital. Whatever the symbolic impact, accelerated colonization threatened to alter demographics in a way that reduced the possibility of political compromise. Disproportionate Sinhalese benefits "intensified the perception among the Tamils that they were being inexorably marginalized even within their own areas" (Shastri 1990, 64).

Demographic dilution of Tamil-majority areas would render any devolution of powers as a solution to ethnic conflict less effective. Indeed, foreign-funded settlement schemes became a flash point of disagreement between Tamil separatists and the government. Just as Tamils demanded devolution of authority over colonization to the province level, the government continued to use the phrase "national settlement schemes" and insisted on a "national ethnic ratio" (rather than a local one) for determining beneficiaries (Peebles 1990, 46). This decision caused considerable dispute in Canadian aid agencies. A senior Canadian diplomat said that the formula "heightened the sensitivity of the Oya project well beyond the local impact." Canada was put in an awkward position: autonomy of nation-states on sensitive issues, such as land resettlement, was a norm of aid, but the diplomat admitted, "we weren't very happy about our money going into something that was going to cause more dissension, and, in fact, to a scheme you could argue simply wasn't fair" (Gillies 1992, 56–57).

The timing of the decision to use a national ethnic ratio for settlement was crucial. President Jayewardene announced the decision just before the All-Party Conference looking for a way to deal with the Tamil national question. The decision put into doubt the good faith of the government going into these critical talks (Gillies 1992, 56). Decentralization of political authority, the compromise position short of creation of a Tamil state of Eelam as demanded by Tamil militants, looked less feasible if the central government could reduce Tamil proportions in areas of Tamil majority in the name of national development.

In symbolic and material terms, Mahaweli loomed large in the UNP regime's vision of Sri Lanka's future. It dwarfed and starved other projects and ultimately proved unsustainable on the ambitious scale of the accelerated scheme. One possible conclusion from Mahaweli is that among projects, small is beautiful (Schumacher 1975), or at least large is not. Mahatma Gandhi distrusted in principle anything large. Large projects have the potential for doing great harm, both directly and indirectly. Of identified alternatives to Mahaweli, all projects had an estimated rate of return higher than the 11 percent projected for Mahaweli, and five of the nine had more than double the expected return. These projects included tank irrigation modernization, village irrigation rehabilitation, extension and research, and other distributable projects.[15] As Mahaweli became the lead project, other projects were scaled back when fiscal constraints forced retrenchment. Such a prestige project attracts both donors and the recipient state, for different reasons, and crowds out other aid projects, which are much more divisible, are spatially separable, and lack the ethnic arousal component of reestablishing the glory of Sinahla kings on Tamil territory.

Recognition of the implications of Mahaweli for ethnic relations was not entirely absent, but it did not stop the aid business from continuing as usual at critical junctures. The U.S. ambassador to Sri Lanka in the early period of Mahaweli, Howard Wriggins, was aware of the ethnopolitical tensions but felt that the case for national development—in terms of power, food production, and irrigation—seemed overwhelming. Wriggins was concerned that the North Central feeder canal that was to water Tamil areas was canceled early on in the project's history—officially on technical grounds. Whatever the technical grounds, budget deficits forced some scaling back of early ambitions for the project; but canceling the canal undermined the government's claim to speak for inclusive national development. Though Ambassador Wriggins was continually reassured by the government of plans to allocate sufficient lands to Tamils in new projects, he "never saw published reports that might have reassured the Tamils."[16]

After failing in its effort to convince the government to avoid ethnically provocative policies, Canada eventually withdrew its support for Mahaweli, but only after much of the damage had been done. Robert Gillies investigated the politically contested positions within the Canadian government agencies that produced this "principled decision," interviewing the participants. The government of Sri Lanka was reluctant to agree to compromises proposed by Canada. Long arguments ensued over two years. One diplomat said in retrospect that the Sri Lankan government's position was "you sign the cheques, fella, let us deliver the goods" (Gillies 1992, 57). Canadian concerns included human rights and were influenced by Tamil groups in Canada arguing for a hard-line stance in Sri Lanka. But the Canadian position was compromised by disagreement within ministries. Eternal Affairs wanted to pull out, scale down, and redirect aid to southeast Asia, but the Canadian International Development Agency

(CIDA) resisted. According to Gillies (1992, 58), "There was also visible resentment at CIDA about the intrusion of political issues into the technical problems of aid delivery." CIDA's antipathy to using aid as a political lever was not innocent of domestic politics of aid: CIDA had relationships with politically powerful Canadian firms contracted to work on Mahaweli. Moreover, there were the sunk costs; Canada was already in the project for 100 million dollars, which would be wasted if the project did not go ahead.[17]

But more than bureaucratic politics and commercial interests are involved in aid inertia. Like that of the Sri Lankan government, the donors' discourse was holistic: the nation-state is the unit of analysis. The nation has needs, rice self-sufficiency, electric power, a higher GDP. Imagining this economic abstraction as object of development policy masks internal differentiation experienced by real people on the ground but is central to conventional development discourse.

Constructing Winners and Losers: Local Knowledge

Social scientists have great difficulty in sorting winners and losers in rapid economic change by ethnicity unless the economy is clearly stratified by ethnic status. Nevertheless, publics do regularly construct ethnic economic morphologies. Minorities are often attributed disproportionate wealth, powers, and opportunity. Commercial groups, acting as middlemen who pass on normatively unacceptable market judgments, are especially susceptible. If necessities are too expensive, someone must be to blame.

The Sri Lankan economy is not neatly patterned by ethnicity, as far as good social scientists can tell. The data are simply not collected in ways that facilitate rigorous analysis. But myths of occupational privilege and deprivation have been hotly debated in the context of reinterpretations of history; intellectuals who attempted demystification of national myths and popular stereotypes were bitterly attacked by ethnic chauvinists. Attacks on "Western social science," particularly that funded from abroad, and the very notion of objectivity, appeared in heated newspaper debates. Social scientists working at demystification were dismissed as self-interested: the argument was that "little intellectuals *(cula ugatun)* were selling the country to foreigners for dollars" (cited in Tennekoon 1990, 212).

Objectively, economic position did not track ethnicity closely, with the exception of plantation laborers in the tea sector, who are disproportionately Tamil. "Indian" Tamils were, however, not significant politically in the ethnic escalation. Tamils in the rest of the country are occupationally dispersed. Disproportionate Tamil presence in the professions and civil service had long been a Sinhalese complaint and the source of reverse discrimination in favor of Sinhalese in educational policy. Tamil farmers of the north are especially concentrated in import-substituting agriculture, which did well under the protectionist United Front regime and was hurt by liberalization. But there is no neat ethnic division of labor.

Perceptions of ethnic winners and losers, however, have been constructed and deployed politically. These perceptions are more politically important than any set of objective indicators, which are little noted and not much believed by anyone other than social scientists.

The interethnic Committee for Rational Development attempted to lay to rest popular ethnic myths in a search for mutual understanding following the pogroms of 1983, but in the process it discovered how deeply they are entrenched, how contradictory are the data, and how little social science is trusted. The committee reported (1984, 15), "there is a perception that the private sector of the economy is dominated by Tamil interests"; the committee went on to dispute this perception but admitted that interlocking directorates and foreign ownership patterns make decisive answers impossible.[18] The committee's report did find some overrepresentation of Tamils at the top of the private sector. Contrary to popular perceptions, the committee argued that Tamils were not overrepresented in public sector jobs and that unemployment among Tamil youth was worse than among Sinhala youth. Likewise, the report contested the myth that bank credit was controlled by Tamil interests.

With the economic expansion of the late 1970s, it was widely believed that the extraordinary real-estate boom disproportionately benefited Tamils. One often heard the comment "Eighty percent of the real estate of Colombo is owned by Tamils." I can find no confirmation of or source for this figure, yet it was widely repeated. More generally, there was a perception that the dramatic expansion of international trade disproportionately benefited Tamils because of their superior connections to the international economy, both through Tamil compatriots in India and through the extensive Tamil diaspora in the West. The president of the Sri Lanka Small Industrialists Association said in an interview with *Divayina* (September 11, 1983), "As a society which allocates first place to commerce evolved, commercial power got alienated from the majority Sinahla and went to the minority national groups" (quoted in Gunasinghe 1984d, 211). Reciprocally, dislocation in import-substituting manufacturing from liberalization, particularly in weaving, was believed to fall most heavily on Sinhalese workers.

The origins of ethnic insurgency, however, were in the Tamil areas around Jaffna, originating in youth radicalism. Prospects for young Tamils there had been deteriorating for decades. The perception that

Tamils were relatively privileged in access to higher education—and thus to lucrative professions—prompted populist affirmative action for Sinhalese. The effects can be seen in terms of university admissions: in 1945, 38.9 percent of Tamil applicants were successful; by 1973–74, only 9.7 percent were successful. Tamils constituted about 40 percent of admissions to the much-coveted science-based courses of study as late as 1969–70, but only 19 percent by 1975.[19] Given the agricultural and industrial limitations of the Jaffna Peninsula, erosion of educational and thus professional opportunities and the skewing of development projects to Sinhala areas together exacerbated the anger of young Tamils.

The Committee for Rational Development concluded (1984, 16): "The recent agitation over statistics on Tamil dominance avoids one inescapable fact. At present the Sinhalese are in *absolute* control of national economic policy. Very few Tamils can receive jobs through state patronage, they can only succeed in private self-employment or in the professions. With control over national economic policy, Sinhalese have the absolute power to direct the course of our economic future." Such statements by peacemakers were countered: "Anglicized intellectuals were accused of building their fame and fortunes on the shame and ruination of the Sinhala" (Tennekoon 1990, 218).

Perceptions of loss were cultural as well. Despite symbolic catering to a Sinhala Buddhist identity by the regime, some radical monks associated themselves with the Janata Vimukti Peramuna (JVP, or National Liberation Front). These monks were distrustful of liberalization on cultural and religious grounds; consumerism, Western influence, drugs and prostitution, the decadence of the tourist industry—the monks believed that all these factors undermined the ideational commitments to Buddhism just as the regime reduced the collective political power of Buddhist monks through a distancing from the *sangha*.[20] Economic change symbolized to many a Westernizing project that threatened the cultural identity of the Sinhalese Buddhist community.

Whatever the objective base of these economic and cultural perceptions, new economic policies almost certainly produced more insecurity and inequality. To the extent that economic insecurity itself produces anger susceptible to scapegoating and new needs for security of identity, we may expect more raw material for ethnic conflict. Global integration of the economy certainly produced more public ostentation in consumption by the rich and more insecurity at the bottom of society as safety nets were cut—a higher level of experienced inequality.

One strand of the celebration of Sri Lanka in the mid-1970s as a success story in terms of providing basic human needs was the reduction of income inequality for the decade 1963–73.[21] Data from the 1981/82 Consumer Finance Survey indicate increased inequality between 1973 and 1981/82; the Gini coefficient, which had fallen to 0.41 in 1973 and was precisely the same in 1978 as in 1963 (0.49), increased to 0.52 in 1981/82, the highest level since the surveys began in 1953. After 1977, property income increased, tax concessions were granted to capital, and indirect taxes were increased, so income inequality after taxes and before subsidies has almost certainly increased. Moreover, the real value of food subsidies was significantly eroded by inflation. Likewise, the management of public sector enterprises has historically had a purposive redistributive impact (Lakshman 1980, 22), which was contrary to the new economic strategy after 1977.

Public guarantees of food security had long been criticized by international development agencies (e.g., World Bank 1953, 123). In June 1978, targeting reduced significantly the eligible population. Subsequent targeting limited the new food stamp program to those with incomes less than Rs 300 (then $12) per month (Oberst 1985). Subsidies were cut further by refusal to index either the income criterion or stamp values to counter inflation. Despite accelerated economic change, new additions to the rolls were forbidden. Between the inception of the program and July 1981, the purchasing power of a typical family's food stamps had been cut in half (Sri Lanka 1981, table 3). Subsequent inflation cut the benefits in real terms even further. In the poorest decile of the population, food stamps accounted for 22 percent of purchases (Edirisinghe 1985). An evaluation by the government found that the effect of policy changes was deterioration of the nutritional status of preschool children and an increase in the number of cases of serious malnutrition (Sri Lanka 1981, 30; see also Sahn 1983). An analysis of consumption data from the periodic Consumer Finance Surveys concluded that between 1978/79 and 1981/82, the calorie intake levels of the bottom 20 percent of the households had "undergone serious deterioration" (Edirisinghe 1985, 49; see also Sanderatne 1985).

So serious a deterioration in public entitlements for the most vulnerable sections of the population would be expected to produce political consequences, particularly in a society characterized by mobilization around of "rice politics" historically. Quiescence is difficult to explain. One possibility is that insecurity and anger were displaced to ethnic animosity.

Quiescence and Displacement

There have been persistent arguments that structural adjustment—particularly under IMF auspices—requires an authoritarian regime, both because elected politicians are reluctant to impose severe hardships on their constituents and because repression of resulting social conflicts is more easily accomplished when the state is not constrained by norms of liberal democracy.[22] Joan Nelson (1984, 1005) counts Sri Lanka as one of the successful cases of stabilization politically, noting that there were no violent protests despite the fact that "subsidies and rations were successfully slashed."

The dominant reason for the exceptional quiescence of Sri Lanka's population through an adjustment episode is its departure from neoliberal orthodoxy. The traditional IMF medicine of inducing a recession while cutting subsidies was offset in the aggregate by a Keynesian expansion, funded from internal deficits and external largesse. Unorthodox fiscal policy contributed to higher levels of growth and employment than had been the norm for the preceding decade. To some extent, increased income inequality and nutritional insecurity were counterbalanced by increasing job opportunities and imported goods. In Sri Lanka, as in much of Southeast Asia, adjustment was associated with growth, not contraction. Moreover, repression often works. An ambitious strike in 1980 was effectively crushed, union organizers lost their jobs, and the government-sponsored Jathika Sevaka Sangamaya began to rule work sites in place of independent workers' unions.

But if an externally funded Keynesian expansion and political repression go far in explaining quiescence in the aggregate, there were nevertheless pains and frustrated expectations in Sri Lanka's very politicized society. Mass protests at cuts in the social wage were also blunted in Sri Lanka by, I believe, diversion of frustration into ethnic hostility in a large enough fraction of the population to induce terror in the minority and render ethnic compromise untenable. Scapegoats are commonly victimized during periods of economic stress. The open economy provided both symbolic materials and exacerbation of real cleavages to facilitate scapegoating.

The riots of 1983 in Colombo—the largest pogrom against Tamils in the nation's history and a turning point in the escalation of regional conflict to civil war—were, in Gananath Obeyesekere's account (1984, 153), driven by urban "lumpen" elements, characterized "by the hatreds and frustrations that slum dwelling breeds everywhere." S. J. Tambiah (1986, 57) likewise attributes the increase in ethnic violence to "political manipulation" of marginalized populations "in protest of their lumpen proletariat condition." Precisely this population was most vulnerable to increased insecurity from cuts in safety nets urged by external development agencies. This population is also markedly incapable of exercising autonomous political power through other means.

The argument that liberalization proper—as opposed to erosion of safety nets—contributed to ethnic conflict was made by Newton Gunasinghe in a controversial series of articles (1984a–d). The argument depends on an assumption that the psychoanalytic phenomenon of displacement is applicable to groups of people, an assumption that is difficult to verify empirically but almost certainly true. To summarize a more diffuse argument, Gunasinghe reasoned as follows: The regulated economy allowed many Sinhalese businessmen with connections to establish themselves—via the permit-quota-license system, mediated through patronage—in niches that a market economy would not have provided. Tamil entrepreneurs largely lacked patronage and connections. Liberalization of the external boundary produced competition that wiped out many of the inefficient or simply small businesses that had survived behind protective regulation of the economy. Margins thinned and firms failed. The anger in the business community was partly directed into anti-Tamil chauvinism.

Gunasinghe used the match industry as an example to illustrate his thesis. Firms in the match industry represented three paths of response to liberalization. The strongest, largest firm met international competition (from India and China) with investment for modernization and survived. The second-largest firm lacked such deep pockets and survived only by modernizing as a subsidiary of foreign capital. The smallest firm simply went under (Gunasinghe 1984b, 17). All three scenarios are disruptive, but for the firms unable to adjust, both workers and owners constituted a new social base of anger. Gunasinghe explained (1984d, 212), "The middle and small level industrialists who were being ruined by the operation of the open economy, perceived the profits accruing to the traders as an unduly large slice of the cake." The July pogroms were seen as a solution to the perceived stranglehold of ethnically distinct middlemen in some quarters. After the July pogroms, the Sinhala paper *Divayina* published a series of articles headed "After the Fall of the Pettah [Central Market] Dictatorship," clearly referring to traders identified with Tamil ethnicity as the erstwhile dictators, which urged the government "to consolidate by administrative and legislative means the gains secured for Sinhala merchants during the July days" (Siriwardena 1984, 227).

At the bottom of society, the urban poor experienced increased opportunity as well as increased insecurity. There was a great deal of internal class differentiation and movement from a culture of "shared poverty" to the "colour TV in the slum tenement" syndrome (Gunasinghe 1984c, 10). New material consumption possibilities fed new relative deprivation and anger. Economic change "converted the urban poor into inflammatory material." Since markets were seen as the source of both insecurity and mobility, Gunasinghe implied, the state became less the object of anger: the anger that had historically been directed against the state became available for the "political manipulation" of which S. J. Tambiah writes (1986, 57).

A critical condition for this scenario to be credible is political organization. Mick Moore (1990), while skeptical of the thesis, notes that the clearly evident ethnic antagonism was nurtured and exacerbated by a member of Jayewardene's cabinet who utilized virulent anti-Tamil nationalism in the business community to cement and augment his political base. Intraparty and intraregime competition for power provided leadership and material support for chauvinist mobilization (Bush 1994, chap. 3). Gunasinghe (1984d, 198) noted "organized attempts on the part of certain chauvinistic elements both within and outside the regime to ignite an anti-Tamil pogrom with the express intention of breaking the economic base of Tamil entrepreneurs, which resulted not only in attacks against small Tamil shop-keepers but also in attacks against major industrial establishments."

New definitions of national identity and threats to the same, as well as a business class and politicians with something to gain, led, in this argument, to targeting and redirecting anger. It was widely believed that Tamils in Colombo were benefiting under liberalization because of their position in real estate and connections to international trade. Their association with India was accentuated by the use of India's Tamil Nadu State as a guerrilla haven. Resentment was fed by views similar to those represented in the Sinhala newspaper *Divayina* that "Tamil entrepreneurs [were] getting rich at the expense of the Sinhala." Pogroms allowed for the literal elimination of competition, a coincidence of material interest and cultural mobilization. In summary, Gunasinghe argued (1984c, 12):

> As the economic role of the state appeared to them to be marginal, some other object of hostility had to be discovered to be held responsible for the current malaise. It is precisely here that the Sinhala chauvinist ideology, which first emerged from the ranks of the middle-level traders, found a fertile ground, engulfing numerous social strata among the Sinhala.

The plausibility of this scenario is strengthened by evidence of a funding connection between small-scale Sinhala businessmen and the radical Sinhala chauvinist JVP (which figured heavily in blocking government options through terrorism after 1987): "These merchants often had Tamil rivals or had experienced difficulty obtaining credit from banks in which they sensed disproportionate Tamil influence."[23] In Serena Tennekoon's analysis of "newspaper nationalism" (1990, 217), there is a connection back from economic policy to cultural challenge: "The Sinhala press—and the *Divayina* in particular—has frequently bemoaned the rapid commercialization and westernization of Sinhala society (produced by the 'Open Economy' policies introduced by the UNP government in 1977) and the concomitant destruction of 'traditional' culture and moral values."

On the reverse side of the coin, liberalization hurt Tamil agriculture in the Jaffna area (Moore 1985, 109–10). Tamil insurgents in the north were convinced that the external flows were being pocketed by Sinhalese supporters of the regime, that virtually all of the carrots of developmental projects were accruing to the Sinhalese community, and that the extensive irrigation and settlement program funded from abroad was introducing Sinhalese incursion on their historic homeland, making decentralization a less viable solution to ethnic disputes. Any coalition of disaffected Sinhalese and Tamils against liberalization became an impossibility as new cleavages dominated political practice. Moreover, the resurrection of the insurgent JVP in 1987 was likewise framed in terms of a nationalist and xenophobic discourse triggered by the Indo-Sri Lankan accords.

Diversion or displacement of frustration induced by economic distress and uncertainty is by no means automatically political or collective. A robust economy creates the special pain of seeing fortunes made while being unable to provide for one's family. With clear evidence of boom all around, it is difficult to focus collective protests and psychologically easy to blame an ethnic outgroup or oneself. If we believe politicians to be especially perceptive observers of popular moods, the antipoverty themes of the UNP in 1988 and 1989 indicate that alternative sources of quiescence were wearing thin.

The puzzle, then, of why a democratic government (albeit less democratic) weathered a period of adjustment and retrenchment and experienced no "IMF riots" has several interrelated answers. First, the IMF was extraordinarily tolerant of budget deficits in Sri Lanka. Second, this tolerance and extraordinary financial concessions from abroad fueled a Keynesian expansion rather than recession; aid projects allowed both more employment and politically targeted payoffs, as well as opportunities for rent-seeking bureaucrats. Third, the escalation of ethnic conflict created both scapegoats for mass frustration and at least some perception among the Sinhalese majority that "our government" is besieged by Tamil insurgents and deserves support. Political discourse and cleavage were substantially remade. Ethnic divisions disabled class politics. Fourth, democratic processes permitted the reassertion by political elites in 1988–89, in a very Polanyi-like fashion, of promises that traditional safety nets for those ground to the bottom by market mechanisms would be reestablished.

Finally, mass protests of any kind confront repression and thus significant risk for the individual; the government showed itself to be quite tough on threats to the economic miracle it claimed to be unfolding. As economic success was the legitimation of the regime, and as business confidence, or investment climate, became the means to that end, protests could not be tolerated. The protests common in liberalization episodes were then blunted by force from the state and by obstacles to collective action across ethnic lines after 1983. Ethnic anger, however, was legitimated and fed by politics within the regime.

The Autonomy of Political Process: Making
Ethnic Conflict

There is no space here for a full treatment of the politics of this period; this section of this chapter aims to emphasize that an autonomous sphere of politics made decisive contributions to the tragic escalation of conflict. Politically, there were reasons for some Tamils and some Sinhalese to perceive themselves to be losers. The most important analytical lesson for politics is that these communities were divided; the terms *Tamils* and *Sinhalese* are dangerous shorthand devices for politically complex communities that were by no means monolithic or communities in any real sense. As some Tamil politicians came back into the fold of electoral coalitions and politics in the 1990s, others continued to wage a war of intermittent terror and armed conflict. Intragroup dynamics were in many ways more important than intergroup dynamics in explaining the escalation of ethnic conflict (Bush 1994, chap. 3). One of the tragic consequences of the late 1970s and early 1980s was to essentialize ethnicity—to speak of Tamils as a whole and the Sinhala as a whole, to attribute collective characteristics to individuals. Essentializing communities serves no useful purpose but rather feeds into the stereotyping strategies of chauvinists. Concrete political interests were served by this distortion; the political consequences were catastrophic.

Beginning with language policy in the 1950s and the constitutions of 1972 and 1978, along with consistent state support of Buddhism, the independent Sri Lankan state could easily have been perceived as an ethnic champion of the majority. Yet Tamils and other minorities had been courted by the UNP before the 1977 election. President Jayewardene began the liberalizing episode having generated expectations in the Tamil community. Whatever the president's intentions, policy was derailed by hard-liners within the regime and the incremental reframing of secessionist protest in Jaffna as terrorism, generating "a growing sense of peril in the Sinhala community" (Little 1994, 87). This was not a groundless fear, though it was a localized one—the mayor of Jaffna had been assassinated by radicals in 1975. But the attribution of terrorism to the Tamil community generally elided important differences. Radical Tamil groups were engaged in both competition and mutual assassination. Moderates held out for political compromise short of violence. There was a vigorously contested spectrum of political opinion among Tamils. Nor were Sinhalese political positions united. Most extremely, after 1987, the government was in effect fighting two wars—with Tamil Tigers in the North and with the Sinhala JVP in the South.

Once the political demands of Tamil youth were perceived in terms of terrorist threat, mirror images of ethnic entities hardened. The United Front government in 1971 had reacted with extraordinary measures of repression to an insurgency of Sinhala youth in the JVP, and it did so again after 1987. But terrorism in the late 1970s and early 1980s became conjoined with Tamil ethnicity. One heard comments suspecting utterly apolitical Tamil individuals of being at least sympathetic to, if not supportive of, the insurgency in the North, as if a common language connoted political position.

The Prevention of Terrorism Act was legislated in 1979. This draconian act—and the *de facto* occupation of Jaffna by armed forces—hardened opinion in the North that the state was threatening and intractable. Combating terrorism is never gentle. Torture, disappearances, denial of due process, and human rights violations were attributed to forces of the state, widely publicized by international nongovernment organizations, and frequently raised with the government in negotiations with the Aid Sri Lanka Consortium, particularly by Nordic donors and Canada. This international discourse in itself helped shape and harden ethnicities. International opinion clearly held Tamils to be victims, enhancing the Sinhala feeling of being isolated and beleaguered; there was a certain amount of rallying around the state. Despite harsh international criticisms, the regime continued to garner critical external support in the aggregate.

Sequencing of escalation followed a familiar political spiral—separatist militancy, state opposition, escalating protests and repression, military occupation, allegations of systematic torture, and extension of terrorist acts. Jayewardene won a second term as president in 1982 amid allegations of fraud. The president then decided to extend Parliament's term for six more years without elections. This unprecedented extension by referendum—"marred by force and fraud" (Moore 1990, 345)—contributed to the feeling that there would be no political solutions available soon. The former prime minister, Mrs. Bandaranaike, had been disenfranchised in 1980. Student councils were dismissed in 1982. In 1983, the JVP, which had emerged from underground to make a strong showing in both local and presidential elections, was proscribed. The more moderate voice of Tamil interests, the Tamil United Liberation Front, was effectively barred from Parliament in 1983. Democratic avenues of redress and compromise were disappearing.

Pogroms in July 1983, which the forces of the state at least condoned and allegedly assisted, turned a conflict between the state and radical Tamil youth into an ethnic war. Struggles within the ruling group clearly were associated with hardening of lines against terrorists and fomenting civil discord (Bush 1994, chap. 3); a hard line on the ethnic question was a recognizable political strategy that for a time benefited cabinet minister Cyril Mathew. Within the Sinhala community outside government, a more radical Sinhalese identity premised on an even harder line was expressed by the JVP; threats from the JVP further reduced the space for compromise. These threats were neither idle nor inconsequential; the JVP launched a debilitating and demoralizing terrorist campaign against the state after the government agreed to intervention of an Indian military peacekeeping force in Tamil areas in 1987.

Political escalation of ethnic conflict was not caused by foreign aid or structural adjustment. Indeed, official repression was criticized by the development community. But criticism did not preclude continued international support for the government. Given the dependence of the government and its economic miracle on foreign resource flows, external demands for reconciliation must certainly have had more potential purchase than was realized; it is doubtful that the regime could have continued had it been abandoned by the development community. But collective action among donor nations was impeded by intragovernmental conflict over aid objectives, commercial interests of donors, and coordination problems (Gillies 1992). Moreover, the target economy was growing.

Conclusions: Overdetermination and Materialist Explanation

> Sri Lanka twice defeated India in the World Cup. But
> that was about good cricket. Economic liberalization had
> nothing to do with it.
> —Ravana Club, 1996

What we call "ethnic conflict" is so complex and overdetermined a phenomenon that any parsimonious account is unlikely to be robust. The purpose of this chapter is to illuminate contributory factors from the sphere of economic policy and foreign resource flows that are missing from the discourse on endogenously ethnic causes of ethnic conflict. The argument for external flows rests on layers of plausible causation. At the most general level, most oblique in causative power is rapid economic expansion or contraction characteristic of marketizing adjustment. The impossibility of successful consumerism for everyone simultaneously is obvious even in the most vigorous episodes of economic change, even in the richest countries. This impossibility confronts the identity of large populations with new definitions of what is to be valued, what it means to succeed, what it means to win and to lose. Karl Polanyi (1957) stressed long ago the threats to social identity and integration inherent in the "great transformation" to market society. Market-driven outcomes have no inherent intersubjectively shared legitimacy.

Neoliberal prescriptions backed by both carrots and sticks accelerate the transformation to a more market-driven allocation system. The forging of a new moral economy is inherently destabilizing. Between 1977 and 1983, growth in per capita income doubled over the rate of the previous regime. Though modest by world standards, this rate of growth was extraordinary for Sri Lanka; it was a boom. Is there an optimum rate of growth for any society at any historic juncture? What rate of growth will permit adaptation to new circumstances? Unprecedented bursts of consumerism in particular carry potential for creating "unfulfilled dreams [and a] profound sense of alienation and deprivation" (Rupesinghe 1992, 5). Restructuring necessitates new notions of right and wrong, of legitimate aspirations and acceptable explanations of relative and absolute deprivation. This is fertile ground for scapegoating, envy, and rage.

The argument for development policy's contribution to ethnic conflict more broadly depends on interrelated threads of possible causation: that in an ethnically divided economy, induced pain will exacerbate existing grievances; that pain from adjustment may be displaced or used politically in ethnically charged ways; that regimes supported by international lenders develop mutual dependencies with agencies, allowing repressive regimes to survive and exacerbate tensions in society through refusal to establish governance in place of rule; and, most indirectly, that accelerated globalization produces cultural challenges amenable to scapegoating and assertion of virulent ethnic chauvinism.

The specific incarnation of policy reform in Sri Lanka both resonated with and departed from these possible dynamics. Compared to many adjustment episodes in poor countries, mass protests in Sri Lanka were blunted by a Keynesian boom led by extensive project spending and atypical leniency in demands for fiscal austerity. Nevertheless, there were losers at the bottom of the income pyramid and widespread evidence of ostentatious consumption by winners. These changes were made especially salient by the nation's history of restraining consumption inequality and securing basic needs with extensive social safety nets.

The expanded flow of benefits enabled by aid was skewed. Expanded patronage worked largely within the majority community, either in Sinhala areas or in disputed areas where resettlement altered the local balance of forces. The Mahaweli project aggravated ethnic territoriality after the contested decision to employ national ethnic ratios rather than local ratios for settlement. Cancellation of the feeder canal that would have taken Mahaweli waters north to Tamil areas symbolized ethnic exclusion from aid benefits.

Costs were also skewed, but not as dramatically. Tamil farmers were hurt by price competition from liberalized imports in an area of few alternative economic opportunities, reinforcing the perception that the future of Jaffna was bleak. Liberalization likewise hurt some Sinhalese workers and entrepreneurs—engendering free-floating anger and a social base for ethnic chauvinism available for scapegoating—though there were selective compensatory gains from new projects resulting from foreign aid and expansion of employment. Costs of inflation on the general public were accompanied by the familiar scapegoating of market middlemen, with an ethnic coloring.

Political options for resolving conflict were reduced by project territoriality. Accelerated colonization projects threatened to dilute or nullify decentralization as a solution to territorial autonomy demands of militant Tamil politics. Simultaneous deployment of ethnically charged symbols of the glories of ancient Buddhist Sinhalese civilization around foreign-funded projects complemented demographic threats from colonization by Sinhalese settlers in areas considered Tamil territory. Political repression and exclusion—justified as necessary for success of the economic miracle—further reduced political options for the minority.

Indeed, authoritarian rule in general reduced the possibilities for heading off escalation. Business confidence became a meta-agenda of policy and a rationale for both increased centralization of political authority and reduced tolerance for dissent. Avenues of registering dissent—elections, union activity, student councils, referenda—were constrained, rigged, or eliminated. A culture of political violence to enforce conformity with regime objectives further radicalized antagonists. Regime capacity to retain power throughout these episodes was critically underwritten by external flows. Official complicity with and encouragement of newly virulent ethnic forces in the pogroms reinforced the perception in the minority community that the state could be dealt with only through violence.

What implications do we draw from this account? Though recent literature on ethnogenesis appropriately stresses the fluid and emergent nature of ethnicity,[24] the dynamics treated throughout this chapter depend on a specific history—not a history of ethnic war or primordial antitheses, but a history that provides raw materials for reconstructing a narrative of ethnicity. Absent a map of past grievances and glories, of rightful territory, much of the perception of skewed costs, benefits, and threats would have been difficult to conjure or would have had minimal social resonance. These conditions are generalizable only at a fairly high level of abstraction from social circumstances that matter. In the Sri Lankan case, stereotypes of an ethnic division of labor, resources, power, space, and opportunity mattered more than reality—which was in any event disputed empirically. Political culture weighed heavily as well: if people believe that cronyism and patronage are modes of allocation, new largesse deepens perceptions of special advantage to the group that holds power. The irreducibly local phenomenology of ethnicity matters more than its objective mapping onto the political economy.

The Sri Lankan case also illustrates structural unity across the conventional distinction between aid projects and programs. Enhanced project assistance often accompanies stabilization and structural adjustment. A government that meets the criteria for one is a good candidate for the other. Moreover, the political sustainability of adjustment may necessitate carrots to soften the blow of sticks. To the extent that international actors want a regime to survive, recognition that genuine restructuring will produce pain (especially in a nation characterized by "premature welfarism"), carrots become a necessary political condition for a government surviving any significant reformation of the economy.

Contrary to the IMF-riot model, the Sri Lankan case suggests how the carrots of foreign assistance may be as disruptive as the sticks. The literature on IMF riots has stressed induced pain as a cause of political unsustainability; Sri Lanka was, in comparative terms, spared pain through lenient treatment. More orthodox restructuring might well produce more ethnic mobilization if the pain falls along ethnic lines. The most generalizable finding may be that the cognitive frame of development agencies—of aggregate phenomena defined by growth rates in gross national product—elides differential distributions of insecurity and opportunity, differences that may be perceived in ethnic terms and thus productive of ethnic conflict. To have large effects, skews need be neither widespread nor large in objectively measurable terms. Triggering events such as the pogroms of 1983 can fundamentally alter the trajectory of conflict. The numbers involved in those horrific riots were comparatively small; the consequences were cataclysmic.

Finally, no materialist account can explain the depths of rage and desperation that cause neighbors to turn on one another. Likewise, no aggregate account can explain the many acts of compassion, tolerance, and heroism in both communities. There is no easy explanation for political failure; President Jayewardene himself once said on reflection that he had "lacked courage." It is not knowable—given political divisions among militant opponents of the regime—what alternative routes to compromise could have succeeded when there was less blood under the bridge. But to assume that international development flows have consequences only within the technical and neutral frame professionals draw for them would be inexcusably naive.

NOTES

1. An excellent summary of the secondary literature on the riots is provided in Bush 1994, chapters 3, 5. See also the contributions to Manor 1984 and the excruciating accounts in Roberts 1994.

2. For a brief overview of the history of collective identities, see Kumari Jayawardene 1984; Roberts 1979; Roberts 1994, especially 249–69; Roberts 1997. Coding simply by language, minority Tamils—Sri Lankan and "Indian" (the latter term is applied to descendants of plantation laborers brought to Ceylon during the colonial period and disenfranchised soon after independence)—are about 18 percent of the population; Sinhalese are about 74 percent of the population. Though there are "religious" differences across these assignations—Sinhalese are more than likely to be Buddhist; a majority of the Tamils, Hindu (Little 1994)—and significant conflicts within these language groupings, the ethnic character of conflict became intersubjectively important after 1983.

3. Using *jatika* to mean "national" has some currency in more intellectual circles; see Tennekoon 1990, 205, on this point, and passim for the rooting of contemporary ethnic discourse in imagined histories of antagonistic "Aryans" and "Dravidians."

4. Horowitz (1985, 141) borrows an episode from Leonard Woolf's novel *The Village in the Jungle* to illustrate the appropriation of ethnic stereotypes as grounds for group identity. Woolf was a colonial officer in Hambantota District before assuming his literary career. Horowitz's example illustrates that cultural integration coexisted with ethnic interpretation at the village level, specifically through Sinhala worship of a Tamil deity.

5. I was personally convinced of this position by wrenching conversations with Tamil professionals and intellectuals after the pogroms in 1983. In their view, there were no compromises left; the Sinhala mobs had demonstrated such ferocious hatred of Tamils, and the state had so openly aided rioters, that the only recourse was war.

6. For example, by the criterion of the physical quality-of-life index (PQLI; composed of equally weighted measures of literacy, infant mortality, and life expectancy), Sri Lanka in the mid-1970s ranked higher than much richer nations,

such as Venezuela or Chile, with a life expectancy near that of some European countries and far greater than its subcontinental neighbors India, Pakistan, Nepal, Afghanistan, and Bangladesh, and with a composite score somewhat better than China (see Herring 1994, table 1). To contextualize these data, consider that Sri Lanka's PQLI of 82, with an annual GNP per capita of about $200, came closer to that of Sweden (97) or the United States (95) than to that of India (42) or Afghanistan (17). See also World Bank 1980c, 90; Jayawardena 1974; Isenmen 1980; Herring 1987.

7. The strategy was launched during an unusually auspicious economic juncture; the terms of trade, which had experienced a trend decline since 1950, showed a 35 percent improvement in 1976, 31 percent in 1977; tea prices experienced an unprecedented rise of 80 percent, contributing to an unprecedented current account surplus of Rs 1,259 million. Real gross national product (GNP) grew at a rate of 8.2 percent in 1978, a very high rate by historical standards, then slowed to 6.2 percent in 1979, 5.5 in 1980, 3.9 in 1981, 5.0 in 1982, and 4.0 in 1983. The rate of growth in real national income fluctuated widely, however, because of subsequent deterioration in the terms of trade; it was 0.4 percent in 1985.

8. The finance minister predictably responded that "external factors beyond our control" were responsible and that cuts in the investment program would dampen the enthusiasm the government had worked so hard to instill among investors (*Asian Wall Street Journal Weekly,* June 6 and July 20, 1981).

9. While not high by contemporary poor-world standards, the debt-service ratio eventually exceeded the historic high experienced during the "oil shock" period of 1973–74, standing at 26.2 percent in 1986 (Central Bank of Ceylon 1987, 228). By 1990, the debt-service ratio had declined to 13.8 percent; foreign debt to GNP hovered near 74 percent. Over 70 percent of the external debt is on concessional terms (Economist Intelligence Unit, *Sri Lanka Country Report,* no. 1 [1992]: 3, 22).

10. Though budget deficits were large (10 percent of GDP in 1984, 19 percent in 1985), it is important to remember that the deficit reached 26 percent of GDP before the real beginnings of internal war in 1983. Rather than being a simple reflection of growing militarization, budget deficits were a reflection of ambitious development projects premised on increased availability of foreign funds on the expenditure side and severe responses of revenues to falling export prices on the income side.

11. Moore (1990, 370) discusses the wide range of projects available for patronage—given "competition" among the many aid donors seeking "viable projects" to fund—and the resultant emergence of "project chasers" as an archetype of new UNP members of Parliament.

12. See Farmer 1957. For a discussion of the functions of colonization schemes as a means of reducing agrarian discontent, see Herring 1983, chapter 4 and passim.

13. This sentence, based on Gillies's account, elicited unexpected confirmation from John Harriss, who, on reading the penultimate draft of this chapter, commented, "It has reminded me very strongly of the time that I spent as a somewhat

reluctant member of the Victoria Dam Appraisal Team in 1978 . . . when, as I never cease to tell students when I talk about development projects and 'planning,' the dam had started to be built even before the team which was supposed to be appraising the project had arrived in the country."

14. Little (1994, 84) believes that irrigation and power projects without the overlay of celebration of rebuilding the ancient glory of the Sinhala Buddhist kingdoms might have been less inflammatory, but in the event the two were linked.

15. Levy 1989, 446–47. U.S. Ambassador Howard Wriggins argued the danger of Mahaweli's crowding out smaller projects and explicitly warned the president of what happened to Menderes in Turkey as a result of inflation initiated by overly ambitious public works projects (personal communication with author, December 30, 1999).

16. Personal communication with author, January 1996.

17. One CIDA official admitted that the firms "with bags of political influence" were "hinting at litigation if the project stalled." Commercial interests also hindered Canada's ability to get other donors to agree on imposing conditionality on the government of Sri Lanka. See Gillies 1992, 58.

18. See also Kumari Jayewardena's article (1984, 117–18) on the prevalence of perceptions that minority-owned or foreign-owned businesses thwarted the development of Sinhalese business and that non-Sinhala had all the good jobs.

19. The pioneering work was done by C. R. de Silva. See his "Education" in *Sri Lanka: A Survey*, ed. K. M. de Silva (London: C. Hurst), table 8, and "The Politics of University Admissions," *Sri Lanka Journal of Social Sciences* 1, no. 2 (December 1978): 105–6. For a discussion in the context of Tamil grievances, see V. Nithiyanandan, "An Analysis of Economic Factors behind the Origin and Development of Tamil Nationalism in Sri Lanka," in *Facets of Ethnicity in Sri Lanka*, ed. Charles Abeysekera and Newton Gunasinghe (Colombo: Social Scientists Association, 1987).

20. Little 1994, 93–94. The accounts in Manor 1984 give perhaps the best account in terms of phenomenology of the participants in this political struggle. See also Moore 1990.

21. As measured by the Consumer Finance Surveys (Jayawardena 1974). The reality of that phenomenon has, however, been called into question, generating a serious empirical dispute (Lee 1976, 1977; Dahanayake 1979; Lakshman 1980). See Herring 1987.

22. See Sheahan 1980, 267–91. Sheahan notes that though authoritarian regimes of the twentieth century show markedly different characteristics, they typically are in the beginning supportive of free markets and opposition to inflation. See also Sheahan 1986, 174–75. For a review of plausible mechanisms, see Moore 1990, 341–46.

23. Horowitz 1985, 115. The JVP first exhibited its anti-Tamil positions in the period leading up to the insurgency that it launched in 1971. It initiated a wave of terror in Sinhala areas against the government after the accords of 1987 brought in the Indian peacekeeping force.

24. See discussion in chapter 1. Discussing Sri Lanka specifically, Samarasinghe

and Coughlan (1991, 7) stress the "malleable and emergent character of ethnic group identity."

REFERENCES

Brow, James. 1990. "Nationalist Rhetoric and Local Practice: The Fate of the Village Community in Kukulewa," in *Sri Lanka: History and Roots of Conflict,* ed. Jonathan Spencer. London and New York: Routledge.

Bush, Kenneth D. 1994. "The Intra-group Dimensions of Ethnic Conflict in Sri Lanka and Northern Ireland." Ph.D. diss., Cornell University.

Central Bank of Ceylon. 1978. *Annual Report.* Colombo: Central Bank of Ceylon.

———. 1979. *Annual Report.* Colombo: Central Bank of Ceylon.

———. 1982. *Review of the Economy.* Colombo: Central Bank of Ceylon.

———. 1984. *Economic Performance in the First Half of 1983.* Colombo: Central Bank of Ceylon.

———. 1985. *Annual Report.* Colombo: Central Bank of Ceylon.

———. 1987. *Annual Report.* Colombo: Central Bank of Ceylon.

Committee for Rational Development. 1984. *Sri Lanka: The Ethnic Conflict.* New Delhi: Navrang.

Dahanayake, P. A. S. 1979. "Growth and Welfare: Some Reflections on the Effects of Recent Development Policy Reforms in Sri Lanka." *CBC Staff Studies* 9, nos. 1/2 (April/September).

Dell, Sidney. 1984. "Stabilization: The Political Economy of Overkill." In *The Political Economy of Development and Underdevelopment,* ed. Charles K. Wilber. New York: Random House.

Dreze, Jean, and Amartya Sen. 1989. *Hunger and Public Action.* Oxford: Clarendon Press.

Economist Intelligence Unit. 1992. *Sri Lanka Country Report* 1.

Edirisinghe, Neville. 1985. *Preliminary Report on the Food Stamp Scheme in Sri Lanka: Distribution of Benefits and Impact on Nutrition.* Washington, DC: International Food Policy Research Institute.

Farmer, B. H. 1957. *Pioneer Peasant Colonization in Ceylon.* Oxford: Oxford University Press.

Gillies, David. 1992. "Principled Intervention: Canadian Aid, Human Rights and the Sri Lankan Conflict." In *Aid as Peacemaker: Canadian Development Assistance and Third World Conflict,* ed. Robert Miller. Ottawa: Carleton University Press.

Girvan, Norman. 1980. "Swallowing the IMF Medicine in the Seventies." *Development Dialogue* 2.

Gunasinghe, Newton. 1984a. "The Open Economy and Its Impact on Ethnic Relations in Sri Lanka." Part 1. *Lanka Guardian* 6, no. 17 (January 1).

———. 1984b. "The Open Economy and Its Impact on Ethnic Relations in Sri Lanka." Part 2. *Lanka Guardian* 6, no. 18.

———. 1984c. "The Open Economy and Its Impact on Ethnic Relations in Sri Lanka." Part 3. *Lanka Guardian* 6, no. 19 (February 1).

————. 1984d. "The Open Economy and Its Impact on Ethnic Relations in Sri Lanka." In *Sri Lanka: The Ethnic Conflict*, by the Committee for Rational Development. New Delhi: Navrang.

Gurr, Ted Robert. 1993. *Minorities at Risk: A Global View of Ethnopolitical Conflicts*. Washington, DC: United States Institute of Peace.

Herring, Ronald J. 1983. *Land to the Tiller: The Political Economy of Agrarian Reform in South Asia*. New Haven: Yale University Press; Delhi: Oxford University Press.

————. 1987. "Food Policy in a Dependent Welfare State." In *IPE Yearbook*, vol. 3, *Pursuing Food Security*, ed. W. Ladd Hollist and F. LaMond Tullis. Boulder: Lynn Rienner.

————. 1990. "Some Notes on Social Science and Catastrophe: The Case of Sri Lanka." Paper presented at the roundtable "Where Did We Go Wrong on Sri Lanka" held by the Association for Asian Studies, Chicago, April 4–7.

————. 1994. "Explaining Sri Lanka's Exceptionalism: Popular Responses to Welfarism and the 'Open Economy.'" In *Free Markets and Food Riots*, ed. John Walton and David Seddon. Oxford: Basil Blackwell.

Horowitz, Donald L. 1985. *Ethnic Groups in Conflict*. Berkeley: University of California Press.

International Monetary Fund (IMF). 1977. *IMF Survey* 6. Washington, DC: IMF.

————. 1980. *Government Finance Statistics Yearbook*. Vol. 4. Washington, DC: IMF.

————. 1984. *Government Financial Statistics Yearbook*. Washington, DC: IMF.

Isenmen, Paul. 1980. "Basic Needs: The Case of Sri Lanka." *World Development* 8, no. 3 (March).

Jayatissa, R. A. 1982. "Balance of Payments Adjustments to Exogenous Shocks during 1970–1981." CBC *Staff Studies* 12, no. 1 (April).

Jayawardena, Lal. 1974. "Sri Lanka." In *Redistribution with Growth*, ed. Hollis Chenery et al. London: Oxford University Press.

Jayewardene, Kumari. 1984. "Ethnic Consciousness in Sri Lanka: Continuity and Change." In *Sri Lanka*, ed. Committee for Rational Development. New Delhi: Navrang.

Kemper, Steve. 1990. "J. R. Jayewardene: Righteousness and *Realpolitik*." In *Sri Lanka: History and Roots of Conflict*, ed. Jonathan Spencer. London and New York: Routledge.

Krueger, Anne O. 1981. "Loans to Assist the Transition to Outward-Looking Policies," *World Economy* 4, no. 3.

Lakshman, W. D. 1980. "Income and Wealth Distribution in Sri Lanka: An Examination of Evidence Pertaining to the Post-1960 Experience." International Development Center of Japan Working Paper 16. International Development Center of Japan, Toykyo.

Lee, E. L. H. 1976. "Rural Poverty in Sri Lanka, 1963–1973." World Employment Programme Working Paper. International Labour Office, Geneva.

————. 1977. "Development and Income Distribution: A Case Study of Sri Lanka and Malaysia." *World Development* 5, no. 4.

Levy, Brian. 1989. "Foreign Aid in the Making of Economic Policy in Sri Lanka, 1977–1983." *Policy Sciences* 22:437–61.

Little, David. 1994. *Sri Lanka: The Invention of Enmity.* Washington, DC: U.S. Institute of Peace.

Manor, James, ed. 1984. *Sri Lanka in Change and Crisis.* London: Croom Helm.

Marga Institute. 1981. *An Analytical Description of Poverty in Sri Lanka.* Colombo: Marga Institute.

Mattis, Ann R. 1978. "An Experience in Need-Oriented Development." *Marga Quarterly Journal* (Colombo) 5, no. 3.

Moore, Mick. 1984. "The 1982 Elections and the New Gaullist Bonapartist State in Sri Lanka." In *Sri Lanka in Change and Crisis,* ed. James Manor. London: Croom Helm.

———. 1985. *The State and Peasant Politics in Sri Lanka.* Cambridge: Cambridge University Press.

———. 1988. "The Ideological History of the Sri Lankan 'Peasantry.'" *Modern Asian Studies* 22, no. 4.

———. 1990. "Economic Liberalization versus Political Pluralism in Sri Lanka." *Modern Asian Studies* 24, no. 2:341–83.

Nelson, Joan M. 1984. "The Political Economy of Stabilization." *World Development* 12, no. 10.

Oberst, Robert. 1985. "The Food Stamp Scheme in Sri Lanka." Paper presented at the Wisconsin Conference on South Asia, Madison, November.

Obeyesekere, Gananath. 1984. "The Origins and Institutionalization of Political Violence." In *Sri Lanka in Change and Crisis,* ed. James Manor. London: Croom Helm.

Peebles, Patrick. 1990. "Colonization and Ethnic Conflict in the Dry Zone of Sri Lanka." *Journal of Asian Studies* 49, no. 1 (February).

Pieris, G. H. 1982. *Basic Needs and the Provision of Government Services in Sri Lanka.* Geneva: International Labour Office.

Polanyi, Karl. 1957. *The Great Transformation.* Boston: Beacon Press.

Roberts, Michael. 1994. *Exploring Confrontation.* Switzerland: Harwood Academic Publishers.

———, ed. 1979. *Collective Identities, Nationalisms, and Protest in Modern Sri Lanka.* Colombo: Marga Institute.

———. 1997. *Sri Lanka: Collective Identities Revisited.* Vol. 1. Colombo. Marga Institute.

Rupesinghe, Kumar, ed. 1992. *Internal Conflict and Governance.* New York: St. Martin's.

Sahn, David E. 1983. *An Analysis of the Nutritional Status of Pre-School Children in Sri Lanka, 1980–81.* Washington, DC: International Food Policy Research Institute.

———. 1986. *Malnutrition and Food Consumption in Sri Lanka: An Analysis of Changes during the Past Decade.* Washington, DC: International Food Policy Research Institute.

Samarasinghe, S. W. R. de A., and Reed Coughlan, eds. 1991. *Economic Dimensions of Ethnic Conflict: International Perspectives.* London: Pinter.

Sanderatne, Nimal. 1985. "The Effects of Policies on Real Income and Employ-ment." In *Sri Lanka: The Social Impact of Economic Policies during the Last Decade.* Colombo: UNICEF.

Schumacher, E. F. 1975. *Small Is Beautiful: Economics as if People Mattered.* New York: Harper and Row.

Shastri, Amita. 1985. "Politics of Constitutional Development in South Asia in the Seventies: A Case Study of Sri Lanka." Ph.D. diss., Jawaharlal Nehru University, New Delhi.

———. 1986. "Limits to the Nationalist Revolution in Sri Lanka: The United Front Regime, 1970–77." Paper presented at the annual meeting of the Association for Asian Studies, Chicago, March.

———. 1990. "The Material Basis for Separatism: The Tamil Eelam Movement in Sri Lanka." *Journal of Asian Studies* 49, no. 1 (February).

Sheahan, John. 1980. "Market-Oriented Economic Policies and Repression in Latin America." *Economic Development and Cultural Change* 28, no. 2.

———. 1986. "The Elusive Balance between Stimulation and Constraint in Analysis of Development." In *Development, Democracy, and the Art of Trespassing: Essays in Honor of Albert O. Hirschman,* ed. Alejandro Foxley, Michael S. McPherson, and Guillermo O'Donnell. Notre Dame, IN: University or Notre Dame Press.

Siriwardena, Reggie. 1984. "National Identity in Sri Lanka: Problems in Communication and Education." In *Sri Lanka: The Ethnic Conflict,* by the Committee for Rational Development. New Delhi: Navrang.

Sri Lanka. 1979. "The New Tax Policy." Speech of the Minister of Finance and Planning in Parliament, Colombo, April 4.

———. 1980a. "Budget Speech, 1981." Speech of the Minister of Finance and Planning in Parliament, Colombo.

———. 1980b. *Performance.* Colombo: Ministry of Plan Implementation.

———. 1980c. *Public Investment Programme, 1980–84.* Colombo: Ministry of Finance and Planning.

———. 1980d. *Report of the Presidential Commission of Inquiry into the Incidents Which Took Place between 13th August and 15th September, 1977.* Sessional Paper VII-1980. Colombo: Government of Sri Lanka.

———. 1981. *Evaluation Report of the Food Stamp Scheme.* Colombo: Ministry of Plan Implementation.

———. 1982. *Sri Lanka Yearbook.* Colombo: Department of Census and Statistics.

———. 1983. *Statistical Pocket Book of the Democratic Socialist Republic of Sri Lanka.* Colombo: Government of Sri Lanka.

———. 1984. *Public Investment, 1984–1988.* Colombo: Ministry of Finance and Planning.

Tambiah, S. J. 1986. *Sri Lanka: Ethnic Fratricide and the Dismantling of Democracy.* Chicago: University of Chicago Press.

Tennekoon, Serena. 1990. "Newspaper Nationalism: Sinhala Identity as Historical Discourse." In *Sri Lanka: History and Roots of Conflict,* ed. Jonathan Spencer. London and New York: Routledge.

Uphoff, Norman. 1992. *Learning from Gal Oya.* Ithaca and London: Cornell University Press.

Vittachi, Tarzie. 1958. *Emergency '58: The Story of the Ceylon Race Riots.* London: Andre Deutsch.

Walton, John, and Charles Ragin. 1990. "Global and National Sources of Political Protest: Third World Responses to the Debt Crisis." *American Sociological Review* 55 (December): 876–90.

Walton, John, and David Seddon, eds. 1994. *Free Markets and Food Riots.* Oxford: Basil Blackwell.

Warnapala, W. A. Wiswa. 1979. "Sri Lanka 1978: Reversal of Policies and Strategies." *Asian Survey* 19, no. 2 (February).

World Bank. 1953. *The Economic Development of Ceylon.* Baltimore: Johns Hopkins University Press.

———. 1975. *The Assault on World Poverty.* Baltimore: Johns Hopkins University Press.

———. 1979. *World Development Report, 1979.* [New York]: Oxford University Press.

———. 1980a. *Annual Report.* Washington, DC: World Bank.

———. 1980b. *World Debt Tables.* Washington, DC: World Bank.

———. 1980c. *World Development Report, 1980.* [New York]: Oxford University Press.

Wriggins, W. Howard. 1960. *Ceylon: Dilemmas of a New Nation.* Princeton: Princeton University Press.

CHAPTER 7

Foreign Assistance as Genocide: The Crisis in Russia, the IMF, and Interethnic Relations

Stephen D. Shenfield

For a long time, Russia has been at the center of attention of a large section of the international development community. Huge sums have been poured into the maw of Russian reform. Politicians and officials in Africa, Asia, and Latin America complain that their countries are being starved of assistance because the former Soviet Union and Eastern Europe are getting all the development attention. Yet reform in Russia has, by and large, proven a dismal failure. Despite the external resources committed to Russia during the 1990s, the Russian economy remains in deep crisis and the people of Russia continue to suffer grievously. Standards of living and health have sunk to abysmal levels, and the dominant mood has become one of personal frustration and national humiliation.

Western advisers and institutions, notably the International Monetary Fund (IMF), offering to help Russia effect its transition from a centralized command economy to a market-based economy, have intervened in Russian economic policy. But in doing so they have imposed a neoliberal model unsuited to Russia's circumstances, exacerbating rather than resolving Russia's problems.

For many Russian politicians and opinion makers, however, Russia's current plight is not the outcome of error or accident. Since the westerners are presumed to act rationally, they must have intended the consequences of their advice and pressure. Their objective was to impoverish, weaken, and divide Russia—in more extreme versions, to perpetrate genocide against the Russian people. Furthermore, these Russian politicians charge a group of operators, mostly Jewish, with serving as willing agents, or compradors, of their Western masters. The Jews are alleged to have enriched themselves by robbing the fruits of the past labor of Russian people, consigning them to hunger, misery, and degeneration. Traders and criminals belonging to the peoples of the Caucasus are likewise accused of exploiting the plight of the Russians to their own profit. In this way, Western assistance and policy advice have actually inflamed ethnic tensions in the Russian Federation.

The first part of this chapter is devoted to an analysis of the socioeconomic crisis in Russia, its social causes and effects, and the role played by Western advisers and institutions in bringing it about. I begin by demonstrating the depth of the crisis and the extent of the suffering of the people of Russia as the country enters the twenty-first century. I then outline the major reasons why the post-Soviet transition has led to such dismal results, and I consider who might be held responsible for the failure of Russian reform. I consider the differential sectoral, geographical, and ethnic impact of the crisis on Russia's population, as well as the role played by those who have profited most from the economic transformation: the "new Russians" and the oligarchs.

In the second part of the chapter, I shift focus from the crisis itself to the way in which it is perceived by moderate and extreme Russian nationalists. I discuss the hostile intent toward Russia that they attribute to the West, their perceptions of Russia's comprador elite and alien oligarchy, and their concept of "russophobia." Another key concept of contemporary Russian nationalism, the genocide of the Russian people, is analyzed in greater depth as a case study. I then direct attention to the way in which the more extreme Russian nationalists perceive the ethnic dimension of the crisis, as an attack on the Russians by the Jews.

In the third part of the chapter, I present some of my own reflections concerning the phenomenon of the oligarchs and its bearing on Russian-Jewish relations. I also briefly consider another aspect of interethnic relations in contemporary Russia—namely, the tensions between the Russians and the peoples of the Caucasus, especially the Chechens. In conclusion, I sum up the causative connections that exist between the interethnic tensions in today's Russia and Western assistance and engagement.

The Crisis in Russia

The Depth of the Crisis

While most people in the West know that Russia is going through difficult times, few appreciate the full depth of the Russian economic crisis.[1] Judging by such criteria as gross national product (GNP), the level of industrial and agricultural output, and the real incomes of the population, the Russian economy has contracted by at least one-half in the course of the 1990s. Russia now occupies a marginal position in the world economy, accounting for about 1 percent of world trade and less than 1 percent of foreign direct investment.

Annual per capita GNP is widely used as a general indicator of a country's level of economic development and standard of living. Ten years ago, Russia came about 30th in a ranking of countries by this indicator. It has now sunk to about the 70th place, below not only the Western countries and almost all of Eastern Europe but also many developing countries. For example, Russia's per capita annual GNP, at around $3,000, is one-half that of Brazil.

There are several reasons to be pessimistic concerning prospects for the recovery of the Russian economy over the medium and long term, although limited and temporary upturns can occur in response to such short-term factors as fluctuation in the world oil price. One reason—namely, the weakness of Russia's institutions and the difficulty of strengthening them—will be discussed in the next section. A second reason is that Russia is deeply in debt, with repayments devouring a large proportion of the state budget. The foreign debt of the central government alone has reached about $174 billion (Ivanova 1999), not counting debt owed by provincial governments. Moreover, the debt burden must be considered in conjunction with the most serious problem of all, Russia's urgent need for massive new investment. The country's stock of productive capital—even in the oil industry, gas being the only major exception—and of infrastructural assets (railroads, power stations, the electricity network, etc.) has been starved of investment during the 1990s and is rapidly aging. Further degeneration of the economy and the society can therefore only be averted by undertaking without delay a massive program of industrial and infrastructural investment, but Russia is in no position to mobilize the huge sums that are needed, estimated by the Expert Institute in Moscow at $2 trillion over twenty years (Expert Institute 1999, 5).

A very large proportion of Russia's population is deeply impoverished. It is officially estimated that in the period immediately preceding the financial crash of August 1998, 23 percent of Russia's population, or 33.5 million people, were living below the subsistence minimum. In the wake of the crash, the corresponding figure rose above 40 percent—that is, 60 million people. In late 1999, 34 percent, or 50 million people, were living below the subsistence minimum (*Ekonomika i zhizn'* 1999, no. 50). Roughly half of those living below the subsistence minimum at any time are below the survival minimum, defined as one-half of the subsistence minimum, which means that they are starving.

Until recent years, unemployment was held at a relatively low level, but it is now increasing rapidly. In April 1999, 10.5 million, or one-seventh of the economically active population, were registered as unemployed.

Specialists estimate that the real unemployment rate is about 20 percent. Many employed people receive their wages only in part or after long delays.

The population's average food intake of about 2,000 calories per day is well below that necessary for the maintenance of good health. Bread and potatoes predominate in the diet of the majority; the consumption of protein and vitamins is severely deficient. As a result, many of the classical diseases of poverty have reappeared. Most dramatic is the rapid spread of tuberculosis, with which at least two million people are now thought to be infected. Syphilis and other venereal diseases are also rampant, in part due to the spread of prostitution. AIDS was relatively rare until recently but is now rising sharply, mainly as a by-product of widespread drug addiction. According to the projection of epidemiologist Dr. Vadim Pokrovsky, 10 percent of Russia's population will be infected with HIV by 2005, and most of that 10 percent will be dead by 2010 (Feshbach 2000). Conditions are maturing in the south of Russia for a large-scale outbreak of malaria (Serenko 1999). Alcoholism remains a serious threat to health, as does continuing reliance on abortion as the main means of birth control. Stress, anxiety, and despair exact their toll in the form of ever more heart attacks, fatal accidents, and suicides.

Worst affected are children, whose growth is stunted by the terrible conditions of life in today's Russia. Rickets and anemia are common. The occurrence of birth defects is alarmingly high. Only a minority of children are in good health. A large proportion of the two million or so homeless are children who have either ran away from or been abandoned by their parents. Many are drawn into criminal gangs or exploited as prostitutes or slave laborers.

The epidemiological situation has dramatic demographic consequences. Since 1992, the death rate in Russia has exceeded the birth rate. On the one hand, mortality has greatly risen, at all ages and for both sexes, but most sharply for men. Life expectancy for adult males has fallen below what it was in tsarist times. A century ago, in 1896–97, 56 out of every 100 16-year-old boys in the provinces of European Russia could expect to reach the age of 60, while in 1997 the corresponding proportion was 54 out of 100.[2] On the other hand, the birth rate has sharply fallen, to the extent that classes for the youngest age-groups no longer exist in many schools. Understandably, Russians are unwilling to have enough children to replace the current population: 24 percent of the women of childbearing age questioned in a 1994 survey did not want to have any children; and of women who already had one child, 76 percent did not want a second ("Eto" 1998).

Russia is undergoing a process of depopulation unique in the contemporary world (except for similar processes in neighboring Ukraine, Belarus, and Kazakhstan). Russia's demographic loss from 1992 to 1997 has been estimated at eight million, made up of three million premature deaths and a shortfall of five million births—more than twice the loss experienced by the USSR in 1929–34, the period of forcible collectivization and famine (Glaz'ev 1999, 13). For a number of years, the natural decrease was partly compensated for by the immigration of Russians from the other post-Soviet states, but as this migratory movement tails off, the rate of population decline is accelerating. It is anticipated that Russia will lose a large proportion of its current population in the course of the twenty-first century. The foremost American specialist in Russian health and demography, Professor Murray Feshbach of Georgetown University, argues that "a projection of eighty million by the year 2050 is not out of line," implying a decline of 50 percent over 60 to 70 years (Feshbach 1999).

Causes of the Crisis

The crisis in Russia has multiple interacting causes. Here I shall outline only those causes that seem to me the most significant.[3]

The abrupt freeing of prices by the new reform government of prime minister Egor Gaidar in January 1992 was a crucial miscalculation. The inflation it set in motion, much more severe and prolonged than had been anticipated, wiped out the savings of the population and bankrupted most of the emerging small-business sector (Medvedev 1998, 84–89). The industrial structure inherited from the USSR was dominated by giant monopolistic enterprises, which responded to price deregulation by raising prices and constricting output. Ideally deregulation would have been implemented by stages, in step with state action to restructure industry, promote competition, and create effective market institutions.

Other causes of the sharp contraction of output that began in 1992 were direct consequences of the breakup of the Soviet Union. Customary supply links across the new borders were broken before the market was able to replace them. In the early years, before the newly independent states introduced currencies of their own, both Russia and its post-Soviet neighbors continued to use the ruble, but without coordination of monetary emission by the national banks of the various states. The inflationary effect was felt particularly badly by Russia. Policy makers were nonetheless reluctant to dismantle the "ruble zone," which they valued as a symbol of Russian regional influence. It was clear, moreover, that in the absence of a properly functioning system of interstate banking, separate currencies would be a serious impediment to trade. The issue was finally resolved when the ruble zone came to an end in the mid-1990s.

The reform was also accompanied by the accelerated criminalization of the economy. Russia's judicial and law enforcement agencies were (and still are) ill-adapted to the requirements of a market economy. The police failed to protect private enterprise, which they continued to regard as illegitimate; debts could not in practice be collected, or contracts enforced, through the courts. Under these circumstances, the entrepreneur had no safe alternative to taking shelter under the "roof" of a criminal gang. The tribute paid to organized crime is a heavy burden on the economy. Equally important, criminals use violence to control open-air markets and prevent price competition.

Besides open crime, the Russian economy is riddled with corrupt practices and fraudulent dealings that are not actually illegal in Russia, though they would be considered so in the West. For example, one of the ways in which the oligarch Boris Berezovsky made his fortune was by selling shares in a prospective car manufacturing plant that never materialized; the numerous shareholders never received any compensation. In the course of privatization, Berezovsky and other oligarchs acquired valuable productive assets at absurdly low prices at auctions rigged in advance by their friends inside the government (Khrushchev 1999). Some former Western advisers to the Russian government who enriched themselves by using inside information on privatized enterprises now face prosecution— not, however, in Russia, but in the United States.

The impact that such "crony capitalism" has had on Russian public finance is especially germane to an understanding of the relation between foreign assistance and the crisis. Tax rates and import and export duties are high, even punitively so. At the same time, collection is inefficient. Companies have several ways open to them of avoiding the payment of tax altogether—for instance, by diverting income into legally separate front companies (Hendley 1999). Organizations ranging from sporting associations to the Russian Orthodox Church have the right to import alcoholic drinks free of duty. The privatization of industry could have contributed a great deal of money to public coffers; as already noted, this chance was lost through corruption.

The state budget, however, is undermined by corruption not only on the income side but also with respect to expenditure. Funds allocated to one or another specific purpose often disappear without a trace, the theft of the money intended for the postwar reconstruction of Chechnya being one of the better-known examples. Yeltsin's reelection campaign of 1996 was financed from the state budget. Account needs also to be taken of the fact that the Russian government does not directly manage its own budgetary funds but entrusts this task to authorized banks controlled by the oligarchs. The state lends these banks public money at a low rate of interest, so that they can immediately relend it at a high rate of interest and pocket the difference.

For quite some time, this extremely corrupt and inefficient fiscal system was kept going thanks to the infusion of supplementary state income obtained by borrowing, both from the IMF and other foreign lending institutions and through the issue of high-yield treasury bonds (called in Russian "gosudarstvennye kreditnye obligatsii" [GKOs], or "state credit obligations"). The IMF was paying not so much for reform as for the enrichment of corrupt Russian officials and their business friends.[4] Sooner or later, of course, the system had to collapse, as the level of repayments rose above that of new borrowing. The beginning of the collapse came with the financial crash of August 1998, when Russia partly defaulted on its GKO debt. The next stage will occur when the Russian government is forced (assuming the absence of debt forgiveness on a massive scale) to default on its foreign debt.

The price for fiscal corruption has been paid above all by the ordinary people of Russia, who have had to cope with the deterioration of education, health care, and other social services that have been progressively starved of budgetary funds. The highest price has been paid by the weakest groups, who are the most dependent on state support: these include the elderly, children in care, and the physically and mentally handicapped. The residents of most institutions for such people are starving. The price has also been paid by millions of state employees, from physicians and schoolteachers to scientists and army officers, who have been driven to desperation (and in many cases to suicide) by prolonged nonpayment of their salaries and the unbearable conditions in which they have to work. Whatever other cuts might have to be made in the state budget, the IMF always insists that repayments due on foreign loans must be made in full and on time. At the same time, pressure has been exerted on the Russian government to keep the budgetary deficit within narrow limits.

That large-scale Western assistance has not safeguarded Russia from ruin also becomes less surprising when one takes into account the massive flight of Russian capital abroad. This has been estimated at $63 billion for the period from 1992 to 1995 (Tikhomirov 1997) and at $77 billion for the period from 1996 to 1998 (Expert Institute 1999, 5)—about $150 billion over the decade as a whole. Capital flight dwarfs foreign loans, aid, and investment taken together. Bearing in mind that Russian capital invested in the West helps to support Western economies, one might well conclude that on balance Russia has been aiding the West in the 1990s rather than vice versa.

In recent years, the crisis has been exacerbated by a new transmutation of the Russian economic system. Wishing to dampen the high inflation of the early 1990s but failing to understand its source, the IMF imposed on Russia its standard recipe, constriction of the money supply. This had a consequence that the IMF was not intellectually prepared to anticipate— the demonetization of the Russian economy. Economic actors did their utmost to preserve their customary patterns of interaction by resorting increasingly to the use of barter, promissory notes, and other monetary surrogates. This "virtual economy" is now deeply embedded in the fabric of Russian life, operates in accordance with its own poorly understood laws, and can be overcome only with difficulty and over a long period.[5] While the virtual economy does allow the survival of millions of people who would otherwise perish as a result of the arbitrary shortage of money, barter entails transaction costs far in excess of those of normal market exchange.

Besides the main structural causes of the crisis, mention should be made of policy decisions made by both the Russian and Western governments that may not have played a decisive role but that have made Russia's situation even worse than it might otherwise have been. The two wars against the separatist regime in Chechnya have been a considerable expense. (However, the Chechen separatists inflicted significant damage on the Russian economy by stealing oil, perpetrating bank frauds, and making their airport available for customs-free import and export.) An example of a harmful Western policy is the insistence from the outset that Russia take over the foreign debt of the Soviet Union, which even today constitutes a substantial portion of Russia's foreign debt (roughly $32 billion out of $174 billion). In the opinion of some observers, one reason for the deficiencies in Gaidar's reform plan may have been his distraction at a critical moment by the time-consuming negotiations on the Soviet debt (Hedlund 1999, 119–21). Another example is the pressure that has been brought to bear on Russia not to take measures to protect its domestic producers from the overwhelming competition of cheap Western imports. The Russian government has often been pressed to reduce or eliminate import duties on products that American firms export to Russia, such as poultry, while U.S. food aid to Russia has had little effect beyond providing support to American farmers needing to dispose of their surpluses and further undermining the shaky market position of Russia's own farmers.[6]

The most significant single factor underlying all the specific causes of the crisis is undoubtedly the weakness of the institutions of post-Soviet Russia. Neither the banks nor the tax collection agencies, neither the courts nor the police adequately carry out the tasks required of them for the proper functioning of a market economy. In principle, it is up to the state to shape the needed institutions, but the state itself has been weakened and privatized to such an extent that it will be an uphill struggle to reconstitute it for any public purpose.

Responsibility for the Crisis

From the preceding discussion, it is clear that responsibility for the crisis in Russia is shared by several actors: the Russian government and its Western advisers, corrupt officials and business operators, Western governments, and the IMF and other lending institutions. Given the ultimate source of the crisis in the precipitous and chaotic collapse of the Soviet Union, one might also lay blame on those Soviet politicians who helped to make that collapse more precipitous and chaotic than it needed to have been, including the organizers of the August 1991 putsch attempt, on the one hand, and Boris Yeltsin and the "democrats," on the other.

Thus, the IMF cannot be cast as the sole villain—and perhaps not even as the chief villain—of the piece. The initial reform plan that was set in motion in January 1992 was the work of Prime Minister Yegor Gaidar and his team, influenced to a certain extent no doubt by their recently appointed Western advisers. (Anders Aslund [1995, 2] became an economic adviser to the Russian government in November 1991.) At that time, the IMF was only just beginning to get involved. Later, however, Russia was to become increasingly dependent on IMF loans and was therefore left little choice but to accept IMF conditions. The IMF orthodoxy thereby came to play an important role in exacerbating and prolonging Russia's crisis.

The contribution of the IMF to the creation of the virtual economy has already been noted. The IMF compounds its initial error by devising its policy goals for Russia without taking proper account of the existence of the virtual economy. In general, the reforms that the IMF advocates would be economically rational in the context of an already effectively functioning market economy, but their implementation under the conditions of the virtual economy could only wreak further havoc and cause worse misery.

Housing reform provides a good example. Under the Soviet regime, the tenants of state-owned apartments paid nominal rents and charges for municipal services, such as heating and sewage. Even if payment was not made, eviction was unheard of. In most parts of Russia, this arrangement still exists. The subsidies place a heavy burden on local government budgets, leaving little money for other categories of expenditure. The situation is exacerbated by the fact that increasing numbers of tenants, receiving their own wages only after long delay or in the form of barter, have stopped paying even the subsidized rents and charges. In a normal market economy, a housing reform that raised rents and charges to an economic level and enforced the eviction of those who persistently failed to pay might make good sense. In Russia, it would lead only to the abandonment of much of the existing stock of housing and to a huge expansion of the already substantial ranks of the homeless. For that reason, plans for housing reform have encountered strong resistance, although experiments with it have been conducted in some places (such as St. Petersburg).

A similar issue is the procedure for taxing the sale of industrial products. The Russian press reported that in September 1997, Lawrence Summers, undersecretary of state at the U.S. Treasury, sent Russian finance minister Anatoly Chubais a letter containing "a direct instruction" to abandon the principle of taxing output at the time of cash payment and instead to extract tax at the point of delivery. Under the conditions prevailing in Russia, there is often a long delay between delivery and cash payment, so the change advocated by Summers would deprive Russian enterprises of scarce circulating capital, dooming many of them to bankruptcy (Sulakshin 1998, 37–38).

Of course, the remit of the IMF has traditionally been to safeguard the stability of the world financial system. Nothing in the experience of the organization had intellectually prepared it for the quite different task of assisting in the transformation of a centrally administered system into a market economy. The IMF was first brought into Russian affairs when Western governments decided in December 1991 to entrust it with the matter, raised by Yeltsin, of providing a stabilization fund to support the ruble. This decision served a purely domestic purpose—that of making the anticipated burden on Western taxpayers politically less visible (Hedlund 1999, 119–21). It might be argued that the fault for the failure of the transformation lies not with the IMF but with the governments that assigned the IMF a task for which it was ill prepared, rather than creating a special body equipped with the necessary expertise.

The Differential Impact of the Crisis

While the great majority of the people of Russia have suffered from the crisis to one extent or another, they have shared the burden far from equally. Certain social strata, occupations, regions, ethnic groups, and age-groups are exposed to much worse conditions than others.

The contrast between people employed in different sectors of the economy, for example, is striking. The average monthly wage in September 1999 was 1,684 rubles ($66 at the current rate of exchange). However, the corresponding figures for those working in the lucrative export branches of the fuel (oil and gas) industry and nonferrous metallurgy were 4,836 rubles ($190) and 3,756 rubles ($147), respectively. The average monthly salary in the financial sector also exceeded 3,000 rubles ($119). At the same time, those employed in the state-funded spheres of education, culture, health care, and social services, as well as catering personnel, received on average 900–1,000 rubles ($35–39) a month. The figure for light industry was 897 rubles ($35), and that for agriculture was only 721 rubles ($28) (*Ekonomika i zhizn'* 1999, no. 50).

Regional differences arise mainly from differences in climate, accessibility, and regional economic specialization. Most of Russia's North has been devastated by the crisis, with the exception of areas rich in natural resources, such as Tiumen' (oil) and Sakha-Yakutia (diamonds). Moscow has enjoyed a highly privileged position, due in large part to its concentration of financial assets, although this has been rather less the case since August 1998. Many differences in the position of various ethnic groups derive in turn from regional contrasts: the Tatars and the Yakuts, for instance, tend to be less poor than the Buryats and the Tuvans.

The overall extent of economic inequality in post-Soviet Russia is very high by comparison with either the Soviet past or the West. In this respect, Russia resembles the Third World. The average income of the top 10 percent of the population has been estimated to exceed that of the bottom 10 percent by a factor of over 13 to 1.

"New Russians" and Oligarchs

Vast fortunes have been accumulated in the hands of a few hundred "new Russians." Many of these are former top Soviet officials, such as Komsomol (Communist Youth) functionaries and ministers in charge of valuable raw materials, who have converted their political power into material riches. Others are leading regional politicians; others are freelance operators who have put their good personal connections inside government to profitable use. Very few are entrepreneurs who are genuinely independent of the state (Medvedev 1998, 214–50).

Among the most wealthy of the "new Russians," one finds a small group of so-called oligarchs who combine enormous wealth with great political influence.[7] The term *oligarch* is used in two different senses. Some use it to refer only to a clique of big bankers, the most notorious of whom is Boris Berezovsky. Alluding to the period in Russian history known as "the rule of the seven boyars" *(semiboiarshchina),* they describe the present time as "the rule of the seven bankers" *(semibankirshchina).* Others use *oligarch* to refer to a somewhat broader group, including the seven bankers but also a number of other individuals, primarily the leading figures of the oil and gas industries (the oil and gas barons). Moscow mayor Yuri Luzhkov also counts as an oligarch in this conception.

Where did the oligarchs come from? The oil and gas barons created their empires by exploiting their positions as top managers in the Soviet oil and gas ministries. Some of the bankers also received a head start from their positions in the Soviet party-state bureaucracy: Potanin emerged from the Soviet Ministry of Foreign Trade, while Khodorkovsky was the most successful of the Komsomol functionaries turned entrepreneurs. The other bankers come from a variety of professional backgrounds: Berezovsky is by training a mathematician; Gusinsky worked as a theater director; Smolensky was in construction; Vinogradov was in the nuclear power industry. In these cases, personal ties with high officials in the reform government played a crucial role. Some observers believe that these top government officials hoped to become leading businessmen themselves after leaving state service and that their banker associates were intended to serve as their proxies but proved more difficult to control than they had expected.

The power of the oligarchs is not unlimited, and they are by no means the sole power in contemporary Russia. Nevertheless, they do possess great power. Yeltsin was in the practice of calling on groups of selected oligarchs to advise him at critical moments, and some oligarchs, notably Boris Berezovsky and Roman Abramovich, belonged to the inner circle known as "the Family" (which included Yeltsin's daughters and specially trusted officials of the presidential administration). The oligarchs were also able to exert their influence over the various governments that Yeltsin appointed during his presidency. The single exception was the government of Prime Minister Yevgeny Primakov, who reportedly issued instructions that Berezovsky not be allowed into the building where Primakov had his office. Moves were apparently afoot at this time to have Berezovsky arrested: he went abroad, and he returned only when assured that he would not be arrested. This may, however, be considered the exception that proves the rule, as within a matter of months Berezovsky prevailed on Yeltsin to replace Primakov.

The oligarchs also influence Russian politics in other, less direct ways. They have provided large-scale financial backing to candidates for public office who are prepared to accommodate their interests. A well-known example is the deal that General Alexander Lebed made with Berezovsky—a deal that presumably solved Lebed's money problems but that tarnished his reputation as a patriot and a fighter against corruption (Polikarpov 1996). In 1999, some oligarchs used their money to become Duma deputies themselves, by promising electors in the constituencies where they stood to bring in investment and raise their standard of living.[8] Entry into the Duma gives them immunity from any future risk of criminal prosecution. Last but by no means least, the oligarchs exert a substantial (though not, of course, unlimited) influence on Russian public opinion through the print and electronic media empires that they own and control.

The power of the oligarchs is, moreover, widely perceived as illegitimate. Firstly, nobody has elected the oligarchs: their power is difficult to reconcile with the officially proclaimed values of democracy, and for this reason alone it is surrounded by secrecy. Secondly, the oligarchs are regarded as extremely immoral and rapacious people. Boris Berezovsky is viewed as a particularly unsavory individual. He has been accused of making his fortune by means of speculation, fraud, and corrupt insider deals, as well as of hiring criminals to murder those who have stood in his way. There is good reason to suspect that these accusations are true.

How Many Oligarchs and "New Russians" Are Jewish?

Oligarchic power is perceived as illegitimate for a third reason: the oligarchs are believed to be mostly of non-Russian, specifically Jewish, origin. How much truth is there in this?[9]

If we restrict ourselves to the seven bankers, then there is little doubt that most of them are of Jewish origin. However, Vladimir Potanin of ONEXIMBANK is an ethnic Russian, and there does not seem to be any reason to think that Vladimir Vinogradov of INKOMBANK is not an ethnic Russian. That leaves us with five "Jewish" bankers: Boris Berezovsky, Vladimir Gusinsky (MOST), Alexander Smolensky (SBS-AGRO), Mikhail Khodorkovsky (MENATEP), and Mikhail Fridman (ALFA-BANK).

If we include the oil and gas barons among the oligarchs, we get a somewhat different picture. The most powerful oilman is Vagit Alekperov, head of the LUKoil company, who is an Azeri by origin. A survey of the twenty most prominent figures in the oil industry reveals a variety of ethnic backgrounds. There are a couple of Jews among them: Roman Abramovich of Sibneft (Siberian Oil) and Semyon Vainshtok of Transneft (the pipeline company). In addition, Khodorkovsky acquired in 1995 a controlling stake in the YuKOS oil company. On the whole, however, it is obvious that Jews do not predominate. And the two men in the gas industry who may be regarded as oligarchs, the present head of the gas monopoly, Gazprom Rem Vyakhirev, and its previous head (and a former prime minister), Viktor Chernomyrdin, are ethnic Russians.[10]

Of the oil and gas barons, the only ones with a clear claim to be counted as oligarchs are Alekperov, Vyakhirev, and Chernomyrdin. Arguably Abramovich should be included on the grounds that in recent times he has been part of "the Family," although he remains dependent on Berezovsky.

Among those commonly labeled oligarchs are two other men: Pyotr Aven, also of ALFA-BANK, a Jew; and Moscow mayor Yuri Luzhkov, a Russian. So we end up with thirteen oligarchs altogether—seven Jews, five Russians, and one Azeri.[11] While the oligarchs cannot be said to constitute a predominantly Jewish group, a disproportionately large number of them are Jewish.

When the net is cast a little wider to cover a broader cross section of "new Russians," the same tendency is visible, though less marked. Of the 211 prominent businesspeople and managers featured in one work of reference, only 60 to 70 percent have recognizably Russian names, although ethnic Russians comprise 80 to 85 percent of Russia's population; the second largest group is formed by 18 individuals (about 9 percent) with recognizably Jewish names (Amirov and Pribylovskii 1997).

How Russian Nationalists Perceive the Crisis

The Hostile Intent of the West

A Russian nationalist, reading the analysis of the causes of Russia's crisis that I have just given, would find in it a great deal with which he (or she) could agree. He would, however, be sure to regard the analysis as apologetic—or at best naive—in one crucial respect. Assuming that westerners are rational and intelligent beings, he would argue that if their actions led to certain consequences—say, the weakening and destruction of Russia's economy—that was not because they did not understand what they were doing but because they intended precisely those consequences and considered them to be in the interests of the West. In short, he would presume hostile intent.

To take one of many possible examples: I have argued that if one takes capital flight into account, the net flow of resources during the 1990s has been from Russia to the West and not vice versa. I did not take the next step and say that Western policy makers, with a view to supporting Western economies, deliberately strive to bring about a situation in Russia that will entail massive capital flight. The Russian nationalist does not hesitate to take this step. Alexander Samoiloff, a former KGB officer and businessman from Khabarovsk in the Russian Far East, writes:

> I don't think that the top political circles of the West did not understand Yeltsin's policy and where all the borrowed funds disappeared to. They closed their eyes because this process favored their own national interests. (Samoiloff 2000)

He supposes, in other words, that the IMF continued to channel funds to Russia despite knowing full well that they would be stolen, because it saw this as part of an arrangement that was in overall accordance with Western economic interests. Such ignorance of the way in which the IMF operates is typical of the vast majority of the Russian public: a poll conducted by the Public Opinion Foundation on July 11, 1998, found that 51 percent of respondents were unable to give any answer to the question "What does the IMF do?"

The specific hostile aims most commonly attributed to the West follow, in increasing order of radicalism.

- To deprive Russia of its rightful status as a great power and of its natural sphere of influence in the post-Soviet region.
- To undermine Russia's economic and political sovereignty and independence. International organizations are said to pursue this aim by using assistance to globalize Russia's economy, making it more dependent on the world market (Malyshev 1999).
- To destroy Russia's indigenous technological capacity, thereby reducing Russia to a "raw-materials appendage" of the West (Polikarpov 1996), like many Third World countries, unable to compete effectively with Western companies on the world market (or even on its own domestic market) for industrial goods, and also unable ever again to pose a strategic challenge to Western global hegemony.
- To eliminate Russia as a single state by promoting the fragmentation of its territory into a collection of petty local states that will be more easily controlled by the West.
- To eliminate the ethnic Russians as a people—that is, genocide. I shall consider this belief at greater length below.

The results of other opinion surveys indicate that a majority of the Russian public now attributes hostile intent to the West. A survey of 1,500 people in 40 provinces, conducted in 1999 by the ROMIR polling agency, found 79 percent of respondents prepared to agree with such statements as "The West wants to split Russia up and destroy it altogether" or "The West is trying to reduce Russia to a Third World country," with only 15 percent willing to give the West credit for providing Russia with economic and political support.[12]

The Comprador Government

In the perception of Russian nationalists, post-Soviet Russia has fallen under more or less direct foreign control. Yuri Goryachev, governor of Ulyanovsk Province in the Volga region, put it in the following way:

In the villages, I am often asked: "Who is ruling us? In the past we knew that the politburo was in charge." Now we are still ruled by the politburo, but it is located in a foreign land and is called the International Monetary Fund. (*Russian Regional Report* 5, no. 1, January 12, 2000)

Many Russian nationalists believe that Gorbachev and Yeltsin were recruited at an early stage as agents of influence on behalf of the Western powers and have followed the instructions of their controllers in accordance with a master plan to weaken, break up, and ultimately destroy first the USSR and then Russia. A fictionalized vision of a Western plot to "capture" Gorbachev and destroy the Soviet Union was presented by Alexander Prokhanov in his novel *The Angel Flew Past* (Prokhanov 1994).

A more sophisticated version, most systematically developed by Sergei Baburin, leader of the Russian All-People's Union, revolves around the concept of a comprador elite—a stratum of businessmen, politicians, officials, and specialists who are willing to cooperate with Western strategies directed against Russia (Baburin 1996). The compradors are said to be willing to betray their own country in this fashion partly because their own interests are inextricably bound up with those of the West and partly because many of them have been brainwashed into Western ways of thought and feeling. According to proponents of this theory, the brainwashing is carried out to a large extent by means of ostensibly nongovernmental organizations and contacts, "through which desired personnel for the institutions of power are selected, official decisions are drafted, and policy is actually made" (Glaz'ev 1999, 123).

One implication is that Western control over Russia is a fairly recent phenomenon, which had its beginnings in the late 1980s but took clear shape only in the course of the 1990s. In a pamphlet eloquently entitled *Treason,* Stepan Sulakshin (former deputy chairman of the Duma's Committee for Industry, Construction, Transportation, and Energy; a Luzhkov supporter; and by professional background a nuclear and laser physicist) outlines how under Yeltsin Russia has "lost its state sovereignty" as "a mechanism for controlling Russia from abroad" has been set up, a mechanism that is now fully functional (Sulakshin 1998, 13, 91). Western advisers, lending institutions (such as the IMF) whose detailed conditions determine Russian socioeconomic policy, and direct relations between members of the Russian and American governments all play a part in the working of the control mechanism.

The Alien Financial Oligarchy

The financial oligarchs (the seven bankers) are regarded by Russian nationalists not only as ruthless and rapacious men but also as constituting an antinational force.

[The oligarchy] presents itself not under a national but under a piratical flag. It is not united with the people but confronts it, [using] all the methods of the previous regime: bribery, theft, bureaucracy, authoritarianism, and moral cynicism. (Bogdanov and Shakhunyants 1999)

The idea of the antinational character of the oligarchs is often given an ethnic coloration, with stress on the fact that all but one of them are Jews (the recognized exception being Vladimir Potanin). The rule of the seven bankers, who are also thought to be linked to Western financiers, is thus often seen as a contemporary form of Jewish domination. The parallel with the issue of "Jewish bankers" in Weimar Germany is striking (Feldman 1995).[13] Those writers who use *oligarch* in a broader sense, to include also Luzhkov and the oil and gas barons, are less likely to stress the theme of Jewish domination.

Russophobia

But why should aliens and westerners seek to bring about the destruction of Russia? "Patriotic" writers suggest a variety of possible motives, some of an economic or geopolitical character, but one important recurring concept is that of "russophobia." Many members of non-Russian ethnic groups in Russia and the former Soviet Union, as well as many influential westerners, are said to have been inculcated with a deep fear, hatred, and contempt of Russians. Russians are feared as barbarians, despised as inferior beings, and hated as the bearers of a primitive, collectivistic mentality and spirituality. Especially important for the worldview of the Russian nationalists is the russophobia that they believe to have animated the ethnically alien German or Jewish state elites who have at various times in history—under Peter the Great, under the Bolsheviks, and under Yeltsin's reformers—ruthlessly imposed painful social transformations on the Russian people.[14]

Case Study: The Genocide of the Russian People

Before me lie two Russian books. They are by different authors, and the subtitles are different, but they have the same title: *Genocide.* The front cover of the first book displays a reproduction of Goya's famous painting of a pyramid of human skulls in a wasteland. The identities of the perpetrator of the genocide and its victim are revealed in this book's subtitle, "The West Annihilates the Russian People." The cover of the second book is not illustrated, except that a large red patch, presumably representing a bloodstain, spreads out from the title. Its subtitle, "Russia and the New World Order," is more scholarly in tone.

The first book bears the names of Vladimir Zhirinovsky, the famous Russian nationalist politician who leads the Liberal Democratic Party of Russia (LDPR), and his party colleague Vladimir Davidenko. This is unlikely to shock the reader, for Zhirinovsky is well known as an extremist. More remarkable is the authorship of the second book. It is by Sergei Glazyev, a professional economist generally regarded as a centrist or moderate nationalist. In the early 1990s he was Russia's minister of foreign economic relations, until he resigned in protest at Yeltsin's violent suppression of the Supreme Soviet. Since 1994 he has been a prominent parliamentarian, first as chairman of the Duma Committee on Economic Policy, then as head of the Information and Analysis Directorate of the Federation Council (the Parliament's upper house). He has been an adviser to General Alexander Lebed, to Moscow mayor Yuri Luzhkov, and to the leadership of the Communist Party of the Russian Federation. Yet, like Zhirinovsky, this intellectual pillar of the respectable opposition also holds that the West is "annihilating the Russian people."[15]

Genocide of the Russian people is a central concept and rallying cry for a broad section of the Russian nationalist movement in contemporary Russia. "The Russian question, as it is now posed," proclaims Alexander Prokhanov (1998), editor of the Russian nationalist newspaper *Zavtra*, "is the question of the genocide of our people." The cry of genocide of the Russian people is also a call to Russians to resist their tormentors, to organize themselves, to carry through a national revolution, and to mete out just punishment on the aliens and traitors who have sought to destroy them.

The idea of an ongoing genocide of the Russian people by the Jews appeared in the propaganda of extreme Russian nationalist and monarchist groups, such as *Pamyat'*, at least as early as 1990. At that time, however, the word *genocide* was used to refer to famine, repression, and the destruction of Russian culture under the Bolsheviks, not to physical annihilation in the literal sense (Buckley 1993, 287–88, 291–93). The idea was given a literal reinterpretation from about the middle of the 1990s, as the process of demographic decline attracted increasing attention.

The concept of genocide of the Russian people may be broken down into two main components: first, the idea that the Russian people are dying out or undergoing extinction; second, the idea that their extinction is the deliberate goal of a hostile force. Russian nationalist authors begin their treatment of the theme of the extinction of the Russian people by reviewing the facts of Russia's current population decline. When the trends that prevailed in the 1990s are projected forward, they point toward extinction within the space of a few generations. Drawing a parallel between the Russian demographic implosion and another exponential process, radioactive disintegration, a number of writers refer to the half-life of Russia's population—that is, the period of time needed for it to decline by 50 percent. According to Glazyev, the half-life is in the range of 60 to 80 years (Glaz'ev 1999, 14). Another demographer suggests a half-life of 50 to 55 years (A. I. Koreshkin in *Natsional'nye* 1997, 122).[16]

The analogy with radioactive disintegration may seem to imply that the number of Russians is expected to go on falling until there are hardly any left. That, however, is not necessarily the argument being made. What is feared is that the severely reduced Russians will be supplanted in their own homeland by more fecund peoples immigrating from the south and east, the most numerous being the Chinese. By the middle of the twenty-first century, warns one "patriotic" forecaster, Russians will no longer constitute a majority in Russia; they are then likely to be absorbed culturally by immigrant groups and disappear as a distinct people. Thus, areas of the Volga and Urals regions that were predominantly Moslem before the sixteenth century, such as Astrakhan, Chelyabinsk, and Orenburg, may become so once again (N. E. Titova in *Natsional'nye* 1997, 131–32).

A number of writers stress that the demographic decline is a process specific to the ethnic Russians (e.g., Koreshkin 1998, 11). The other ethnic groups living in Russia, it is alleged, are much less affected. The point is made that the population of many of the ethnoterritorial autonomous provinces and republics, where a high proportion of inhabitants are non-Russian, is still increasing; therefore, the situation in the ethnically Russian provinces must be even worse than in Russia as a whole. Moreover, the true scale of the demographic decline among ethnic Russians has been masked by the large-scale migration to Russia since 1991 of Russians from the Caucasus, Central Asia, and the other post-Soviet states (D. D. Benediktov in "Eto" 1998; Koreshkin 1998, 12). Once this migration reaches completion, the full extent of ethnic Russian demographic decline will become evident.

That demographic decline can arouse the fear of extinction even in a large ethnic group is confirmed by the experience of Weimar Germany, where rampant disease (to a large extent, the same diseases as in Russia today, especially tuberculosis and syphilis) and falling birth rates were widely perceived as *Volkstod* (death of the people) (Thaler 1996).

The transition from the idea of extinction of the Russian people to that of genocide is an easy one for many Russians to make. Under the Soviet regime, it was constantly drummed into people's heads that important things do not happen by mere chance: one should always ask who stands to gain from them. Thus, explanation in terms of genocide makes the prospect of extinction more comprehensible, plausible, and meaningful. We may observe this mental mechanism at work in the speech of Academician Benediktov. "We have a type of reproduction characteristic only of countries that have long been at war," he notes, comparing conditions in Russia with those in such war-devastated countries as Afghanistan and Ethiopia. He goes on to ask the apparently logical question "Who is at war with us?" ("Eto" 1998).

One recurring answer is that a concrete plan of genocide has been worked out by Western foundations and think tanks. This plan is based on the calculation that fifty million Russians will suffice for the economic purposes of the West, the primary such purpose being the exploitation of Russia as a "raw-materials appendage." The remaining one hundred million Russians are therefore to be destroyed "as excess ballast" (Polikarpov 1996).[17] Baburin takes the view that the annihilation program is inherited from Hitler by Western and pro-Western Russian politicians: it has the twin goals of replacing the USSR and then Russia by "petty nationalist states under Western control" and of reducing the Russian and other Slavic peoples "to such a demographic condition that they will die out in two or three generations" (Baburin 1997, 286).

In their expose, Zhirinovsky and Davidenko survey some of the methods used by the West to annihilate Russians. They argue that besides economic exploitation and other conventional methods, the West pursues its genocidal goal by inciting Chechens and other non-Russian minorities to kill Russians, by kidnapping young Russian men and women to extract their bodily organs for export to Israel and the United States, by promoting family planning in Russia, and by introducing sex education in Russian schools to corrupt the youth (Zhirinovskii and Davidenko 1997, 11–12, 15–17, 18–20, 41–44).[18] Writer Edward Limonov, head of the National Bolshevik Party, argues (1998) that the "logical conclusion" of the genocidal process will be "to dismember our bodies and eat us."

Glazyev's account of the genocide is more mundane, focusing on the effects of impoverishment and disease. He also casts some doubt on whether "the ideologists and purveyors of the genocide policy" really do intend to bring about the extinction of the Russian people: their subjective motives may be nongenocidal or even benevolent, but objectively they are perpetrating genocide (Glaz'ev 1997, 11, 46–47). Glazyev is clearly aware that intent on the part of the perpetrator is one of the elements of the definition of genocide in international law, but he considers that point unimportant. Even if the conscious goal of the perpetrators is social engineering rather than genocide as such, they are unwilling to change course when it turns out that the extinction of millions of people is the actual result of their policy. Being russophobes, they regard Russians as inferior beings whose fate is a matter of little or no account.

More precisely whom do the Russian nationalists identify as the perpetrator of the genocide? The main subject of the genocide, writes Glazyev, is "the natural symbiosis of radical [internal] anti-Russian extremists dreaming of the destruction of independent Russian statehood, and external forces supporting them that have traditionally striven to weaken Russia" (Glaz'ev 1997, 47–48). The leading external force is identified as the United States. Glazyev warns against understanding the symbiosis in conspiratorial terms, although he does hint in a footnote that shadowy Jewish and Masonic forces may stand behind Russia's overt enemies (Glaz'ev 1999, 106–10).

In literature of a more extremist slant, "the Jews" are unequivocally identified as the perpetrators of the genocide, and the governments of Russia and the Western powers are portrayed as Jewish puppet regimes. For Alexander Barkashov, leader of the nazi Russian National Unity, this crime by the Jews justifies the countergenocide that is to be perpetrated against the Jews once the Russians return to power.[19] In the middle of the spectrum, the Jews may be portrayed as an important but not necessarily predominant component of the anti-Russian West. This appears, for example, to be Zhirinovsky's view.

Implications for Interethnic Relations

The Jewish Oligarchs and Russian-Jewish Relations

To what extent can the conflict between the oligarchs and their opponents be regarded as not just a political but an ethnopolitical conflict? To what extent does the phenomenon of the Jewish oligarchs account for the occurrence of popular anti-Semitism in post-Soviet Russia?

The economic crisis affects Russian-Jewish relations primarily through the widespread perception that Jews are disproportionately or even predominantly represented among the newly powerful and wealthy of post-Soviet Russia—the "new Russians" (most of whom, it is often objected, are not actually ethnic Russians) and, above all, the oligarchs. The charge made against "the Jews" is twofold: firstly, that they are to blame for the ruin of Russia's economy; secondly, that they have benefited the most from the crisis.

The anti-Semitism characteristic of contemporary Russian nationalism—unfair as it is to the majority of Russian Jews, who are neither oligarchs nor "new Russians"—cannot be regarded as a mere manifestation of mental delusion, archaic prejudice, or irrational scapegoating. No doubt old stereotypes of the Jew as a bloodsucking moneylender play a certain role, but those stereotypes could not possibly exert such a strong hold on the popular imagination were they not supported by aspects of present-day social reality—namely, the greater poverty on average of Russians as compared with Jews and, above all, the wealth and power of the Jewish oligarchs.

The main social divide in Russia lies not between one ethnic group and another but between rich and poor. But this social divide is not without an ethnic tinge. The weight of the ethnic Russian element is considerably greater in the masses than it is in the elite, while members of various non-Russian minorities, especially Jews, constitute a disproportionately large section of the elite. This helps to explain why popular protest is often accompanied by the expression of prejudice against non-Russians in general and Jews and "Caucasians" in particular, just as it helps to explain why elite contempt for the masses often takes the form of russophobia. The divide between the elite and the masses in late tsarist Russia had a similar ethnic tinge, with individuals of German descent playing the role now more commonly occupied by people of Jewish origin.

As making this point invariably causes misunderstanding, I add what should go without saying: that to offer a (partial) explanation of anti-Semitism does not mean to excuse it, let alone to justify it. Insofar as the ethnic composition of the elite is not in fact the cause of the people's suffering, prejudice against non-Russians diverts popular attention from the problems that really matter and is easily manipulated in the interest of ethnic Russian sections of the elite or ethnic Russian counterelites. In the nineteenth century, one of the founders of the German and international social democracy, August Bebel, argued this point pithily when he said that "anti-Semitism is the socialism of fools." That is still true in Russia today. And there are indeed some prominent figures among Russian nationalists and communists, such as the famous cinematographer and parliamentarian Stanislav Govorukhin and the communist theorist Boris Slavin, who understand this and take a strong public stand against anti-Semitism.

Why should the proportion of Jews and of some other ethnic minorities that have prospered in the post-Soviet transition be larger than the proportion of ethnic Russians who have done so? This question still awaits serious sociological research. We may, however, plausibly suppose that part of the answer has to do with the specific nature of the stereotypes that various ethnic groups hold about themselves and one another. Such stereotypes are not a priori valid, but by molding what people expect of themselves and of others, they may act as self-fulfilling prophecies.

St. Petersburg sociologist Zinaida Sikevich argues that ethnic Russians tend to hold very similar negative stereotypes about different non-

Russian ethnic groups, who are typically perceived as having such qualities as greed, audacity, arrogance, clannishness, dishonesty, cunning, and hypocrisy (Sikevich 1996, 124–25). By contrast, Russians tend to see themselves as unselfish, modest, honest, naive, and straightforward. Of course, if one is on the other side of the fence, negative qualities can readily be reinterpreted as positive ones and vice versa—audacity as initiative, arrogance as self-confidence, cunning as intelligence, hypocrisy as sophistication, and so forth. In any case, the qualities typically identified as non-Russian are the more conducive to success in a market economy—all the more so under the wild and chaotic conditions of the economic transition—while the qualities typically identified as Russian are bound to impede the individual's adaptation to new and changing conditions. As a result, socioeconomic policies that are expounded in "neutral" technical terms, with no reference to ethnicity, come to be seen as designed for the benefit of some ethnic groups and to the detriment of others.

The Relationship between the Jewish Oligarchs and Russian Jewry

How strong an impact the phenomenon of the Jewish oligarchs may have on Russian-Jewish relations in general clearly depends, inter alia, on the extent to which the Jewish oligarchs regard themselves, and are regarded by others, as symbols, representatives, or leaders of Russian Jews as an ethnic and religious community. To the extent that the stereotypes analyzed by Sikevich hold sway, the oligarchs are prone to be seen in precisely this light, as archetypical Jews. As Sergei Pogorelsky argues, the image of the Jewish banker drowns out the benign alternative images of the Jewish scientist, musician, or physician.

> Who in [the Jewish family] today are its "elder brothers"? Not the composer Shostakovich or the airplane designer Mill. They represented the Jewish family in Soviet times, but their time has passed. Today the "elder brothers" are the bankers. (Pogorel'skii 1999, 53)

In fact, most of the Jewish oligarchs do not appear to attach a great deal of significance to being of Jewish origin. Like the great majority of Jews in Russia, they are highly Russified, and their identity as Jews is weak. They are not religious. (Berezovsky is ostensibly a convert to Orthodox Christianity.) They have shown little or no interest in Jewish causes. In short, the Jewish oligarchs pursue no specifically Jewish goals, only their own aggrandizement.

This generalization does not, however, apply to one of the Jewish oligarchs, Gusinsky, who recently created and financed his own Jewish organization, the Russian Jewish Congress. A widely based Russian Jewish organization, the Va'ad (whose name means "council" in Hebrew) had already been in existence for several years. The Va'ad, an umbrella organization bringing together Jewish communities from across Russia and Jewish groups of varying orientation, was the creation of Mikhail Chlenov, a scholar formerly of the Institute of Ethnology and Anthropology of the Russian Academy of Sciences, who had been the only professional ethnologist specializing in the study of Jewish culture and customs at a time when such a choice of specialization required a certain moral courage. The Va'ad still has a much more valid claim to represent Russian Jews than does any rival organization. When Chlenov objected to the attempted usurpation by the Russian Jewish Congress of the status of the representative body of Russian Jewry, Gusinsky summoned him to a meeting and offered him the choice between "cooperating" or "being destroyed." Now, when Russian or Western journalists wish to quote a "representative of Russian Jews," they interview Gusinsky. Perhaps they do not know that there is such a person as Chlenov, or perhaps they, too, are in thrall to the old anti-Semitic stereotypes.

The repulsive image of the Jewish banker is somewhat blurred by the efforts of Jews who take a public left-wing or "patriotic" stand against the oligarchs. Especially salutary has been the stand taken by Yevgeny Primakov, who is generally known to be of Jewish origin. From this point of view, even Zhirinovsky may be said to play a positive role in Russian politics, for he is widely regarded as Jewish despite the fact that his mother was an ethnic Russian (Shenfield 2000, chap. 5).

That antioligarchic Jews may have had some modest success in holding anti-Semitism in check is suggested by the responses to their public statements that have appeared in the Russian nationalist press. Of some interest is the debate on the "Jewish question" that Yuri Mukhin, editor of the Russian nationalist discussion journal *Duel,* opened in its pages in 1998. Not only Russians but a number of Jews participated in this debate, at the price of exposing themselves to gratuitous insult by subsequent contributors. In closing the debate, Mukhin concluded that "good Jews" do exist, albeit not many of them, and he invited them to "stand side by side" with their Russian fellow patriots. The prominent Russian nationalist philosopher Alexander Dugin has likewise revised his Eurasianist theory to allow for the existence of pro-Russian "Eurasian" Jews. Admittedly, even in the process of making such concessions, these writers continue to sound like anti-Semites. But the virulence of their anti-Semitism is blunted.

The Question of Russophobia

The "patriots" accuse the oligarchs of being russophobes who hate Russia and strive to do harm to Russians. Most believe that the russophobia of the oligarchs is connected to the fact that so many of them are not Russians but Jews, who despise Russians as an inferior ethnic group. As Viktor Ilyukhin, a communist deputy in the last Duma and chairman of its Committee on Defense and Security, argued, "The large-scale genocide would not have been possible if Yeltsin's inner circle had consisted of the main ethnic groups and not exclusively of one group, the Jews." Jews stand accused of being either rootless cosmopolitans—the key slogan of the anti-Semitic campaign of Stalin's last postwar period—or Zionists, loyal to Israel and not Russia. They are alleged to lack a strong feeling of attachment to Russia, to regard Russia merely as a provisional place of residence, as "this country" rather than "our country." The implicit and questionable assumption is that to be a good citizen, it is both necessary and sufficient that one love and feel rooted in one's native soil.

What can we say of the attitudes and motives of the oligarchs, especially of the Jews among them? In a recent article, the Russian-Jewish émigré sociologist Vladimir Shlapentokh marshals impressive evidence that the Russian political elite of the 1990s, or at least the part of it that he calls the "liberal establishment," is indeed pervaded by contempt for the ordinary people of Russia and by indifference and insensitivity to their suffering (Shlapentokh 1999). Moreover, this contempt is often directed specifically at ethnic Russians. A case in point is the scandal sparked by a radio interview given by Alfred Kokh, a former deputy prime minister of Russia and former head of the State Property Committee, on a visit to the United States in October 1998. In the interview, he argued that "the Russian people deserve their miserable fate." Following the publication of the text of the interview in the Russian press, Kokh was widely attacked, for being himself "one of the Jews who have robbed Russia" and for "provoking antisemitism" (Samoiloff 1998). As it so happens, the general assumption that Kokh is a Jew was incorrect: I am reliably informed that he is of ethnic German descent. The concept of "Jew" is rather flexible in Russia.

It might seem logical to assume that russophobic sentiment is particularly rife among those members of Russia's liberal establishment who are themselves of non-Russian origin, but such an assumption is not necessarily valid. One should ideally treat this assumption as a hypothesis to be tested by means of empirical research. Casual observation suggests that prominent politicians, entrepreneurs, and media people who are themselves of ethnic Russian origin are also prone to speak in disparaging terms of "the Russians," implying either that they are contemptuous of themselves or that they consider themselves atypical Russians (or a bit of both).[20] Similarly, the behavior of the oligarchs and "new Russians," including those among them who really are ethnic Russians, is hardly that of people who cannot bear to be separated from their native land. They buy residences for their families in the West, stay there themselves whenever they can, and have their children educated in private schools abroad (Korostikova, Chernikov, and Chernikova 1999). Yeltsin's grandson goes to a private school in England.

Among ordinary people, there may well be a tendency for Jews, on average, to feel less strongly rooted in Russia than do ethnic Russians. They are more likely to have family ties with other countries, and the experience of feeling rejected as somehow different naturally generates feelings of alienation from Russia. A survey conducted by sociologist Dmitry Furman in 1991 confirmed that Jews are indeed the most Western-oriented of Russia's ethnic groups. The statement "The best of possible societies has been created in the West, and we must imitate the West" evoked agreement from only 13 percent of ethnic Russians but from 52 percent of Russian Jews (Pogorel'skii 1999, 57).

But once again, relative differences between ethnic Russians and Russian Jews should not be absolutized. Furman's survey also shows that almost half of Russian Jews are not oriented toward the West. There are many political activists of Jewish origin whose loyalties lie with the left-wing and/or Russian nationalist sectors of Russia's political spectrum. Such individuals tend to have a strong dual identity as both Russians and Jews, so that they feel offended equally by russophobia and anti-Semitism (Shlapentokh 1998).

The accusation that the Jewish oligarchs lack patriotic feeling toward Russia may therefore have a certain basis, but primarily because they are oligarchs, not because they are Jews.

The Topol-Berezovsky Exchange

A number of the points made in this chapter are illustrated in a revealing exchange that took place in 1998 between Berezovsky and Eduard Topol, a popular Russian-Jewish writer known primarily for his detective fiction. Topol interviewed Berezovsky in connection with a book he is writing about Russia at the end of the twentieth century. Topol then made public some excerpts from their conversation as part of an "open letter to Berezovsky, Gusinsky, Smolensky, Khodorkovsky, and the other [Jewish] oligarchs" that appeared in the popular magazine *Argumenty i fakty* under the title "Love Russia, Boris Abramovich!" (Topol' 1998).

Topol, by his own account, confronts Berezovsky in the following terms:

For the first time in the thousand years since Jews settled in Russia, we have acquired real power in this country. . . . How do you intend to use it? What do you intend to do with this country? . . . And do you feel responsibility to our people [i.e., Jews] for your actions?

Topol's confusion is evident here in his switch from the first to the second person: he says, "*we* have acquired power," but he asks, "How do *you* intend to use it?" He imagines that he, too, shares in some kind of Jewish power, but then he suddenly understands how absurd it would be to ask Berezovsky, as if they were equals, "How shall *we* use it?" The power in question belongs, after all, to Berezovsky, not to Topol. Berezovsky replies by regretting the "disproportion" in the numbers of Jewish and Russian bankers and pondering why it should exist. There are Russians with the requisite talent, he opines, but they lack the needed strength of will. He admits that the question of "responsibility to our people" is not one that he or the other Jewish bankers have considered. The question of what Berezovsky intends to do with Russia remains unanswered.

Topol's open letter to the oligarchs was commented on in the leading nationalist newspaper *Zavtra,* in an approving, if slightly condescending, tone, by the Russian "native-soil" writer Vladimir Bondarenko. Bondarenko expressed regret only that Topol opposed the oligarchs more out of fear of the anti-Jewish pogroms that the oligarchs might provoke than out of sympathy for the Russians whom the oligarchs had reduced to penury (Bondarenko 1998).

Thus, the conflict between the oligarchs and their opponents is best regarded as being primarily of a political, rather than an ethnic, character. However, the Jewish origin of a large proportion of the oligarchs inevitably has the effect of giving this political conflict the appearance of an ethnic conflict between Russians and Jews. The strength of this effect varies depending on circumstances. In particular, the effect will be greatly strengthened to the extent that some or all of the Jewish oligarchs come to be recognized as leaders or representatives of the Russian Jewish community, while the public activity of antioligarchic Jews is capable of significantly de-ethnicizing the conflict.

Relations between the Russians and the Peoples of the Caucasus

Not only Russian-Jewish relations have been strained by the economic crisis in Russia. Another important example of the impact of the crisis on interethnic relations is provided by relations between ethnic Russians and members of the peoples of the Caucasus, especially Azeris, Chechens, Georgians, and Armenians. Although there are deep cultural and political divisions between the various peoples of the Caucasus, ordinary Russians have a strong tendency to lump them all together as a single "Caucasian nationality."[21] This may help to justify the convenient, albeit (strictly speaking) incorrect, practice of referring to "Caucasians" and "Russian-Caucasian relations."

Apart from Vagit Alekperov, there are no Caucasians among the oligarchs. However, Caucasians are very prominently represented among two other groups that arouse strong resentment among ethnic Russians.

Firstly, Caucasians dominate the trade in tropical and subtropical fruits and other luxury food products that are transported by air from southern regions for sale in the open-air markets of cities and towns in central and northern Russia. This is one of the main reasons why Caucasians are widely perceived to be "disproportionately concentrated in the most prestigious and lucrative social niches" (*Problemy* 1998, 29). The high prices at which the Caucasian traders sell their products put them well beyond the reach of the impoverished majority of ethnic Russians, whose feelings of outrage against the "speculators" tend once again to assume an ethnic coloration and now and then assume open expression in the form of violent attacks by gangs of Russian youths on Caucasian traders and their stalls.

Secondly, Caucasians are prominent in many of the organized criminal gangs that terrorize and extort tribute from the inhabitants of Russia's cities. More than half of well-known criminal gangs are said to be partly or wholly Caucasian in character. This tendency is especially marked in Moscow, where gangs organized on an ethnic basis predominate, including at least six gangs made up of members of different Caucasian groups: Azeris, Chechens, Daghestanis, Armenians, Georgians, and Ingush. Moreover, Otari Kvantrishvili, who was known as the godfather of the Moscow mafia, was a Georgian (Kryshtanovskaya 1995, 599–600). And I recall how one Russian academic colleague, showing me around an open-air market near his Moscow home, whispered to me conspiratorily, "It looks like [the salespeople] are all Russian girls, but if you pay careful attention you will see that the boss controlling them is an Azeri." Moscow also has well-known ethnic Russian gangs, such as the Solntsevo gang, but this does not suffice to prevent the association in Russians' minds between organized crime and Caucasians, one of the consequences of which is the persecution and abuse of all Caucasians at the hands of the Russian police.

Russians associate Chechens—to a greater extent, perhaps, than any other ethnic group—with criminality. As was mentioned earlier, Zhirinovsky lists the murder of Russians by Chechens as one of the means by which the West carries out its genocidal plans against the Russians. Russian stereotypes characterizing Chechens as cruel, sly, and treacherous date back at least to Russia's war to conquer the Caucasus in the nineteenth century. The contemporary phenomena of Chechen crime, kidnapping, and terrorism appear to confirm these stereotypes, which, together with the fear and hatred they evoke in Russians, have made Yeltsin's decision to launch a second war in Chechnya an effective electoral ploy.

The practically unchecked activity of the "authorities" (bosses) of organized crime, like the power of the oligarchs, is an essential feature of the corrupt system that the West has helped to establish and maintain in post-Soviet Russia. Indeed, from the start, there have been close links between the two groups. It can therefore be argued that just as Western advisers, governments, and financial institutions have made a significant contribution to the tensions in present-day Russian-Jewish relations, so they have contributed to Russian-Caucasian tensions, including the violent conflict between Russians and Chechens.

Conclusion

In this chapter, I have demonstrated how ill-conceived Western policy advice and financial assistance to post-Soviet Russia have inadvertently shored up an extremely corrupt and inefficient fiscal system, postponing its inevitable demise and thereby facilitating the enrichment by dishonest means of a small number of top Russian officials, financial oligarchs, and oil and gas barons. The large proportion of individuals of Jewish origin among those reaping profit from this system has been an important factor in the rise of popular anti-Semitism in Russia. The IMF may therefore be considered to bear indirect responsibility for Russian-Jewish tensions.

At the same time, the deep economic crisis in Russia has also fueled other interethnic tensions, especially in relations between the Russians and the peoples of the Caucasus. The IMF and other Western institutions may be regarded as indirectly sharing in the responsibility for these developments as well.

NOTES

1. For a more detailed survey of the socioeconomic situation in Russia shortly before the financial crash of August 1998, see my report "Russia on the Threshold of Disaster" (July 2, 1998) on the web site of the Federation of Independent Trade

Unions of Russia, <www.trud.org/index7–4.htm>. This report does not on balance give too misleading an impression of the current situation, because the further deterioration brought about by the August crash has been roughly canceled out by the limited recovery that followed.

2. Data of the State Committee for Statistics of the Russian Federation, as reported by Interfax on June 10, 1997.

3. For a general critical scholarly study of the Russian economic transition, see Hedlund 1999.

4. For other critical assessments of the negative consequences of Western assistance to Russia, see Wedel 1998; Williamson 2000, forthcoming.

5. Although a more liberal policy of monetary emission in the early 1990s would have helped prevent the emergence of the virtual economy, it does not follow that such a policy initiated now would automatically lead to the remonetization of the economy. Given the institutional inertia that the virtual economy has acquired, the main result might merely be higher inflation in the monetary sector of the economy.

6. The factor of foreign imports played an important role in the decline of Russian consumer industry in the period up to the financial crash of August 1998. The collapse of imports triggered by the crash has made possible a revival in this branch of Russia's economy.

7. Not all of the superwealthy enjoy the political influence that would qualify them as oligarchs. For instance, Vladimir Bryntsalov, leader of the Russian Socialist Party, is known for his great wealth but is not an oligarch.

8. Berezovsky stood in the Republic of Karachaevo-Cherkessia in the northern Caucasus, a place with which he had no prior connection, while Roman Abramovich, head of Sibneft (Siberian Oil), stood in Chukotka Province in the extreme northeast of Siberia. Both were elected to the Duma. Leading officials in Kayachaevo-Cherkessia later expressed annoyance that Berezovsky had so far done nothing to fulfill his promises to help the local economy.

9. By discussing this matter in print, I am breaking a taboo. Even Russian and Western sociologists who specialize in the study of the post-Soviet Russian elite, such as Olga Kryshtanovskaya (Institute of Sociology of the Russian Academy of Sciences) and David Lane (University of Birmingham, U.K.), never so much as touch on the ethnic composition of the elite. This is not, unfortunately, because the subject is genuinely considered irrelevant: those who avoid referring to it in public are quite happy to talk endlessly about it around the kitchen table.

I first wrote about the ethnicity of the oligarchs in some remarks posted on Johnson's Russia List in early 1999. Some of those who responded did not so much criticize my ideas as object to my writing about the subject at all. One Russian Jew, a teacher of English in a provincial city, upbraided me as follows: "Speech is silver, but silence is golden. Every Jew in Russia knows it. Why don't you? Because you do not live there, and don't even care to put yourself in others' shoes."

I understand my correspondent's preference for silence as a reflex learned under the Soviet regime, when it may really have been the case that speech could only make matters worse. But I do not understand why it should still be necessary to keep silence now that speech has become possible in Russia. To do so means to give the anti-Semites a monopoly on discussion of the subjects concerned, to leave their arguments unrefuted, and in effect to "admit" that they are right.

It is difficult to analyze the ethnic composition of the Russian elite, because the taboo impedes the collection of reliable information. Thus, reference handbooks provide detailed information about Russia's leading entrepreneurs, including their hobbies, but do not indicate their ethnic origin (Amirov 1996; Amirov and Pribylovskii 1997). Nor is such information to be found in either journalistic or scholarly works about the oligarchs (e.g., Chernikov and Chernikova 1998; Medvedev 1998; Khrushchev 1999; Korostikova, Chernikov, and Chernikova 1999; Tsyganov 1999). The information given in works by Russian nationalists is not to be trusted. One is forced to resort to making judgments based on people's names, a very unreliable method inevitably resulting in numerous errors. I am grateful to my colleague Sergei Khrushchev for giving me the benefit of his personal knowledge concerning the ethnic origin of the oligarchs.

10. For an analysis of Russia's oil elite, though without any reference to ethnic composition, see Lane 1999, chapter 3.

11. There is no sharp dividing line between the narrow category of oligarch and the broader category of wealthy and prominent businessman (or the very occasional businesswoman). Sometimes other individuals apart from those listed are referred to as oligarchs. An example is Anatoly Chubais, current head of the electricity network United Energy System of Russia. It is uncertain, however, whether Chubais is either wealthy or powerful enough to qualify as an oligarch. If too many individuals are included, the term begins to lose its specific meaning.

12. As reported by Reuters and posted on Johnson's Russia List, no. 3640.

13. In this chapter, I do not discuss the question of the analogy between post-Soviet Russia and Weimar Germany beyond pointing out a couple of striking parallels. I acknowledge that the Weimar/Russia analogy is not without its weaknesses. For fuller discussion of the strengths and weaknesses of the analogy, see the debate between Stephen Hanson, Jeffrey Kopstein, and myself in Hanson and Kopstein 1997, Shenfield 1998, and Kopstein and Hanson 1998; see also the last chapter in my forthcoming book on Russian fascism.

14. The classical exposition of the concept is the essay entitled "Russophobia" written by the Russian nationalist dissident Igor Shafarevich in the early 1980s (Devlin 1999, 10).

15. See Zhirinovskii and Davidenko 1997; Glaz'ev 1997. Shortly before the Duma elections of December 1999, Davidenko left the LDPR to form the Spas (Salvation) bloc, which served as a cover for the Russian National Unity, the nazi movement led by Alexander Barkashov. Glazyev's book has now been published in English translation by the Executive Intelligence Review News Service (Glaz'ev 1999). Glazyev was reelected to the Duma in December 1999 as a nonparty candidate on the Communist Party list.

16. Koreshkin derives from his model a maximum, a medium, and a minimum projection. The medium projection gives Russia a population of 65 million in the year 2045—that is, a reduction of 45 percent compared to 1995.

17. Like the nazis, explains Yevgeny Mikhailov (1995, 7), LDPR governor of Pskov Province, the West "plans the extermination of the Russian people down to a population level established in advance by various international foundations."

18. The operations to extract organs for export are allegedly performed on the victims at a secret Moscow clinic, the exact location of which is given by the authors. This is a rather unusual claim; attacks on family planning and sex education are more common (see, e.g., Orlov 1998).

19. "Inasmuch as the genocide [of the Russians] has been on a scale unprecedented in the history of humanity, and the planning of anti-Russian activity has been global in character, the responding measures of the Russian state must be on a corresponding scale and of a corresponding character" (Barkashov 1994, 99).

20. I am grateful to Vladimir Shlapentokh for clarifying his view of this matter in personal correspondence with me.

21. The police in Moscow and other Russian cities customarily make use of the expression "persons of Caucasian nationality."

REFERENCES

Amirov, Anvar. 1996. *Naibolee vliiatel'nye predprinimateli Rossii* (The most influential entrepreneurs of Russia). Moscow: Panorama.

Amirov, Anvar, and Vladimir Pribylovskii. 1997. *Rossiiskie biznesmeny i menedzhery: Biograficheskii spravochnik* (Businessmen and managers of Russia: Biographical handbook). Moscow: Panorama.

Aslund, Anders. 1995. *How Russia Became a Market Economy.* Washington, DC: Brookings Institution.

Baburin, S. N. 1996. *Rossii nuzhna antikompradorskaia revoliutsiia* (Russia needs an anticomprador revolution). Moscow: ROS-Informbiuro.

———. 1997. *Rossiiskii put': Utraty i obreteniia* (The Russian way: Losses and gains). Moscow: Novator.

Barkashov, A. P. 1994. *Azbuka russkogo natsionalista* (ABC of a Russian nationalist). Moscow: Slovo-1.

Bondarenko, Vladimir. 1998. "Strakha radi . . ." (For the sake of fear . . .). *Zavtra* 40 (October).

Bogdanov, Vladimir, and Aleksandr Shakhuniants. 1999. "Etika izbiratel'noi kampanii" (Ethics of the electoral campaign). *Nezavisimaia gazeta,* November 20, 3.

Buckley, Mary. 1993. *Redefining Russian Society and Polity.* Boulder: Westview.

Chernikov, G., and D. Chernikova. 1998. *Kto vladeet Rossiei?* (Who owns Russia?). Moscow: Tsentrpoligraf.

Devlin, Judith. 1999. *Slavophiles and Commissars: Enemies of Democracy in Modern Russia.* New York: St. Martin's.

"Eto—genotsid" (This is genocide). 1998. *Zavtra* 5 (February).

Expert Institute. 1999. "Investitsionnyi klimat v Rossii" (The investment climate in Russia). *Voprosy ekonomiki* 12 (December): 4–33.

Feldman, Gerald D. 1995. *Jewish Bankers and the Crises of the Weimar Republic.* Leo Baeck Memorial Lecture 39. New York: Leo Baeck Institute.

Feshbach, Murray. 1999. "A Sick and Shrinking Nation." *Washington Post,* October 24, p. 4.

———. 2000. "An AIDS Catastrophe." *Moscow Times,* January 14, p. 1.

Glaz'ev, Sergei. 1997. *Genotsid: Rossiia i novyi mirovoi poriadok* (Genocide: Russia and the new world order). Moscow: Egra.

———. 1999. *Genocide: Russia and the New World Order.* Washington, DC: Executive Intelligence Review News Service.

Hanson, Stephen E., and Jeffrey S. Kopstein. 1997. "The Weimar/Russia Comparison." *Post-Soviet Affairs* 13, no. 3 (July–September): 252–83.

Hedlund, Stefan. 1999. *Russia's "Market" Economy: A Bad Case of Predatory Capitalism.* London: University College London Press.

Hendley, Kathryn. 1999. "How Russian Enterprises Cope with Payments Problems." *Post-Soviet Affairs* 15, no. 3 (July–September): 201–34.

Ivanova, Anastasiia. 1999. "Dolgu dolog vek" (A century long in debt). *Nezavisimaia gazeta—Politekonomiia* 18 (December 21): 3.

Khrushchev, Sergei. 1999. "Russia's Gambling Capitalism: Players and Fools." *Mediterranean Quarterly* 10, no. 1 (winter): 15–55.

Kopstein, Jeffrey S., and Stephen E. Hanson. 1998. "Paths to Uncivil Societies and Anti-liberal States: A Reply to Shenfield." *Post-Soviet Affairs* 14, no. 4 (October–December): 369–75.

Koreshkin, A. I. 1998. *Demografiia sovremennoi Rossii: Analiz i prognoz* (The demography of contemporary Russia: Analysis and forecast). St. Petersburg: International Slavic Academy of Sciences, Education, Arts, and Culture.

Korostikova, Tatiana, Gennadii Chernikov, and Diana Chernikova. 1999. "Oligarkhy posle krizisa" (Oligarchs after the crisis). *Argumenty i fakty* 965 (April).

Kryshtanovskaya, Ol'ga. 1995. "Russia's Illegal Structures." In *Post-Soviet Puzzles: Mapping the Political Economy of the Former Soviet Union,* vol. 3, ed. Klaus Segbers and Stephan De Spiegeleire, chapter 19. Baden-Baden: Nomos Verlagsgesellschaft.

Lane, David, ed. 1999. *The Political Economy of Russian Oil.* Lanham, MD: Rowman & Littlefield.

Limonov, Edward. 1998. "We Will Eat You, Westerners, Dearest Yankees, and Arrogant Europeans." *eXile,* June 4–18.

Malyshev, Valerii. 1999. "Byla li doperestroechnaia Rossiia razvivaiushcheisia stranoi?" (Was preperestroika Russia a developing country?). *Nezavisimaia gazeta—Politekonomiia* 18 (December 21): 7.

Medvedev, Roi. 1998. *Kapitalizm v Rossii?* (Capitalism in Russia?). Moscow: Prava Cheloveka.

Mikhailov, Evgenii. 1995. *Bremia imperskoi natsii* (The burden of an imperial nation). Moscow.

Natsional'nye interesy russkogo naroda i demograficheskaia situatsiia v Rossii (The national interests of the Russian people and the demographic situation in Russia). 1997. Moscow: Shtrikhton.

Orlov, Aleksandr. 1998. "Oppozitsiia v kontekste obshchei situatsii" (The opposition in the context of the general situation). *Duel* 1, no. 48 (January 13).

Pogorel'skii, Sergei. 1999. *Russkie i evrei: Shans dialoga* (Russians and Jews: Chance for a dialogue). Moscow: Informpechat'.

Polikarpov, Andrei. 1996. "'Lebed': Strategicheskaia ugroza Rossii" (Lebed: A strategic threat to Russia). *Zavtra* 34 (August).

Problemy natsional'nogo samosoznaniia russkikh: Etnicheskie stereotipy naseleniia (Problems of Russians' national self-consciousness: Ethnic stereotypes of the population). 1998. Moscow: Institute of Scientific Information on the Social Sciences of the Russian Academy of Sciences.

Prokhanov, A. A. 1994. *Angel proletel: Roman* (The angel flew past: A novel). Moscow: Sovremennyi Pisatel'.

———. 1998. "Sibirskie manevry" (Siberian maneuvers). *Zavtra* 22 (June).

Samoiloff, Alexander. 1998. "A Provincial View on Statement of Kokh." *Hello Russia* 12, November 15.

———. 2000. "My View of the West's Policy Toward Russia." Hello Russia 54, June 15.

Serenko, Andrei. 1999. "Gosti s iuga" (Guests from the South). *Nezavisimaia gazeta,* November 24, 16.

Sikevich, Z. V. 1996. *Russkie: "Obraz" naroda* (Russians: Image of a people). St. Petersburg: Izd-vo S.-Peterburgskogo Universiteta.

Shenfield, Stephen D. 1998. "The Weimar/Russia Comparison: Reflections on Hanson and Kopstein." *Post-Soviet Affairs* 14, no. 4 (October–December): 355–68.

———. Forthcoming. *Russian Fascism: Traditions, Tendencies, and Movements.* New York: M. E. Sharpe.

Shlapentokh, Dmitry. 1998. "'Red-to-Brown' Jews and Russian Liberal Reform." *Washington Quarterly* 21, no. 4 (autumn): 107–26.

Shlapentokh, Vladimir. 1999. "Social Inequality in Post-Communist Russia: The Attitudes of the Political Elite and the Masses (1991–1998)." *Europe-Asia Studies* 51, no. 7 (November): 1167–82.

Sulakshin, Stepan. 1998. *Izmena* (Treason). Moscow: Foundation for the Development of Political Centrism.

Thaler, M. Michael. 1996. "Medicine and the Rise and Fall of the Weimar Republic: Health Care, Professional Politics, and Social Reform." *German Politics and Society* 14, no. 1 (spring): 74–79.

Tikhomirov, Vladimir. 1997. "Capital Flight from Post-Soviet Russia." *Europe-Asia Studies* 49, no. 4 (July–August): 591–615.

Topol', Eduard. 1998. "Vozliubite Rossiiu, Boris Abramovich!" (Love Russia, Boris Abramovich!). *Argumenty i fakty* 938 (September 16).

Tsyganov, Yuri. 1999. "Political Background of the Economic Crisis in Russia." In *Anatomy of the 1998 Russian Crisis,* ed. Vladimir Tikhomirov, chapter 10. Carlton: Contemporary Europe Research Centre, University of Melbourne, Australia.

Wedel, Janine R. 1998. *Collision and Collusion: The Strange Case of Western Aid to Eastern Europe, 1989–98.* New York: St. Martin's.

Williamson, Anne. 2000. Testimony to the House of Representatives Committee on Banking and Financial Services, submitted September 21, 1999. In *Document 106–38: Russian Money Laundering,* House of Representatives Committee on Banking and Financial Services. Washington, DC: U.S. Government Printing Office. <www.house.gov/banking/92199wil.htm>.

———. Forthcoming. *Contagion: The Betrayal of Liberty; Russia and the United States in the 1990s.*

Zhirinovskii, Vladimir, and Vladimir Davidenko. 1997. *Genotsid: Zapad unichtozhaet russkii narod* (Genocide: The West annihilates the Russian people). Moscow: Voenizdat.

CHAPTER 8

"Indian Market": The Ethnic Face of Adjustment in Ecuador

Alison Brysk

On February 5, 1999, Ecuador's president Jamil Mahuad decreed the latest in almost two decades of austerity programs, seeking from the International Monetary Fund (IMF), World Bank, and Inter-American Development Bank $700 million in loans needed to pay the interest on Ecuador's $15 billion foreign debt. This year's program included cutoffs of state subsidies on cooking gas, electricity, and drinking water; layoffs of state employees, including teachers; a new regressive tax on financial transactions; and food price increases of 15 percent per month. By March, the administration had frozen Ecuadorans' bank accounts and imposed a 60-day state of emergency suspending civil rights. In response, an opposition coalition headed by Ecuador's Indian rights movement launched a national strike, blockading the Andean nation's highways for almost two weeks. On March 18, the beleaguered president agreed to a compromise truce suspending some of the adjustment measures. Specifically, the government agreed to the indigenous federation's demands for an increase in funds for bilingual education, electricity rate preferences for Indians and peasants, and the release of indigenous activists jailed in antiausterity protests. By January 2000, ethnic conflict had escalated, as a coaliton of Indian protesters and military officers attempted to overthrow the civilian government. After they briefly seized power, President Mahuad stepped down in favor of his vice president. The new leader intensified adjustment by linking the national currency to the U.S. dollar. Protest resumed.

How does the increasing presence of market forces and development assistance differentially affect indigenous peoples in Ecuador? What are the political and economic responses to economic change by ethnic communities? How successful are these responses in meeting the challenges of globalization? What are the implications of new economic forces and behavior for ethnic mobilization and ethnic conflict?

The impact of development assistance on ethnic conflict must be seen in the wider context of the diverse economic changes affecting ethnic communities and the overall framework of adjustment policy that has dominated Latin America's political economy for over a decade (Haggard and Kaufman 1992). The Washington consensus of the 1980s, which saw market integration as a long-term good that would eventually benefit all sectors, is increasingly questioned; the evidence of a generation now suggests that market adjustment is often partial and distorted, that markets tend to increase inequality, and that market integration is filtered through preexisting distributions of power and resources (Bulmer-Thomas 1996; Przeworski 1993; Smith and Korzeniewicz 1997; Inter-American Development Bank 1998/99). While some private or even bilateral aid may have a redistributive tilt toward the poor, the larger multilateral programs, such as World Bank loans, try to assist the poor by enhancing the role of the market—resulting in ethnic "IMF riots" (Walton 1989). The presence of social safety nets has significantly mitigated the impact of economic liberalization in some cases (e.g., Bolivia), but compensatory social programs have been sporadic, corrupt, or ineffective in most of Latin America (Fox 1994). What remains is the uneven introduction of unregulated market forces in societies distorted by external dependency and internal racism. As Esman reminds us (1994, 232): "Individual competition and market processes tend to reward those who enter the level playing field with superior resources. This applies to ethnic collectivities as well as to individuals."

Development assistance alone has not played a highly significant or linear role in Ecuador but has been part of a complex of larger market forces that have affected ethnic inequality and possibilities for ethnic conflict. In Ecuador—a very poor country with a 1999 per capita gross national product of $1,679—dominant market forces include export dependency (it is a literal "banana republic"), high foreign debt, and international agencies' adjustment programs. Not only do market forces tend to increase inequality and differentially disadvantage the poor, but they have specific effects on ethnically distinctive populations whose values, institutions, and behavior may be socially functional but economically dysfunctional. These include such factors as communal production patterns, use of minority languages, community religious practices, and nonlinear knowledge systems. The best that aid can do in this situation is to ameliorate market processes and conserve cultural resources.

Although the structural dynamics of market integration set the parameters for poverty and conflict, policy does matter. In the negative sense, nationally specific corruption and disastrous leadership in the mid-to late 1990s have exacerbated Ecuador's economic problems beyond the regional trend. In 1995, Ecuador's vice president Alberto Dahik, an enthusiastic partisan of market adjustment, was indicted on corruption charges and fled to Costa Rica with a portion of the national treasury. Two years later, the next administration's president, Abdala "El Loco" Bucaram, was removed from office by popular outrage over his privatizations, corruption, and mental instability. In addition, some of the putative beneficiaries of aid, notably a few Amazonian Indian leaders, have also misused resources and abused the trust of their communities. But positive models of policy response—from the Inter-American Foundation's cultural revival development programs to the creative responses of some ethnic communities, like Ecuador's Shuar—show that some of the challenges of adjustment can be overcome. And recent protests against privatization show a promising emergence of transethnic popular sector coalitions that emphasize common policy grievances over cultural difference; the 1999 national strikes included (largely mestizo) taxi drivers, teachers, oil workers, and labor unionists alongside Indian peasants.

Thus, overall development assistance buffers some economic changes, accelerates others, and produces various social side effects. But none of these economic changes leads directly to conflict; in every case, the social impact of economic change is conditioned by the *response* of ethnic communities to market forces. Furthermore, in Ecuador the predominant form of ethnic conflict has been with the government rather than among communities, although interethnic violence has been more costly (see chap. 1 in this volume). Rapid economic change does tend to produce social conflict, but social conflict does not inevitably take the form of interethnic violence. In the terms laid out in chapter 1 by the editors of this volume, an ethnically differentiated political economy and structurally ethnic state strategies of allocation militate toward conflict, but the incidence and form of conflict hinge on the dynamic element of the formation of ethnic identities—in, against, and around the market.

Indian responses to economic challenges range from passive participation to political mobilization to economic mobilization. The type of response chosen is a combined product of the form of economic challenge and the availability of political and economic channels for response (as Brysk and Wise 1997 proposes for the comparative cases of Mexico, Peru, and Bolivia). Conventional views of ethnic conflict tend to equate the political mobilization response with the creation of conflict, but violent ethnic insurgencies in Latin America—such as those in Mexico, Nicaragua, Guatemala, and Peru—have occurred when Indians are most thoroughly marginalized from conventional political channels, not competing through them (as in postcolonial Asia and Africa). Although political mobilization makes ethnic conflict more visible in the short run, passive participation in distorted, inequitable markets may ultimately create the structural basis for deeper, long-term conflict and violence. Throughout Latin America, the latter half of the 1990s has seen increasing antiadjustment protests, food riots, land invasions, and rising crime rates, which are harbingers of structural violence.

Background: Ethnicity in Ecuador

Approximately 30 to 40 percent of Ecuador's 10 million citizens identify themselves as indigenous; Indian population in the region varies from a clear majority in Bolivia to less than 1 percent in Brazil. The markers of indigenous identity include physical features, non-Western dress, use of Quichua or an Amazonian language, peasant status, and urban poverty. The ethnic composition of Ecuador includes a dominant minority of Hispanic "whites" (around 10 percent), a middle- and working-class strata of culturally defined mestizos (around 40 percent), Indians (more than 30 percent), an impoverished minority of Afro-Ecuadorans concentrated on the coast (3 to 5 percent), and a handful of urban Asians (mostly entrepreneurs).[1]

The vast majority of the Indian population lives in the highlands, speaks Quichua as well as Spanish, and has been in contact with the state and market forces since the Spanish conquest. However, since the Inca Empire dominated Ecuador for less than fifty years before the arrival of the Spanish, regional differences among highland groups remain more pronounced here than in other parts of the Andes. About 300,000 Amazonian Indians constitute a fraction of the national population but a (60 percent) majority within the lowland rain forest region. A half dozen distinctive ethnic groups—the Shuar, Achuar, Cofan, Huaorani, Siona-Secoya—have been incorporated in national life for a generation or less. In Ecuador's third geographic-demographic zone, the coastal region, several very small indigenous groups subsist on isolated traditional lands, marginalized from the political, social, and economic life of the nation.

Historical ethnic conflict has resulted from chronic Indian resistance to economic and political incorporation by the dominant Hispanic culture. Pan-Indian identity was actually created by this opposition. While the Spanish conquest had been facilitated by previous intra-Indian conflicts (e.g., Cañari resistance to the Incas, which resulted in Cañari collaboration with the Spanish), colonial priests unwittingly unified Indian communities by promoting the use of Quichua as a lingua franca for evangelization. Periodic Indian rebellions against both colonial and republican rule often focused on new economic impositions (e.g., taxes and forced labor). As late as 1764, highland indigenous rebels sought to reestablish pre-Hispanic and pre-Inca forms of traditional government (Moreno and Figueroa 1992, 19). Localized groups of Amazonian natives violently resisted territorial encroachment and economic competition from foreign, mestizo, and highland Indian colonists and "development agents" throughout the nineteenth and twentieth centuries. Perhaps the most resistant group—the Huaorani—attacked and killed foreign and Ecuadoran mestizo missionaries, black and highland Indian oil workers, and Quichua and Shuar colonists through the 1980s (the missionaries were often linked to the oil companies [Labaca 1988]).

Given this ethnic panorama, how and to what extent is the political economy ethnically differentiated? Class and ethnicity are intimately related in Ecuador, with a clear hierarchy correlating proximity to Hispanic identity with wealth and privilege (whites-mestizos-Indians-blacks). The majority of Indians are poor (about 35 percent in "critical poverty," about 45 percent in "relative poverty" [Bebbington et al. 1992, 9]), and a high proportion of the poor are Indians (of the bottom quintile, 23.4 percent speak an Indian language in the sierra, 88.4 percent in the Oriente [Fierro 1995, 16]).[2] Indians are concentrated in the countryside, the urban informal sector, and unrewarding low-status service occupations—such as maids and porters. The World Bank (1996, 11) finds a 33 percent wage gap for indigenous language speakers after other qualifications have been factored out. While several waves of land reform (1964, 1973) changed the formal dominance of "blanco-mestizo" haciendas in the countryside, rural highland Indians generally still depend on Hispanic or mestizo landowners and shopkeepers for agricultural inputs, marketing, transport, consumer items, employment, services, and sometimes water. In one indicator of the impact of this interethnic dependency, rural transport (provided by mestizos) may often consume 30 percent of the final price for rural products (sold by Indians) (Trujillo 1994, 97).

In the Amazon, by contrast, native groups still seek allocation and demarcation of traditional territories, as well as access to resources within those territories. Since oil—a key export and the largest source of state revenue—is located in Indian rain forest areas, a series of struggles have developed among Indian organizations and their environmentalist allies, the state (which retains subsoil rights), and multinational corporations and international agencies invited by the state to develop oil-producing areas. Oil earnings have comprised 12 to 17 percent of gross national product during the 1990s (Sierra 1994). Indigenous peoples generally seek recognition of the use value of contested territories, compensation for environmental damage, and development assistance. (The Cofan are currently suing Texaco in the United States, while the Huaorani have negotiated the construction of schools with Maxus Oil). Ecuador also displays a pattern found throughout the Amazon River basin, in which agricultural colonization of fragile rain forest lands has been tolerated or encouraged by the state, with the dual purpose of relieving land pressures in the highlands and introducing export-oriented agriculture.

Unlike in regions where group mythologies have fueled conflict, in Ecuador perceptions of ethnic economic differentiation largely mirror the objective distribution of resources. The social psychology of ethnic conflict arises more from attribution of causes and solutions than from distorted assessment of hierarchies. For example, construction of ethnic difference plays a role in explaining the anomalous economic success of a handful of indigenous groups, by denying social barriers to market participation, while simultaneously strengthening those barriers by condemning ethnic competitors who exhibit adaptive market behavior (Zubritski 1990; Meisch 1987).[3]

While the state has been captured by one ethnic-class elite in most Latin American polities, government is not necessarily the dominant arena for ethnic conflict. This fact results from an ironic combination of tradition and modernization. By tradition, Indians were so firmly excluded from the state that there was no opportunity to compete for civil service positions or local development projects. Although in Ecuador Indian mobilization and the state's development role increased during the 1980s, economic crisis and state-shrinking modernization had eclipsed government as a development arena by the 1990s. For example, one bilateral assistance program alone (the Inter-American Foundation) had an annual budget in Ecuador 50 percent higher than the state development agency FODERUMA (Bebbington et al. 1992, 3). Furthermore, nongovernment organizations (NGOs) play an increasing role in Ecuador, and an increasing proportion of bilateral and multilateral aid is channeled directly through NGOs rather than through (or alongside) state agencies. By the mid-1990s Holland, one of the leading bilateral funders, began working mainly through UN agencies or NGOs, not state counterparts.

The Impact of Market Forces

Ecuador signed 14 standby agreements with the IMF between 1961 and 1989, a period that coincided with a structural process of agricultural modernization and increasing trade penetration. Economic adjustment intensified during the 1980s because Ecuador's principal export (oil) and investment declined; debt, debt service, and deficit increased; and newly democratic governments (after the transition in 1980 from military rule) were more open to international influence. Between 1974 and 1994, external debt increased from less than $1 billion to more than $13 billion (Sierra 1994, 159). As adjustment continued through the 1990s, adjustment programs mandated privatization of state enterprises, reduction of barriers to foreign trade and investment, elimination of consumer subsidies and price supports, labor code reform, and financial sector liberalization. Although the later IMF agreements have included some attention to social policy, restrictions on state spending have virtually vitiated any safety net. State social spending has declined proportionally more than overall state spending; by the mid-1990s, per capita budgets for social programs had fallen below 1972 levels (ibid., 148, 193), and the World Bank (1996, 229, ix) was reporting "declining and minuscule" social spending along with "alarming levels of malnutrition and child mortality" among indigenous peasants. While it is difficult to distinguish the overall effects of adjustment programs from the general economic stagnation and hyperinflation that caused the UN to label the 1980s Latin America's "Lost Decade," short-term and sectoral pain was not generally balanced by the promised long-term gain (Pastor 1987; Ramirez 1991). The trends of low growth, falling real wages, trade deficit, and inflation continued into the 1990s.

During the 1980s adjustment programs, Ecuador as a whole showed declines in growth, investment, and purchasing power, coupled with increases in unemployment and underemployment (Bebbington et al. 1992, 22–23). By 1999, formal sector urban unemployment in Ecuador stood at 15.6 percent, with urban underemployment at an additional 51.3 percent; and the rural situation, though undocumented, was generally estimated as worse (Banco Central del Ecuador; "Pulso Latinoamericano" 1995; Sierra 1994, 182). Inequality increased in all sectors through the 1990s (Inter-American Development Bank 1998/99; Fierro 1995, 17; Larrea 1995). Debate rages on the distribution of decline: although groups tied most closely to the market (e.g., the urban poor) probably suffered the most proportionally, more severely impoverished (mostly rural) Indians have clearly experienced negative consequences of adjustment, and the decline in indigenous welfare may even be greater in absolute terms. For example, rural households cut food consumption during the 1990s (World Bank 1996, 183). Whatever formal latitude for equitable distribution of costs may have existed in the adjustment programs was obviated by the debt service imperative to support sectors and activities that generate foreign exchange, the state incapacity to extract alternative revenues and administer social programs, and the systematic lack of political representation and leverage by Indians and the poor.

Economic liberalization adversely and differentially affected Indians as an ethnic community through cuts in social programs, changes in rural property relations, privatization of public services, loss of subsidies on consumer items, and increased state openness to the presence of multinationals in indigenous territories. Indians suffer more from adjustment because they are poor and disproportionately dependent on social services and state subsidies (although Indian communities are consistently disadvantaged in access to services and subsidies, these inputs, whenever present, comprise the margin for survival among the very poor and isolated). Indigenous highland areas show levels of poverty and infant mortality 50 percent higher than corresponding mestizo zones, while public spending in indigenous areas is around 60 percent of local budgets in Hispanic-majority cantons (Zamosc 1995, 44). One study shows that residents of Indian areas are four times as likely to be illiterate (41 percent), that they are 50 percent more likely to be malnourished (64 percent vs. 45 percent), and that only 6 percent of them have access to sewage systems (compared to a 38 percent national average [Fierro 1995, 16]). Overall poverty has grown with adjustment (Larrea 1995, 19; Grijalva Jiménez 1994, 120–22). By 1992, infant mortality in Ecuador was worse than in El Salvador—a poorer country that was then emerging from a civil war (World Bank 1996, 25).

As everywhere, the poor are more dependent on the government subsidies that are cut by adjustment programs. In Ecuador, a 1987 study showed that 68 percent of those in absolute poverty depended on government subsidies for a majority of their incomes (Gonzalo Bustos in Racines 1993). From 1982 to 1993, public spending on education has fallen from 5.1 percent to 2.7 percent; health has gone from 2.2 percent to 0.7 percent (Larrea 1995, 20). This has side effects for vulnerable populations, such as a series of strikes in public schools and hospitals, which have periodically eliminated all access to these services for indigenous communities. Programs of special significance to Indian communities have suffered disproportionately: funds for bilingual education were cut 30 percent in 1995 alone (interview with Directorate of Bilingual Education, August 24, 1995), while the Rural Social Security program, which provided the only health care in many poor, Indian parts of the sierra, has declined dramatically and was almost eliminated in 1995. These changes have a variety of negative effects on the welfare of Indian communities. At the aggregate level, an Ecuadoran research institute study shows a 70 percent increase in rural malnutrition from 1990 to 1995 (CAAP, June 22, 1995). At a microlevel, an indigenous community leader from the southern highlands explained to me (interview, July 20, 1995) how the liberalization of prices for cooking gas impacts his village: as households return to cooking with wood, the labor of women and children increases, respiratory problems intensify, and deforestation accelerates. Even the World Bank's 1996 report on Ecuador concludes that government subsidies should be better targeted, phased out, or replaced with income support for the poor. But the larger thrust and political distortions of adjustment have resulted in uncoordinated and unbuffered cuts in subsidies and services.

Market forces also change production and consumption patterns in a way that disadvantages Indian communities. In general, rural communities have become increasingly dependent on market inputs, for both production and consumption (Triyillo 1994, 83–84). However, this has not been matched by viable patterns of agricultural production. In fact, both yields for food staples and the rural-urban terms of trade have declined (Moreno and Figueroa 1992, 28). During the 1980s, the terms of trade deteriorated for all basic products except rice—which was still subsidized by the state (Martínez Valle 1992, 90). Liberalization has encouraged the production of agricultural exports at the expense of food for internal consumption (Racines 1993, 107). While inflation between 1981 and 1990 reached over 2,000 percent, inflation in food products (which comprise a higher proportion of consumption for the poor) was over 3,000 percent (ibid., 109). One surrogate for urban indigenous sector purchasing power—the real minimum wage—declined 46.5 percent between 1981 and 1990 (ibid., 101). By 1999, real salaries had continued their decline to 89 percent of the 1995 index (Banco Central del Ecuador).

Another adverse effect of market opening is the liberalization of rural property rights. Various adjustment-encouraged modifications of the land reform program and cutbacks in the implementing agency culminated in a 1994 Agrarian Law that halted further redistribution and downgraded the land titling bureaucracy. The 1994 law resulted from a compromise between a ruling-party proposal (written by a think tank funded by the United States Agency for International Development [USAID]) and massive indigenous protest. The general trend of market-oriented reforms has been the erosion of both traditional communal holdings and haciendas in favor of subsistence smallholdings *(minifundios)* alongside commercial agriculture, which ironically offers less employment and security for surrounding Indian communities than the hacienda did. Sociological factors compound the structural effects: rural population growth in the highlands has been much greater in indigenous areas (33 percent in 30 years), producing intense and differential demographic pressure on landholdings (Zamosc 1995, 26). As a result, in 1974, 18.6 percent of production units were less than 20 hectares, but by 1987, 35 percent were smallholders (Galo Ramón in Trujillo 1994, 179). By 1994, 1.6 percent of highland farms controlled 42.9 percent of the land (World Bank 1996, 33). This provides the demographic push for rural-urban migration.

Amazonian indigenous land tenancy has also come under increasing pressure with adjustment. First of all, many highland Indians have responded to the land pressure already outlined by migrating to the Oriente, where they compete and conflict with sparsely settled Amazonian groups in ecologically fragile rain forest areas. As in most of Latin America, this migration was originally encouraged by the state and abetted by multilateral infrastructure projects, such as World Bank–funded roads (Hicks 1990). Second, pressures for debt service have encouraged the state to increase oil exploration and production in the Amazon, since oil revenues through the state company Petroecuador comprise a high proportion of state resources. Most of the oil-producing region falls within traditional areas of indigenous settlement—if not legally allocated territory (Huaorani, Cofan, and lowland Quichua); the adverse effects on indigenous health, welfare, cultural integrity, and environmental conditions are well documented (Kimerling et al. 1991; Kane 1995). Third, debt pressures and adjustment-mandated facilitation of foreign investment have provided the motive and opportunity for an increased presence of multinational corporations engaged in timber, mining, African palm production, and pharmaceutical research in Indian areas (Ashley 1987).

Development assistance interacts with market forces in a variety of roles, which depend somewhat on whether the aid is multilateral, bilateral, or nongovernmental. Multilateral aid generally seeks to further market integration of indigenous peoples, whether indirectly, through World Bank infrastructure projects, or directly, through programs like the United Nations Development Program's craft-marketing initiative (UNDP 1993). However, some bilateral and NGO projects (e.g., the U.S.–funded Inter-American Foundation) try to create alternate modes of market participation (e.g., the NGO Quicha, often translated as "Marketing like Brothers" [MCCH] supports marketing cooperatives). Some NGOs and (mostly European) bilateral programs buffer the effects of adjustment by substituting for lost state services; for example, the German Cooperation Agency (GTZ) has been providing most of the texts for bilingual education, while a Danish NGO's bilingual education budget approximately matches that of the state bilingual education agency Dirección Nacional de la Educación Intercultural Bilingue (DINEIB). The same type of assistance programs help Indian communities to directly confront the structural impacts of adjustment, such as loss of rural property rights. Thus, land demarcation for threatened Amazonian groups is directly supported by Dutch foreign aid, the Danish NGO Ibis, the Italian volunteer service Movimiento Laico de America Latina, the Comité Ecumenico (a consortium of European churches), and others. CARE's Project SUBIR (with USAID support) is training indigenous paralegals to register land claims, while the church-associated Fondo Ecuatoriano Populorum Progreso (FEPP) buys disputed lands in the sierra for Indian communities, using debt-swap funds. Some development workers further argue that any provision of resources to indigenous communities gives them the tools to respond to market pressures on their own terms. As the director of one religious NGO put it, "An Indian who is better fed, better educated, and healthier will fight better against neoliberalism" (interview, June 19, 1995).

Ethnic Responses to the Market

Ecuadoran Indians have chosen three patterns of response to adjustment pressure: passive participation, political resistance, and alternative economic strategies. While in some cases one of these responses clearly characterizes a given community over time (e.g., Otavaleño textile commercialization), they are not exclusive alternatives. Responses may be combined within a community or form a sequence. For example, market absorption and attendant migration have been strong in the southern sierra province of Cañar, but Cañar has also been characterized by a high level of political mobilization (the community is characterized as "poor but proud"). In neighboring Saraguro, migration caused by market pressures and microplots actually catalyzed political mobilization: the highland Saraguros entered the Amazonian homeland of the Shuar Federation (Ecuador's oldest ethnic organization), and the Shuar both inspired and encouraged the formation of Saraguro's own federation.

The type or pattern of response is determined by a combination of the level and kind of economic pressures and the availability of economic and political channels to confront these pressures. Otavaleño economic mobilization was influenced by a traditional role as traders and weavers dating to pre-Inca times, commercial weaving expertise gained from forced labor in Spanish textile factories, a relatively thorough process of land reform, and early foreign aid (ranging from Dutch construction of the craft market to Peace Corps marketing assistance). In general, Amazonian groups have mobilized politically more readily than their sierra counterparts—in response to clear, discrete challenges by outsiders (rather than highland modernization of perennial internal systems of discrimination) and with greater access to international assistance despite geographic isolation.

Market Absorption

The response of passive participation in the market is characteristic of marginalized areas of the highlands and the smaller Amazonian populations. Partial absorption in the market creates increasing dependency on market inputs and consumption without an economically viable pattern of production, diversification, or occupational mobility. This disequilibrium produces high levels of migration, loss of identity, and the disarticulation of community and ethnic organizations. One indicator of disequilibrium is that by 1988, the cost of corn production had risen six times, while sale prices remained relatively constant (Racines 1993, 111). Another is that in 1992 alone, the purchasing power of the minimum wage declined 38 percent (Maiguashca 1993, 445). Shrinking plots with lagging access to technology cannot absorb the rural labor force. Sixty-three percent of indigenous zones in the highlands are populated by subsistence smallholders. Indigenous areas also show much higher Gini indices of inequality and land concentration (Zamosc 1995, 36–39). Differential modernization of agriculture under intensifying market competition leads to an increasing predominance of export agriculture and ranching over subsistence production (Martínez Valle 1992, 84, 90), which reduces job opportunities for Indian peasants. Also, some evidence suggests a loss of nonagricultural employment opportunities during the 1980s (Zamosc 1995, 43).

One result of market absorption is massive temporal urban migration of the primary labor force (males ages 15–45), leaving women, children, and the elderly to manage the subsistence sector. Migration is more likely to occur where traditional agriculture can no longer provide employment, above all from the depressed rural sierra to cities, coastal commercial agriculture, and development projects in the Oriente. By 1990, 37 percent of the rural population drew its main income from services or urban activities rather than agriculture (Martínez Valle 1992, 87). A study of indigenous cantons throughout the highlands found 1992 migration rates of 26 percent (World Bank 1996, 80). As much as half the population of Saraguro has moved to the Oriente (interview with Saraguro community leaders, July 20, 1995). A side effect of the new division of labor is a reduction in supplementary income from production of animals and handicrafts, since women's labor is now wholly consumed with agriculture and domestic work. Permanent migration also occurs, following similar geographic patterns but generally involving entire families. Urban Indian families are occupationally and residentially concentrated, with consistently inferior levels of consumption, health, and education compared to their mestizo counterparts (Cliche and Garcia 1995).

Since both temporary and permanent migration are more likely for the young, single, better-educated, and male (Brea 1991), migration drains traditional highland Indian communities of their most conventionally productive members and potential leaders. In the area of Cañar, observers have noted a decline in organization over time as migration increases (Trujillo 1994, 151). International aid has begun to substitute for the state's role of economic intermediation in these partially market-absorbed sectors and regions, but while aid ameliorates economic losses, it often deepens dependency and further distorts the articulation of ethnic identity. A number of the larger aid programs have policies against supporting regional ethnic associations (which they label "political"), while they channel funds to local base-level organizations that are generally more production-oriented and sometimes compete with provincial federations. Many market-oriented aid projects also increase peasants' risk and dependence on technology as they attempt to rationalize and commercialize production.

Political Mobilization

The contrasting active response of political mobilization has secured changes in state policy—as seen in the 1990 Indian uprising; a 1992 land grant to the Amazonian organization OPIP, which marched on Quito; and 1994 changes in the Agrarian Law following Indian rights movement demonstrations. More recent attempts to integrate ethnically specific economic demands with labor and popular sector opposition to privatization have met with mixed response.

The June 1990 national uprising of Ecuador's Indians—a massive weeklong occupation of public spaces, demonstrations, and blockage of roads and markets—was historically and regionally unprecedented. Almost half of the demands announced by the national Indian rights organization Confederación de Nacionalidades Indígenas del Ecuador (CONAIE) were directly related to adjustment pressures, including land rights, postreform access to water, forgiveness for land debts to state and international agencies, a price freeze on basic consumer products, increased public works, and unregulated import and export for indigenous artisans. In addition, analysts have noted that inflation, the declining terms of rural-urban exchange, and the loss of temporary employment opportunities in the construction industry were important in inspiring the rebellion (León 1994, 19, 71; Zamosc 1994). In the manifesto issued following the takeover of Quito's main cathedral, Indian activists explained:

> We peasants and Indian nationalities are the most affected by the economic crisis and the government's social policies. Even though smallholders of less than 10 hectares provide 80 percent of the grains and roots consumed by the population, the government authorities of the Ministry of Agriculture and IERAC [the land reform agency] give their attention mainly to the large landowners and ranchers. . . . In this manner, they try to privilege agroexport, following an agrarian policy designed by the monopolies and the IMF. The government is

only interested in paying the external debt and applying the Brady Plan to relieve credit for business groups. . . . Because of this we feel obliged to take possession of what historically belongs to us. (Moreno and Figueroa 1992, 62–63)

While one feature of the uprising was to transfer demands to the state that previously had been directed to international aid, Indian organizations in one of the most conflictual areas (Chimborazo) included increased international assistance (UNICEF/World Health Organization health centers) among their demands (Trujillo 1994, 140, 210).

After a series of ethnic protests with an economic component in 1991 (the Amazon March for Territory), 1992 (Anti-Columbus Quincentenary), and 1994 (against the new Agrarian Law), recent waves of Indian mobilization have been explicitly linked to resistance to adjustment. Rural Indian organizations were the major participants in a 1995 general strike called by a labor-peasant coalition to protest cuts in government social programs—since Rural Social Security was slated for elimination. CONAIE is now regularly consulted by the government about new economic policies, and CONAIE's support is considered critical for the success of any popular sector protest. While the 1995 energy sector strike was broken by the military, the 1999 national blockade led to a modification of adjustment policies.

Political mobilization is often in opposition to multilateral aid policies but supported by NGOs. While NGOs do not sponsor, encourage, plan, or manipulate mobilization (as dominant elites in Ecuador claim), the support they provide for social movements builds organizational capacity for protest and resistance. The national and regional Indian rights organizations receive direct operational support from NGOs, such as Oxfam; services, such as newsletter production, from FEPP; and headquarters donated by European church groups. NGO networks provide international publicity and assist in pressure campaigns, like the Amazon for Life coalition of Indians and environmentalists that forced Conoco out of the Oriente.

Economic Mobilization

Economic mobilization may be an alternative to or concomitant of political mobilization. Alternative forms of market participation include production and marketing cooperatives, folklore and craft commercialization, the promotion of ecotourism, and tribal management of ranching or export agriculture. Each of these strategies attempts to use elements of ethnic identity as a factor of production, to establish an ethnic market niche. However, there is in each case an inherent tension between the homogenizing logic of globalization and the very characteristics of collective norms, harmony with nature, and non-Western cultural distinctiveness that constitute Indian ethnic identity. Some of these characteristics impede, and others are transformed by, participation in the market.

In Otavalo, a long-standing strategy of craft commercialization has dramatically improved the welfare of the indigenous community but blunted political mobilization. Otavaleños mass produce sweaters, rugs, and other craft items in family-based workshops, then market them in a weekly local fair that is one of Ecuador's prime tourist attractions; in street stands and shops throughout Ecuador; in the streets of U.S., European, and even Japanese cities; and for wholesale export to Colombia and Chile. Otavalo's 60,000 Indians retain a distinct style of regional dress and market their cultural identity through frequent participation in traditional music groups that perform for tourists and overseas. The Otavalo marketplace was constructed with foreign assistance, and weaving techniques were refined by Peace Corps volunteers during the 1960s. In one estimate, exports amounted to more than $2 million annually by the early 1980s; in 1993, 130,000 foreign tourists visited Otavalo and spent an additional $7 million (Meisch 1987; Hopley 1995). As a result, Otavalo is the most prosperous indigenous community in Ecuador (and perhaps in all of South America). Most of the community is healthy and well nourished, while a handful of successful Otavalans attend universities and own all the consumer accoutrements of the middle class.

But economic success has come at a political and cultural cost: although some Otavaleños are active in Indian organizations as individuals, the community as a whole has been distinctly underrepresented in national political mobilizations (Trujillo 1994, 149–50). Inequality within the community has grown, and most Otavaleños continue to depend on agriculture. The high level of international migration and cross-cultural contact produced by trade has affected identity: the younger generation wears jeans and watches violent American videos, and a surprising number marry foreign women. Even the traditional textiles that formed the basis of Otavaleño success have been adapted to market conditions: many of the rugs now contain Aztec figures or Escher motifs, and some of the clothing retailed is actually made in India or the Phillipines.

Another long-standing experience in economic mobilization is that of the Amazonian Shuar. With the help of Salesian missionaries, the Shuar organized Ecuador's first ethnic Indian federation in 1964. Because traditional lands were considered unused by the Ecuadoran state and thus subject to colonization, the Shuar Federation also launched a massive tribally managed ranching program to retain title. The Shuar have been supported by World Bank loans and various channels of bilateral assistance (e.g., from Holland and the United States). The ranching program has been an economic success: the profits have improved welfare conditions in the community and have also supported the federation's clinics, radio schools, and organization. But animal husbandry is patently unsuited for the rain forest environment and has caused deforestation and erosion. To save their culture, the Shuar had to save their land. To save their land, they entered the market in a way that destroyed their environment and challenged the culture of harmony with nature that they were striving to preserve.

For the typical highland community, marketing cooperatives for existing products are the most direct and viable response to adjustment pressures. In the past ten years, the NGO MCCH has created a nationwide and self-supporting network of 45 grain-marketing centers, 300 community store agricultural outlets, and 160 women's handicraft production groups that export their wares. The organization was founded by an Italian priest, its headquarters were built by an Italian cooperative association, and it has received a loan from the Inter-American Development Bank (a regional multilateral organization). MCCH has a staff of 120, and its businesses gross around $800,000 each month. The organization is expanding into a credit union and popular tourism, and it is linking up with similar ventures in nine other Latin American countries.

Despite its overall success, MCCH has encountered both cultural and market obstacles. MCCH has started a multifaceted training program that now encompasses a significant part of its operations (and is subsidized), because of culturally based problems with production quality, accounting, and management in the communities it serves. On the market side, MCCH continues to struggle with domestic competition through induced demand for imported products and international market saturation of "alternative" products and networks.

Community Responses and Ethnic Conflict

What has been the impact of these ethnic responses to market forces on the incidence and form of ethnic conflict? Does political mobilization promote conflict or self-determination? Is market absorption integrating or unbalancing? Can production alternatives safeguard indigenous identity and standards of living? The Ecuadoran experience examined here provides partial answers to these questions but clearly shows that ethnic conflict can and does result from each response to market forces. Overall, land struggles over property rights—not political mobilization or cultural issues—are the main source of ethnic conflict and the leading cause of violence (Dubly and Granda 1991).

First, we must define the actors in ethnic conflict. Ethnic conflict may involve a majority versus a minority, a marginalized versus a dominant group, interethnic conflict among marginalized minorities, or intra-ethnic conflict within a community about issues of identity and relationship to the wider society. All of these types of conflict have been present in Ecuador, in the forms of the marginalized highland Indian plurality against the dominant Hispanic minority; interethnic conflict among Indian groups, such as Huaorani versus Shuar; interethnic conflict between coastal Indians and Afro-Ecuadorans; and community conflict over identity among rapidly assimilating groups in all regions, such as conflicts between Catholic/traditional and newly evangelical Indians.

Second, we must define the character and indicators of conflict. Conflict may mean anything from vicious graffiti to genocide. When conflict does not involve violence, how do we distinguish legitimate self-assertion or group competition from dysfunctional clashes? At a minimum, indicators of conflict should be labeled according to the following scale: (1) passive resentment, (2) expressed hostility, (3) social discrimination, (4) economic competition, (5) political manipulation for group interests, (6) peaceful extrasystemic mobilization, (7) violence (which should then be distinguished by degrees). These labels may also permit a more differentiated assessment of the character of different types of ethnic conflict: for example, the national-level Indian rights conflict with the Hispanic elite in Ecuador has concentrated on mobilization, but some of the most acute interethnic conflict among Indian groups has combined economic competition with violence.

Third, we must consider whether conflict is inherently negative and dysfunctional. While high levels of violence clearly harm all participants, retard development, and diminish the social cohesion necessary for the realization of any collective project, some level of competition, mobilization, and even hostility may be necessary to achieve the self-determination of historically marginalized groups. Even the universalist goal of equality and a color-blind society displays a Western status quo bias that may not reflect the legitimate aspirations of groups that seek equity and the preservation of difference. Ecuador's Indian rights movement has long sought the constitutional recognition of plurinationality and territorial autonomy in addition to the classic civil rights and group welfare. While it is certainly undesirable for development assistance to promote violence, it may be inevitable that development assistance promotes conflict as it promotes development.

Political mobilization is seen mostly in conflict between Indians and the dominant Hispanic-mestizo society, but it also increasingly draws on Indians' mestizo allies among the poor and displaced. Political mobilization is both a cause and a consequence of ethnic conflict, but the level of violence engendered is largely a function of the response of the dominant group to ethnic challenge. At the national level in Ecuador, Indian mobilization has resulted from a history of "structural violence" through discrimination and political manipulation. Thus far, national mobilization has evoked hostility but surprisingly little violence from the dominant blanco-mestizos: during the 1990 uprising, security forces had orders not to shoot, and fewer than a dozen Indian protesters were killed in a week of nationwide confrontations that included the taking of police, government officials, and landowners as hostages. In general, the *levantamiento* seems to have increased positive ethnic self-identification by Indians and the political space granted by the dominant society for ethnic self-assertion (Trujillo 1994, 52–53).

By contrast, at the local level and subsequent to national protest, anti-indigenous paramilitary groups appeared in contested areas, and there have been violent clashes in several areas, such as Cañar and Chimborazo. For example, a notable presence of paramilitary forces that committed serious human rights violations occurred in Yuracruz; their activities were curtailed by intense international protest. In Cañar, local mestizos attacked and burned down the headquarters of the provincial Indian federation. Several days of street incidents ensued, culminating in the entry of military police to pacify the area.

Development assistance played a number of roles. One motive for the Cañar attack was the poor mestizo population's resentment of perceived preferential treatment of Indians by international funders; CARE was accused of "stirring up the Indians" (interview with CARE, August 4, 1995). A number of NGOs pulled out of Cañar in the wake of the conflict, but the Comité Ecumenico (European church groups) helped to rebuild the indigenous federation's headquarters (interview with Comité Ecumenico, August 8, 1995). The legacy of political mobilization and conflict has also complicated subsequent development assistance: a Cañar dam project funded by bilateral Dutch aid and the multilateral Fondo Interamericano de Desarollo Agricola has foundered on local political resistance and complex mutual recriminations about ethnic control of the project (interview with Dutch aid agency, August 15, 1995).

However, market absorption can also produce conflict between dominant and marginalized groups over land and other resources, among marginal groups pitted against each other in newly competitive markets, and within ethnic communities over strategies for change. In the impoverished and conflictive highlands, Indian land invasions of Hispanic holdings—repressed with varying degrees of violence—are a regular occurrence. Land conflicts have grown through the 1980s, producing at least 33 deaths (Dubly and Granda 1991, 207), including the deaths of several leaders of indigenous organizations—several times the number of deaths produced by political mobilization. In a typical incident, Hispanic landowners preparing to sell their land to a local Indian community were seized and beaten by a rival Indian group that had occupied an isolated portion of the property containing water reserves (interview, September 1, 1995). Various international programs attempt to buy or facilitate landholdings in Chimborazo. A complicating factor is the high level of conversion to evangelical Protestantism in the same region, with widely noted economic consequences—both Protestants and Catholics acknowledge that evangelicals are more economically successful. This difference has played a role in a series of religious conflicts within communities, resulting in several deaths in recent years (interview, July 25, 1995). Similarly, in the Amazon, the Huaorani attacked and killed dozens of mestizo and Quichua oil workers pushed into Huaorani territory by economic displacement from the highlands (Cabodevilla 1994). On the coast, a chronic conflict between the Chachi Indians and neighboring Afro-Ecuadorans over land rights has intensified with the development of timber by the Chachis and shrimping by the blacks. In this case, CARE is studying the Afro-Ecuadorans' land roots to better delimit their claims versus the Chachis, who have a long-standing indigenous reservation (interview, July 11, 1995).

Even apparently successful strategies of economic mobilization can create both interethnic and intra-ethnic conflict. In Otavalo, economic control of the town has shifted from mestizos to indigenous residents. This has caused resentment, hostility, and sporadic racial attacks—in 1994, an Otavalan Indian was murdered by local mestizos. However, Otavaleños who have traditionally served as intermediaries for other indigenous producers resist alternative marketing initiatives, such as MCCH; MCCH vehicles have their tires slashed in the Otavaleños home province of Imbabura (interview with MCCH, August 17, 1995). A similar dynamic exists in the Amazon: successful Shuar ranchers have expanded into Huaorani territory, and several Shuar have been killed as a result.

Conclusions and Recommendations

If economic change produces ethnic conflict, and if development assistance contributes in various ways to both economic change and community response, what can development agencies do to reduce the negative consequences of their presence? First, outside funders must acknowledge that market forces and adjustment pressures appear to be the main causes of declining welfare and increasing differentiation of marginalized groups and, thus, that forms of development assistance that reinforce passive absorption by the market contribute—either directly or unwittingly—to poverty and inequality. Unmitigated, market pressures seem to produce more types and higher levels of ethnic conflict than either political or economic mobilization.[4] Esman asks in the concluding chapter to this volume, "can donors continue to assume an integrated national economy where economic growth will raise all ships, a society of individualistic economic maximizers willing and able to participate in market competition, or a government committed to equity among its diverse citizens and subjects?" Ecuador provides a clear negative answer to these queries.

In general, outside funders should require an explicit assessment of ethnic impacts for both programs and projects. Although the World Bank now attempts to anticipate the effects of structural adjustment programs on vulnerable populations, this recommendation would extend the more comprehensive and institutionalized consideration currently given to communities facing physical displacement and resettlement to all ethnic communities within a project zone, since all face economic displacement. Ethnic impact assessment must not be limited to the current project or program but rather should document the social and political filters through which all outside resources pass: historical patterns of discrimination, group identities, state incentives and limitations. Therefore, such assessments should be prepared by a combination of ethnic community leaders, national experts, and international outsiders, to balance the inherent bias found in each population. Coordination among multilateral, bilateral, and nongovernmental funders working in a region is also crucial to this process.

Second, development agencies must recognize that "apolitical" programs of alternative market insertion also produce conflicts within and among communities, and the agencies must take steps to buffer these effects whenever possible. The solution here is less clear, since many aid agencies already claim to focus on poverty rather than ethnicity but find that the poor are Indians, who have cultural characteristics that must be factored into projects, which creates an ethnic focus to aid. Another limiting factor is that many alternative market initiatives are relatively self-sponsored, taking advantage of, but not relying on, outside aid.

A positive model may be seen in the Inter-American Foundation's promotion of development projects based on community forms of cultural expression (Kleymeyer 1994). Funders should generally attempt to provide parallel but distinct programs for neighboring or competing communities, along with some measures that reward interethnic cooperative projects (especially for mutually beneficial infrastructure and services). "Separate but equal" development projects for their neighbors may ultimately benefit indigenous communities as well. For example, the British Overseas Development Association's alternative timber project has relieved some colonization pressures on Ecuador's Awa Indian reserve. Certain kinds of grassroots development projects provide benefits across communities; for example, the cheese processing facilities of Salinas reward Indian dairy farmers, employ mestizo factory workers, and raise the standard of living for all residents of the community. Projects like these should receive priority.

Finally, development assistance providers should reexamine their role in political mobilization. Agencies that support adjustment may be contributing just as much to the motive for mobilization as do direct funders that provide organizational opportunity. Furthermore, political mobilization does not necessarily produce violent ethnic conflict; state and dominant community response are crucial mediating variables.

Therefore, rather than seeking to avoid or dampen political mobilization, development funders may want to consider mechanisms to encourage constructive interaction among community leaders and a conciliatory state and elite response to mobilization when it occurs. These may include ethnic conditionality for grants and loans, support for human rights monitoring, special funding for state programs for marginalized groups (e.g., bilingual education), and education and exchange programs that raise consciousness among state and ethnic elites. The most effective mechanism of ethnic conditionality is funders' insistence on the inclusion of affected communities in the design, execution, and evaluation of programs. State-sponsored Indian agencies may be appropriately involved but do not substitute for direct representation of civil society. Human rights monitoring is best performed by a combination of insiders and outsiders—especially nonpartisan international NGOs. Project budgets that include support for relevant state institutions (e.g., human rights offices and judiciaries) may strengthen the role of these bodies in future projects and internal policy debates. While leadership socialization alone cannot combat structural pressures, international funders can promote elite consciousness of the value of cultural diversity and alternatives to ethnic suppression by sponsoring educational programs and exercises. Funders should work with international bodies whose resources and clout are brought to bear on international negotiations of civil conflict to foster structured interactions among ethnic communities before large-scale ethnic violence occurs; participation may be a condition for receiving resources.

Above all, development agencies must consult directly with the affected ethnic communities about their needs, identities, rivalries, strategies, and preferences—through their own organizations rather than state, NGO, or expert intermediaries. Furthermore, as Esman reminds us in the concluding chapter of this volume: "[E]xternal assistance can contribute to sustained economic growth only when other conditions are simultaneously present. Among them is political stability." Development programs that treat "the market" as an empty space inhabited by impersonal social forces and interchangeable individuals—instead of human communities with different identities, opportunities, and resources—may end up turning that marketplace into a battlefield.

NOTES

This chapter was originally prepared for a conference on development assistance and ethnic conflict at Cornell University, October 5, 1995. Many thanks to participants in that conference, especially Ron Herring and Milt Esman, for helpful suggestions. This chapter is part of a larger project on the international relations of indigenous peoples in Latin America, *From Tribal Village to Global Village* (2000, Stanford University Press), supported by the U.S. Institute of Peace. The chapter draws on approximately 80 interviews conducted in Ecuador during 1995 as well as secondary sources, and all interviews are referenced by date and translated by the author. Fieldwork in Ecuador was hosted by the Facultad Latinoamericano de Ciencias Sociales, and skillful research assistance was provided by Layne Mosler and Fernando Rivera.

1. These figures represent consensus estimates derived from a variety of sources; no definitive ethnic breakdown of population exists, because census figures are not available by ethnicity—although some attempts have been made by use of Quichua (and many Indians boycott or avoid the census). Ethnic identification is highly contested, and undercounting of indigenous population is likely due to isolation and self-identification whenever possible as "mestizo" to avoid the stigma of being labeled as Indian (for some interesting examples of ambiguous self-identification, see Cliche and Garcia 1995).

2. Statistical information is presented in this chapter in an illustrative fashion rather than as a quantitative demonstration of causality. Economic statistics have been compiled from a variety of sources, which may reflect differing methodologies and a substantial range among sources. However, the sense and trend of statistics is remarkably similar on all key points: Indians are the poorest of the poor, overall and Indian welfare has declined during the period of adjustment, and market participation has generally negative consequences for Indian welfare. Sources for 1998 and 1999 data include the web sites of the Inter-American Development Bank at <www.iadb.org>, the Banco Central del Ecuador, and *Weekly News Update on the Americas* (a summary and translation of Latin American and Euro-

pean wire services, compiled by the Nicaragua Solidarity Network of Greater New York).

3. The highland Otavaleños have achieved unprecedented relative prosperity through the production and worldwide marketing of textiles. Their example is cited by Hispanic Ecuadorans as evidence of the lack of racism in Ecuador (a "model minority"), at the same time that the Otavaleños are stigmatized for the "atypical" industry, thrift, cosmopolitanism, and strong family networks that have fueled their success (several interviewees referred to them disparagingly as "the Jews of Ecuador" in interviews with the author, June 9, 1995).

4. One example of a first step toward analyzing these issues is the Food and Agriculture Organization's "Forests, Trees, and People" Amazonian conflict management program, which has completed seven case studies of development conflicts involving indigenous groups, emphasizing both community participation and the role of outside actors (Varea 1995).

REFERENCES

Ashley, John M. 1987. "African Palm Oil: Impacts in Ecuador's Amazon." *Cultural Survival Quarterly* 11, no. 2:55–60.
Bebbington, Antony, Galo Ramon, Hernan Carrasco, Victor Hugo Torres, Lourdes Peralvo, Jorge Trujillo. 1992. *Actores de Una Decada Ganada: Tribus, Comunidades y Campesinos en la Modernidad.* Quito: COMUNIDEC.
Brea, Jorge. 1991. "Migration and Circulation in Ecuador." *Tijdschrift voor Econ. en Soc. Geografie* 82, no. 3:206–19.
Brysk, Alison, and Carol Wise. 1997. "Economic Adjustment and Ethnic Conflict in Bolivia, Mexico, and Peru." *Studies in Comparative International Development* 32, no. 2 (summer): 76–104.
Bulmer-Thomas, Victor, ed. 1996. *The New Economic Model in Latin America and Its Impact on Income Distribution and Poverty.* London: Institute of Latin American Studies.
Cabodevilla, Miguel Angel. 1994. *Los Huaorani en la historia de los pueblos del Oriente.* Coca: CICAME, Vicariato Apostólico del Aguarico.
Cliche, Paul, and Fernando Garcia. 1995. *Escuela e Indianidad en las urbes ecuatorianas.* Quito: Ministerio de Educación.
Dubly, Alain, and Alicia Granda. 1991. *Desalojos y despojos: Los conflictos agrarios en Ecuador, 1983–1990.* Quito: Comisión Ecuménico por los Derechos Humanos; Editorial El Conejo.
Esman, Milton J. 1994. *Ethnic Politics.* Ithaca: Cornell University Press.
Fox, Jonathan. 1994. "Targeting the Poorest." In *Transforming State-Society Relations in Mexico,* ed. Wayne Cornelius, Ann Craig, and Jonathan Fox. La Jolla: Center for U.S.-Mexico Studies, University of California at San Diego.
Fierro, Luis C. 1995. "¿Qué dice el Banco Mundial?" *Gestión* (Quito), August, 15–18.
Grijalva Jiménez, Agustín, ed. 1994. *Datos básicos de la realidad nacional.* Quito: Corporación Editora Nacional.

Haggard, Stephan, and Robert Kaufman, eds. 1992. *The Politics of Economic Adjustment.* Princeton: Princeton University Press.

———. 1995. *The Political Economy of Democratic Transitions.* Princeton: Princeton University Press.

Hicks, James. 1990. *Ecuador's Amazon Region: Development Issues and Options.* World Bank Discussion Papers, no. 75. Washington, DC: World Bank.

Hopley, Elin. 1995. "At the Otavalo Crossroads." *Inside Ecuador* (Quito), May, 12–14.

Inter-American Development Bank. 1998/99. *Facing Up to Inequality in Latin America.* Washington, DC: Informe Progreso Economico y Social en America Latina.

Kane, Joe. 1993. "Letter from the Amazon: With Spears from All Sides." *New Yorker,* September 27, 54–79.

———. 1995. *Savages.* New York: Alfred Knopf.

Kimerling, Judith, S. J. Scherr, J. E. Gibson, G. Prickett, J. Gale, and L. Fischer. 1991. *Amazon Crude.* Ed. Susan S. Henriksen. New York: Natural Resources Defense Council.

Kleymeyer, Charles David, ed. 1994. *Cultural Expression and Grassroots Development.* Boulder and London: Lynne Rienner.

Labaca, Alejandro. 1988. *Crónica Huaorani.* Napo: CICAME, Vicariato Apostolico del Aguarico.

Larrea, Carlos. 1995. "Pobreza creció con el ajuste." *Gestión* (Quito), August, 19–21.

Maiguashca, Franklin. 1993. "The Role of State and Market in the Economic Development of Ecuador." *Journal of Economic Issues* 27, no. 2 (June): 441–50.

Martínez Valle, Luciano. 1987. *Economía Política de las Comunidades Indígenas.* Quito: Centro de Investigaciones de la Realidad Ecuatoriana.

———. 1992. "El empleo en economías campesinas productoras para el mercado interno." *European Review of Latin American and Caribbean Studies* 53 (December): 83–93.

Meisch, Lynn. 1987. *Otavalo: Weaving, Costume, and the Market.* Quito: Libri Mundi.

Moreno Yánez, Segundo, and José Figueroa. 1992. *El levantamiento indígena del inti raymi de 1990.* Quito: Fundación Ecuatoriana de Estudios Sociales; Ediciones Abya-Yala.

Pastor, Manuel. 1987. *The International Monetary Fund and Latin America: Economic Stabilization and Class Conflict.* Boulder: Westview.

Przeworski, Adam. 1993. "The Neoliberal Fallacy." In *Capitalism, Socialism, and Democracy Revisited,* ed. Larry Diamond and Marc F. Plattner. Baltimore: Johns Hopkins University Press.

"Pulso Latinoamericano." 1995. *El Comercio* (Quito), special supplement, September 15, B6. <www.bce.fin.ec>.

Racines, Francisco. 1993. "De la estabilización monetaria al ajuste estructural: Impactos sociales y alternativas de desarrollo." In *Ajuste Estructural en los Andes,* ed. José Baldivia. Quito: Ediciones Abya-Yala.

Ramirez, Miguel D. 1991. "The Impact of Austerity in Latin America, 1983–89: A Critical Assessment." *Comparative Economic Studies* 33:57–102.

Sierra, C. Enrique. 1994. "Ecuador: La política social en el marco de las políticas de ajuste y de los cambios neoliberales." In *Políticas Sociales y Pobreza*. Quito: Corporación de Estudios para el Desarrollo; Fondo de Inversión Social de Emergencia.

Smith, William C., and Roberto Patricio Korzeniewicz. 1997. *Politics, Social Change, and Economic Restructuring in Latin America*. Miami: University of Miami North-South Center.

Trujillo, Jorge Léon. 1994. "Las organizaciones indigenas: igualdad y diferencia." In *Indios: Una reflexion sobre el levantamiento indígena de 1990*. Quito: Abya-Yala.

———. 1994. *De campesinos a ciudadanos diferentes: El levantamiento indígena*. Quito: Centro de Investigación de los Movimientos Sociales en el Ecuador; Ediciones Abya-Yala.

United Nations Development Program (UNDP). 1993. *Participando en el Trueque de Ideas del Mundo de la Mujer*. Seminar report. Guatemala.

Varea, Anamaría. 1995. *Marea negra en la Amazonia*. Quito: Ediciones Abya-Yala; Instituto Latinoamerica de Investigaciones; FAO; Unión Mundial para la Naturaleza.

Walton, John. 1989. "Debt, Protest, and the State in Latin America. In *Power and Popular Protest*, ed. Susan Eckstein. Berkeley: University of California Press, 299–328.

World Bank. 1996. *Ecuador Poverty Report*. Washington, DC: World Bank.

Zamosc, Leon. 1994. "Agrarian Protest and the Indian Movement in the Ecuadorian Highlands." *Latin American Research Review* 29, no. 3:37–68.

———. 1995. *Estadística de las áreas de predominio étnico de la sierra ecuatoriana*. Quito: Ediciones Abya-Yala.

Zubritski, Yuri. 1990. "Los estereotipos etno-socio-psicológicos y su papel en las relaciones interetnicas en el area Otavalo-Cotocachi." In *Ecuador Indígena: Antropología y Relaciones Interétnicas*. Quito: Instituto Otavaleño de Antropología; Ediciones Abya-Yala.

CHAPTER 9

Policy Dimensions: What Can Development Assistance Do?

Milton J. Esman

In most countries that receive development assistance—in Asia, Africa, and Latin America; in Eastern Europe and the successor republics of the former Soviet Union—ethnic pluralism has become an important (often the most salient) dimension of politics and the principal source of violent conflict. The previous chapters address whether this presents a special challenge to the providers of development assistance and, if so, how they should deal with it. Where ethnic divisions have been politicized, can donors continue to assume an integrated national economy where economic growth will raise all ships, a society of individualistic economic maximizers willing and able to participate in market competition, or a government committed to equity among its diverse citizens and subjects? Or must they reach beyond technical rationality, beyond macroeconomic variables, to the actual structures, values, and political dynamics of the societies in which they intervene? Can economic development proceed under conditions of political turbulence induced by ethnic conflict? If not, must foreign assistance directly confront this reality? And has it the capacity to prevent, alleviate, or help to resolve such disputes?

Three decades ago, the reluctance of development assistance agencies to consider the social impacts of their interventions was held responsible for the failure of many projects and for inflicting needless pain on weak and vulnerable populations. As a result, "social soundness," or social-cultural compatibility, was incorporated into the guidelines of several development assistance agencies (Kottak 1991). Projects and policies were expected to take account of the values, preferences, lifestyles, and capabilities of the publics they affected; the harm inflicted on any group should be held to a minimum. Though social soundness is now a recognized concern of development assistance agencies and is included in their operating instructions, it has yet to be fully institutionalized. It has seldom been extended to such "political" factors as ethnic solidarities and their implications for development assistance.

The Importance of Context

In developing sensitivity to ethnic pluralism, context is critical. Such simplifying abstractions as those that facilitate macroeconomic analysis and prescription are not useful for evaluating social and political realities. Every societal environment is distinctive, and that distinctiveness at national, regional, and local levels must be appreciated if development assistance is to have beneficial rather than detrimental effects on interethnic relations or on relations between ethnic communities and governments. Among the significant contextual factors are identification of the principal ethnic communities; their demography—numbers and geographic distribution; their relative power, economic roles, social status, and relations with government; whether interethnic relations are stratified or segmented (members of all ethnic communities are represented at all socioeconomic levels); the extent to which ethnic communities are politicized, mobilized, or passive; divisions or factions within the ethnic communities; their dominant values and capabilities; evidence of interdependency and of crosscutting affiliations and memberships; recent history of relationships among ethnic communities and between them and the state. In possession of such basic information, development assistance agencies can equip themselves to estimate the impact of proposed interventions on ethnic politics.

By intent or by inadvertence, development assistance produces changes, including changes in economic status, aspirations, and expectations that may increase competition and hostility between ethnic communities. Policies and projects that benefit from contextual evaluation can reduce the uncertainties inherent in foreign assistance and in induced societal change. They may enable the adjustment or revision of proposed intervention strategies so that the resulting changes prevent unintended harm or even ameliorate interethnic relations. This is a precondition for the conversion of ethnic sensitivity to viable intervention strategies.

The Consequences of Development Assistance

The interethnic consequences of development assistance are conditioned by the strategies pursued by aid providers, the orientation of the government, and the predispositions of the ethnic communities that are affected. There is nothing predetermined about the interethnic effects of development assistance. A development assistance project or policy may prove to be irrelevant or have no apparent effect. It may not be perceived as affecting the interests of ethnic parties one way or the other.

Where the impact threatens to be harmful, development assistance may precipitate mobilization along ethnic lines, as Brysk notes in the case of Ecuador (chap. 8), among publics that had previously been relatively passive. The resultant grievances may even stimulate ethnogenesis, as small communities find it expedient to combine their forces in the face of a common threat, as Gibson notes in his chapter on displacement (chap. 2). In that process, the communities may discover or invent similar traits or historical affinities that furnish the raw material for shaping a new collective identity.

Development assistance projects may contribute to aggravating conflict among already mobilized and politicized ethnic communities. This process is outlined by Herring in his analysis of the Mahaweli project in Sri Lanka (chap. 6). That policies sponsored by foreign assistance can have similar negative effects is demonstrated by Herring's account of the effects of economic liberalization on the confrontation between Tamils and Sinhalese. Fiscal austerity, as prescribed by development assistance agencies to check inflation and balance external accounts, tends to reduce government services and eliminate subsidies that benefit lower middle class and low income families. By thus shredding the social safety net, structural adjustment measures increase insecurity and privation. In ethnically divided societies, this may eventuate in violence against members of vulnerable minorities. This pattern of scapegoating has erupted against the Chinese minority in Indonesia and, as Shenfield points out (chap. 7), against Jews in Russia.

Lest the reader despair, there is convincing evidence that development assistance can be managed in ways that avert or mitigate interethnic conflict and even lay the foundation for reconciliation and peaceful coexistence. The divisible character of benefits in a World Bank–sponsored project in Lebanon that located small but efficient waste disposal facilities in regions inhabited by each of the sectarian communities had the effect of averting conflict (Lebanese Republic 1995). The social organization component of the Gal Oya project in Sri Lanka, as analyzed by Uphoff (chap. 5), mitigated what might have become severe tensions between neighboring Tamil and Sinhalese farmers. The United States Agency for International Development's support for ethnic federalism was intended to enable the nationalities in Ethiopia to establish the structural basis for peaceful and consensual coexistence (Cohen 1994).

The Culture and Institutions of Development Assistance

For a half century development assistance has been a significant presence in international affairs (OECD 1999). It has touched nearly all countries as contributors or recipients and generated intense controversy between contributors and recipients and within both contributing and receiving countries. As development assistance institutions, bilateral and multilateral, gained experience in this novel enterprise, they evolved a culture, a set of beliefs and practices, and a special vocabulary that guided their behavior and into which new recruits were inducted and socialized.

A prominent theme in this culture has been its technocratic and economistic bias. As the common goal was believed to be economic development, economic resources and their efficient utilization were seen as the proper concerns of donors, supplemented by the enhancement of skills, transfer of technology, and strengthening of institutions required for economic development. Formal deference to state sovereignty has been a component of this culture; many recipient governments, recently liberated from colonial control, have been especially jealous of the symbols of their sovereignty, while the technicians and economists who staffed the donor institutions were uncomfortable with political matters. While decisions about what countries should be assisted and the volume of assistance have often been based on political, strategic, or commercial calculations, the implementation of development assistance has assumed a decidedly apolitical cast. The multilateral agencies have been especially deterred by their charters from involvement in the politics of their member countries.

There was considerable attention to microeconomic factors, such as the efficiency and output of individual projects, but the master criterion for success was macroeconomic growth. This was warranted by the ascendency after World War II of the Keynesian paradigm and the evidence in Europe and Japan during the two decades after the Marshall Plan that macroeconomic growth seemed, in fact, to lift all boats. When that impressive growth was found to bypass large numbers of people, questions of distribution were introduced into the culture of development assistance. While those protected from harsh distributional consequences may turn out to be members of ethnic communities, this has been, as McHugh concludes (chap. 3), mostly accidental. Explicit ethnic concerns tended to be defined as political, thus beyond the proper purview of development assistance.

The end of the Cold War has introduced into the universe of development assistance fresh themes that challenge its established culture. The culture of foreign aid has begun to make room for political values cautiously and selectively. Such concerns as human rights and democratization are now vigorously promoted by USAID, the Dutch, the Canadians, and the Scandinavian countries. The World Bank fosters improved "governance," the rule of law, and "transparency" in financial affairs. These cannot be written off as nonpolitical. Where human rights violations by weak states are conspicuous and flagrant, as in Kenya, the development assistance community is prepared to impose conditions on aid flows, demanding specific political reforms; where human rights violations, restrictions on democratic processes, or repression of ethnic minorities by more powerful states are similarly blatant, as in China, Turkey, and Indonesia, development assistance agencies have found it expedient to overlook them while continuing to provide substantial assistance, confident perhaps that prosperous market economies are inevitable progenitors of democracy and human rights. When the Indonesian government expelled the Dutch foreign aid agency for protesting human rights violations, an aid consortium chaired by the World Bank made up the loss of Dutch assistance. Following the logic of developmentalism, economic growth superseded the bank's concern for human rights and justice for ethnic minorities.

While some political factors have intruded into the practice of development assistance, this has been challenged as inappropriate interference both by leaders of developing countries and by some staff members of the development institutions. Japan, now the largest aid donor, is reluctant to impose political conditions. Donors are aware that ethnic tensions may undermine their assistance programs, but consistent attention to ethnic concerns has been slow to emerge. USAID has been the lead agency in promoting democratic development, but McHugh (chap. 3) finds that its interest in ethnic politics has not been institutionalized. Brysk (chap. 8) reports that USAID declined to act in a situation that might have promoted democratic development in Ecuador, fearing that intervention in ethnically sensitive situations might be construed as too political. Shenfield (chap. 7) writes that the International Monetary Fund (IMF) and Western advisors, with little understanding of Soviet economic practices or of post-Soviet economic conditions, imposed neoliberal policies on an economy that was unable to accommodate them, with devastating economic and social effects, including the scapegoating of ethnic minorities.

Cohen (chap. 4) speculates from his experience in East Africa that the allergy to political concerns and specifically to ethnic realities is far more evident in institutional headquarters than among field personnel. Headquarters may be constrained by the language of their institutional charters and remoteness from the incidence of conflict, while field staff members must find ways in their daily operations to cope with the realities they encounter. Especially when humanitarian operations encounter ethnic violence, the resourcefulness of field staff is tested to the limit. In the absence of agency policies and guidance on the management of assistance under conditions of ethnic tension and conflict, field staff members are left to their own devices.

Each of the institutions that supply and manage development assistance has its distinctive personality. This depends on their main constituency, the mission they undertake, and their sources of staffing. These differences are reflected in their approaches to ethnic conflict.

The IMF considers its main constituency to be central bankers, finance ministries, and the international investment community. Its main mission is to help governments achieve fiscal stability, manage their external payments accounts, and maintain creditworthiness. Its staff members come from the ranks of central bankers, public finance specialists, and fiscal and monetary economists. Internal distributional questions, including the status of ethnic communities, are not prominent among their priorities. Yet, during the 1990s, the IMF began cautiously to raise with potential borrowers such political issues as official corruption, excessive military expenditures, the rule of law, and violations of human rights (James 1998).

In extreme contrast, the Oxford Committee for Famine Relief (OXFAM) is an international voluntary nongovernmental organization (NGO) whose constituents are mainly concerned with social justice and human rights. Its mission is to contribute to grassroots development especially among poor and disadvantaged publics and to help them assert their human rights. Its staff members are selected from university graduates from the left of center in the political spectrum. While the IMF works only with governments and investors, OXFAM works directly with disadvantaged communities and is sensitive to the needs of ethnic communities that are oppressed or disadvantaged by governments or by the results of development assistance. Thus, OXFAM's institutional personality contrasts sharply with that of the IMF.

OXFAM exemplifies one tendency in the heterogeneous ranks of the NGOs. While some are content to promote humanitarian or development activities in a strictly nonpolitical mode, others have become concerned with distributional equity among the publics they assist, including ethnic communities. Initially apolitical, they have been converted to advocacy for disadvantaged communities by their experiences in the field. Brysk (chap. 8) reports that NGOs in Ecuador facilitated ethnic mobilization against structural adjustment measures and attempted to replace some government services to the poor that had been eliminated. Others warn that some NGOs, notably sectarian agencies, may exacerbate ethnic tensions by favoring one community over another.

Rotberg and his associates propose that since NGOs are present on the ground, they are well situated to provide early warning of impending violence, but that they require more effective means to alert international organizations and their member governments (Rotberg 1996). However, Mary Anderson, a well-informed and sympathetic participant-observer of NGO operations, reaches the surprising conclusion that they have seldom been effective in mitigating interethnic conflicts.

> . . . through operational dilemmas encountered in providing aid, NGOs—whether focused on relief, development, human rights, or peace—have, to a greater or lesser extent, inadvertently exacerbated rather than lessened it [conflict] and its consequences. In some cases the negative consequences have been profound and costly. (Anderson 1995)

Anderson cites as one of many examples the tragedy of the refugee camps in Goma, the Congo, near the Rwandan border. There NGO supplies intended for innocent destitute refugees were distributed through refugee "leaders." These proved to be officers of the Hutu militias whose fighters had recently committed genocidal atrocities against Tutsi civilians. The militias were using the camps and the supplies provided by NGOs as bases for conscription, training, resupply, and sustenance in preparation for the reinvasion of Rwanda (Anderson, personal conversation). In this case, the ethnic context had not been correctly evaluated and had perhaps been overlooked entirely.

When providing relief intended for the innocent victims of conflict, donors often confront a harsh dilemma, the ethnic salience of humanitarian assistance. It seems virtually impossible to escape the perception by one side or the other that donations intended entirely to relieve suffering and preserve life are assisting the enemy at their expense. Whether the goods are distributed by governments or by NGOs seems not to matter. Thus, the contestants feel justified in blocking the flow of relief goods, controlling its distribution, or looting it for themselves or their partisans. This has been the experience in Sudan, Somalia, Congo, Liberia, and Kosovo. Should donors work through the contending organizations to maximize the likelihood that at least some aid will reach the truly needy—and thus be charged with ethnic bias—or should they persist in withholding aid until they can be assured that it will be distributed impartially?

Between the IMF and OXFAM are located most of the government-sponsored development assistance institutions. The World Bank has become the world's largest and most prestigious development agency. Though dominated by engineers and economists who emphasize technical and economic rationality, its ranks include a minority of social scientists who continue to raise social and distributional issues. Thus, as Gibson indicates (chap. 2), the bank's staff is divided between a dominant segment committed to economic rationality and a minority that asserts the importance of institutional and cultural concerns, including the impact of projects on indigenous peoples. These concerns are sometimes reflected in the bank's decision making and in its loan provisions, including its recent emphasis on good governance and on measures to compensate for the detrimental short-term effects of austerity policies on vulnerable groups in countries undergoing structural adjustment. As its charter forbids it to interfere in the internal affairs of member states, its management tends to avoid matters, such as interethnic relations, that might be construed as explicitly political.

USAID has, in the past, been a pioneer in fresh approaches and a bellwether among development assistance institutions. Its main constituency is the U.S. Congress. It uses its diminishing resources in support of a variety of causes that are dear to congressmen of different political persuasions, among them promoting private enterprise, providing humanitarian relief, and most recently promoting democracy and human rights. Its current "Guidelines on Democratization and Governance Programs" refer to ethnic conflicts but provide its staff with scant instructions on how to proceed. It has begun, albeit hesitantly, to grapple with ethnic realities, as in its assistance to the Ethiopian government's efforts to manage ethnic conflict by territorial federalism.

The Scandinavian aid programs, reflecting the social democratic values in these societies, have been prepared to use their resources and their influence to stress social equity and human rights. This includes questions of interethnic equity as a component of democratic political development.

The attitude of Japan's International Cooperation Agency (JICA) toward "political" matters is an expression of Japan's sensitivity toward foreign and especially Asian perceptions of Japan's ambitions, based on harsh treatment of other Asians during its era of imperialist expansion prior to and during the Pacific war. Therefore, JICA prefers to avoid measures that might be construed as political, including ethnic issues. Yet, under pressure from Japanese public opinion and international human rights organizations, it did withdraw from the Sardar Sarovar Dam project in India, which threatened to inflict severe privation on an indigenous "tribal" community.

Because of its "one country, one vote" system of governance, most UN-related agencies remain cautious about matters that might be displeasing to their members. This includes ethnic concerns. The main exception is UNICEF, whose mandate emphasizes services to disadvantaged children and whose constituency includes large numbers of private citizens from whom it raises funds and who are attracted to its people-to-people and humanitarian image. In many respects, UNICEF's outlook resembles the distributional orientation of many NGOs.

Cultures change, usually gradually, as societies are forced to confront fresh problems. So do institutions. The present culture of development assistance and the institutions that embody it contain several components. The largest component is the orthodox, apolitical, technocratic-economistic growth strategy; this strategy continues to underpin the culture as a whole. This is why social soundness concerns are often overlooked. A second, smaller concern is distributional consideration, which claims significant, but minority, support. The smallest element, and one struggling for wider recognition, is made up of concerns to advance democratization/human rights values. To shift the metaphor, the contemporary development assistance culture includes themes that compete for attention and support among decision makers, practitioners, and the publics that finance them. The more distributional and human rights themes succeed in gaining influence, the more likely it is that ethnic concerns will gain legitimacy and be factored into intervention strategies.

The Goals of Intervention

There is an expanding body of knowledge—though no general theory—on the origins and manifestations of ethnic conflict and on processes for its regulation and management. It is based on analysis and evaluation of a large body of experience (Young 1976; Glazer and Moynihan 1975; Horowitz 1985; Brass 1985; Kellas 1991; Gurr 1993; Esman 1994). But the application of this knowledge to the circumstances of specific conflicts, especially when mediated by development assistance institutions (with their special cultures), must be tempered by cautious and informed judgment. Humility and prudence concerning interventions in societies understood imperfectly have not been prominent in development assistance and stabilization operations. Yet humility and prudence are precisely what are needed for interventions designed to influence such complex and uncertain subjects as economic institutions and interethnic relations. The disastrous consequences of the mindless imposition of neoliberal practices on the post-Soviet Russian economy have been described by Shenfield (chap. 7). The dogmatic and zealous prescription of democratic practices, such as majoritarian (winner-take-all) elections, may actually ignite interethnic tensions, as minorities face the prospect, in the name of democracy, of being excluded from political office and denied political influence. This was the fate of the Catholic minority in Northern Ireland during the half century preceding the outbreak of sectarian violence in the early 1970s.

Once the specific context has been evaluated and efforts have been made to consult the parties that might be affected, each instance of intervention should be regarded as a hypothesis about the consequences that might ensue (Rondinelli 1983). Moreover, interventions should be monitored to account for unanticipated consequences and to provide opportunities for timely corrections.

Assuming that donor agencies have gained some sensitivity to the ethnic dimensions of development or have been compelled to confront them, what should be the goal or goals of their interventions? Once violence has erupted, they might be satisfied to limit its scale and intensity and to alleviate human suffering. But given the opportunity to consider longer-term outcomes, there are three possible goals:

- to avoid conflict and ensure peaceful coexistence;
- to achieve equity or rough distributional justice;
- or simply to do no harm to any ethnic community.

Each of these hopeful outcomes is fraught with dilemmas and complications.

Economic growth theorists believe that restraining growth in the interest of distributional fairness is a misguided short-term strategy (Rostow 1990). They contend that development assistance should therefore not be distorted by such political objectives, especially since policies conducive to these ends are surrounded by high levels of uncertainty and may in any case be beyond the capabilities of development assistance. They argue that the best hope for mitigating conflict—class conflict or ethnic conflict—is an expanding economy that permits the distribution of increments of growth to all competing communities. According to their thinking, since the introduction of ethnic criteria is likely to raise project costs or constrain the implementation of liberalization policies, the net effect of such extraneous considerations is to hobble economic growth and, perversely, thwart the one strategy that its proponents think is most likely to mitigate and resolve ethnic conflict in the long run.

Skeptics of this approach, including myself, reply that external assistance can contribute to sustained economic growth only when other conditions are simultaneously present. Among them is political stability, which is unlikely under conditions of intense ethnic conflict. Moreover, there is no convincing evidence to support the conventional wisdom that economic growth necessarily diminishes conflict (Olson 1963; Arndt 1978). Many ethnic conflicts have little to do with economic considerations and much more to do with political control, a recent example being the brutal confrontation between Serbs and Albanians in Kosovo. Competition over the distribution of economic growth may actually aggravate conflict (Majstorovic 1995; Esman 1990).

The objectives of conflict avoidance and of equity are, under some circumstances, contradictory. It may not be possible to pursue both at the same time. Efforts to achieve distributive justice on behalf of low-status, disadvantaged groups may actually prolong conflict and cost lives (Miller 1992). Members of more favored communities charge that affirmative action deprives them of opportunities they have earned by merit and hard work, to benefit the undeserving—bringing about, in effect, reverse discrimination (Nevette and Kennedy 1986). Solicitude by NGOs and other outsiders for depressed communities may provoke envy from those who are only somewhat better off. Brysk (chap. 8) reports the hostile reaction of mestizos in Ecuador to development assistance targeted toward Indians; blue-collar whites in the United States have similarly responded to affirmative action for designated racial and ethnic minorities; upper-caste Hindus have protested violently against reservations of government jobs and university admissions for members of "backward" castes. Such measures aimed at equity can precipitate backlashes that exacerbate grievances and provoke conflict.

Similarly, the apparently minimalist goal of no harm to any ethnic community may have the unintended effect of provoking conflict. Though not harmed in an absolute sense, a mobilized ethnic community, aware that others are gaining at their apparent expense, can readily succumb to the malady of invidious comparison, to a sense of relative deprivation that may produce aggressive reactions (Esman 1990).

Should development assistance activities aim to de-emphasize and even delegitimate ethnic solidarity in the hope that other, presumably less violence-prone, collective identities may emerge as more salient sources of political alignment? Or should they recognize ethnic solidarities as enduring and legitimate allegiances, while promoting measures conducive to peaceful, consensual coexistence? These two approaches are mutually exclusive, since they visualize contradictory political and societal futures. Those who advocate de-emphasis argue that ethnic alignments are inherently unstable and conflict prone, provide incentives for extremist leadership and uncompromising claims, and tend to abridge the rights of individuals to freedom of choice (Horowitz 1985; Sowell 1990). In an effort to attenuate ethnic solidarity, they would promote crosscutting organizational memberships and proscribe ethnic messages and ethnic organization in political campaigns.

Consociationalists and others who argue for legitimizing ethnic solidarities as political actors where ethnic cleavages seem deep and enduring believe they are recognizing political realities and responding to manifest social preferences (Lijphart 1977; McRae 1974; for a critical assessment, see Rabushka and Shepsle 1972). They hope to achieve consensual patterns of power sharing where this is possible and guarantees for minority rights where this is necessary. The Anglo-American confidence that individuals are the only legitimate claimants to human rights cannot and should not be imposed dogmatically on societies where collective solidarities are paramount; in such societies, the emphasis on individual as opposed to group rights cannot be a successful prescription for managing deep-seated ethnic conflicts (Van Dyke 1975).

Since the goals of distributive justice and peaceful coexistence may not be compatible (at least in the short run), donors should be prepared to confront the likely trade-offs. A powerful case can be made for according priority to social peace even at the expense of distributive justice, since peaceful coexistence is prerequisite to the realization of all humane values. By the same token, donors should accept as legitimate existing expressions of ethnic solidarity, instead of attempting to transcend them, as there is little evidence that strategies intended to break down ethnic solidarities, especially when promoted by outsiders, can be effective except over very long periods of time. President Tito's campaign to create an overarching "Yugoslav" identity and allegiance failed completely; the merging of Normans and Saxons into English required more than four centuries.

Policies to Avert or Moderate Ethnic Conflict

These are no standard formulas for managing ethnic conflict. Unlike the IMF formula for economic stabilization that is believed to be equally valid for Bolivia, Uganda, and Russia, one size cannot fit all. Context conditions the effectiveness of interventions. To appreciate the ethnic dynamics of the society in which they intend to intervene, development assistance agencies must first investigate and learn. The first step is to examine the recent history of these relationships; the next is to consult with representatives of ethnic communities that might be affected by the programs they sponsor or support. They can rely on government spokespersons only for the government's often incomplete or biased assessment of underlying realities and of the effects of proposed interventions.

Definitions of fairness by governments, by ethnic communities, and by intra-ethnic factions are likely to diverge. Donors must take care that local consulting firms or NGOs that they employ to clarify these relationships do not harbor biased points of view. Where possible, donors should foster dialogue that involves government agencies and ethnic communities, with the objective of achieving consensus on a fair apportionment of benefits and costs. Proposed projects or policies and methods of implementation may have to be adjusted and modified, and delays may occur as differences are identified and debated. While consensus may not be possible, the communities affected will at least know that an effort has been made to solicit their views and take them into account.

Among the important policy choices for development assistance agencies are allocation principles. Three principles apply both to projects and to policies. The first principle is the search for common interests. The ideal policy or policy set produces positive-sum outcomes for all the parties concerned and mutual confidence that benefits and costs are equitably shared. USAID's support for the rehabilitation of the large Gal Oya irrigation system in Sri Lanka that included both Tamil and Sinhalese farmers successfully incorporated this objective. To be avoided are interventions that, whatever the intended macroeconomic benefits or anticipated economic rates of return, will be perceived as benefiting one community at the expense of the other.

The second principle calls for divisibility. Where ethnic communities occupy territorially separate enclaves, the divisibility of projects may contribute to mutually tolerable results. Thus, the major confessional communities in Lebanon benefited from a World Bank–sponsored project that provided a modern, efficient waste disposal facility in each of their territories. Especially where projects reflect local demand, rather than the preferences of governments or donors, and where communities participate in their design and management and acquire a sense of ownership, the satisfactions produced by development activities contribute to an atmosphere of tolerance that bodes well for peaceful coexistence. Large projects that are perceived as damaging to an ethnic community may be redesigned and divided into several smaller projects that avoid the original damage but achieve similar and often higher economic rates of return. For example, several small-scale, locally controlled water management systems could substitute for a large government-operated dam.

The third principle produces interdependence, where a division of labor between ethnic communities rewards cooperative, rather than competitive, behavior. An excellent example is reported by Anderson (1995). An NGO-sponsored project in Tadjikistan was designed to avert economic competition and create economic interdependence among two hostile ethnic communities. One was given wool-producing machinery, the other carpet-making equipment. Economic interdependence fostered incentives for their joint economic success.

Western donors normally favor allocation of resources and opportunities flowing from their interventions (scholarships, employment, business loans, privatization of state enterprises) according to objective criteria, such as individual market competition or individual merit—no preferences, no discrimination. But where societies are divided along ethnic lines, market-merit processes may have perverse results. While they may overcome the gross favoritism, corruption, and ethnic patronage practiced by some governments, they may also yield allocations that are skewed along ethnic lines, generating grievances among those who feel disadvantaged, left out, or cheated. Members of ethnic groups that are initially privileged by superior education or business experience, such as Tamils in Sri Lanka, Jews in Russia, and Chinese in Indonesia, benefit disproportionately from market-merit competition, widening the original gaps and yielding resentment that fuels ethnic conflict.

One remedy is proportionality, where jobs, licenses, contracts, university admissions, and so on are allocated among ethnic communities according to relative numbers. This may reduce economic efficiency and retard growth but ensure equitable participation. Governments may at times favor compensatory allocations for members of disadvantaged communities and expect donors to comply with this policy. Like proportionality, compensatory policies are vulnerable to the previously mentioned backlash reaction. "Affirmative action" for Sinhalese produced grievances and anger among Tamils that precipitated the Sri Lankan civil war. More skillfully managed, compensatory measures in Malaysia contribute to rectifying previous patterns of ethnic-based economic and occupational inequality at tolerable social cost (Esman 1994).

Individual competition, proportionality, and compensatory preferences are the principal formal criteria for allocation. All have implications for ethnic conflict. None is inherently superior on moral grounds. The effectiveness of each depends on the context to which it is applied. Development assistance agencies should evaluate the trade-offs in consultation with governments and with the relevant ethnic communities to determine which allocation criterion is most likely to be perceived as fair and workable. Some anticipated efficiency and growth may have to be forgone in the interest of more basic values, such as peaceful coexistence and interethnic equity.

Where governments engage in practices that flagrantly discriminate on the basis of ethnic membership and cannot be trusted to change their practices, development assistance agencies may (1) disqualify them for further assistance or even apply economic sanctions, as in South Africa in the 1980s; (2) channel all resources through local authorities or NGOs; or (3) impose their own criteria and rigorously monitor performance. In the Kenyan example reported by Cohen (chap. 4), donors interested in democratization, controlling corruption, and promoting interethnic equity imposed stern measures to prevent deliberate skewing of the distribution of the resources they provide. To repeat an earlier caveat, because of their neocolonialist implications, such interventions should be undertaken with circumspection and only after quiet diplomacy has proved to be futile.

When foreign aid promotes democratization and human rights in ethnically divided societies, their first concern should be, as previously noted, to eschew majoritarian (winner-take-all) elections. If ethnic minorities are to feel secure, they must be convinced that they have some control over their destiny. Where territorial autonomy is feasible, ethnic federalism is an option, as in India. The national minority becomes the majority in its region; the regional government is operated by fellow ethnics; they control the allocation of land and natural resources, credit, and public contracts; its language becomes the language of government and education. At the same time, representatives of the minority participate in the affairs of the central government in decision-making roles. The complications and risks of federalism are well known: federal autonomy may lead to demands for full independence; minority communities within federalized regions may insist on their own autonomy, as have, for example, the Indian communities in Quebec and the Nepalese in West Bengal. Secession or the further division of federalized units may, however, be preferable to prolonged and violent conflict; it may bring government closer to the people and forestall ethnic conflict when peaceful coexistence within a single polity proves impossible.

Where territorial autonomy is infeasible, power-sharing arrangements may enable minorities to control some of their own institutions, including schools; to use their own language in transactions with government; and to hold positions in government in rough proportion to their numbers (Lijphart 1990; Sisk 1996). Less far-reaching than formal power-sharing arrangements, minority rights provide the means for minorities to feel secure in a multiethnic polity, to maintain their cultures and their corporate existence. Minority rights exemplify recognition and respect by government and the majority for their distinctive status, thereby diminishing the sources of conflict (Gurr 1993, chap. 10).

While they are not panaceas for managing conflict, free elections contribute to the legitimacy of governments. Electoral processes should make it possible for minorities to be equitably represented. Proportional representation is one such method. Another is to design the electoral system to favor ethnically moderate candidates and make it more difficult for extremists to be elected. A number of such arrangements have been identified and analyzed (Horowitz 1990). Even where ethnic solidarities are recognized as legitimate and enduring, multimember districts in which voters from all ethnic backgrounds cast ballots for all the seats provide incentives for candidates to appeal for support across ethnic lines. Party and election rules can sanction political organizations and candidates whose campaign appeals are blatantly ethnic and likely to provoke interethnic hostility.

The 1990s have witnessed the ascendency of economic globalism propelled by neoliberal ideology. Private investment has displaced government action as the prime mover of development. Development assistance is expected to promote and facilitate foreign private investment. Like projects financed by foreign aid, foreign private investment activities may have important consequences for ethnic politics. In the Niger delta region of Nigeria, the exploitation of petroleum resources by foreign oil companies has precipitated violent protests by local ethnic communities whose spokespersons complain that few of the benefits from the extraction of their oil have reached their impoverished region in the form of either public facilities or employment, while their environment has been ravaged. Meanwhile, lucrative royalties have been collected by a central government dominated by ethnic groups from other regions of the country. As development assistance facilitates the climate for private investment, the latter should exercise similar circumspection about the ethnic consequences of their operations both to fulfill their responsibilities to their host country and to protect their investments.

Ethnic Conditionality

One of the principal findings in this volume is that understanding of and concern for ethnic conflict among the major development assistance institutions has been hesitant, reluctant, inept, or completely absent. Ethnic solidarities have become politicized in many of the countries in which the institutions operate, and ethnic conflict, often violent, has become a global reality likely to affect the success of their interventions. The tendency to ignore this reality or to address it awkwardly or obliquely represents a culture lag that will have to be overcome.

An analogy may be found in environmental affairs. There, too, most development assistance professionals and Third World governments initially opposed—or were reluctant to complicate their calculations, negotiations, and operations with—still another noneconomic impediment. They were forced to do so by the pressure of determined environmental lobbies and the requirement that environmental impact statements be prepared for projects that might have environmental implications. While the results have often been disappointing to environmentalists, they have greatly increased the salience of environmental values in development assistance operations. Following this precedent, why not introduce ethnic impact statements for policy initiatives or projects that might affect interethnic relations or relations between ethnic communities and governments?

What might ethnic impact statements contain? First, there would be a country or regional background analysis identifying the major ethnic communities and their demography, economic base, and levels of mobilization and solidarity; a recent history of relations among these communities and between them and government; and an account of government policies and practices affecting these relationships. Since the behavior of ethnic communities changes over time in response to perceived threats or opportunities, it would be necessary periodically to update them. Ethnic impact statements would constitute extensions, in effect, of social soundness analysis. They would be not dissimilar to the economic background statements that donor agencies routinely require to inform their economic policy initiatives and project interventions. Armed with this information, donors would be better equipped to estimate the effects of proposed interventions on these relationships—on equity, coexistence, or conflict—and to design interventions accordingly.

These statements would be prepared by qualified social scientists with the participation of indigenous scholars and consultants. Some development assistance professionals would resist these statements, just as they initially resisted similar requirements for environmental analysis, and for similar reasons: that they would increase costs and delay implementation of economically sound projects or policies, divert attention from economic fundamentals, and have the mischievous effect of stimulating ethnic activism among previously passive communities. Governments may also regard this interest by donors in their domestic politics as illegitimate, neocolonialist encroachments on their sovereignty.

Yet it is no longer possible for donors to disregard the reality that dominates public affairs in many of the countries in which they operate. That reality has the potential for disrupting their interventions and might even mean that their activities reinforce or provoke conflict. Even with accurate information, development assistance initiatives will encounter uncertainties and unanticipated consequences, but reliable information can help reduce risks and avoid unnecessary mistakes.

Does ethnic sensitivity by donor agencies imply ethnic conditionality, as suggested by McHugh in her review of USAID's practices (chap. 3)? What is the rationale for any form of conditionality, and would ethnic conditionality meet these tests? Conditionality has been imposed by donors for both instrumental and intrinsic reasons.

First, donors may believe that successful implementation of policies, projects, or humanitarian assistance requires responsive behavior by host governments. A project cannot be expected to succeed unless, for example, certain technical, financial, and administrative procedures are followed and measures are in place to ensure that the project can be sustained after external assistance ends. Such conditions are routinely incorporated into project agreements before they are launched. Infusions of funds intended to achieve fiscal and monetary stabilization may be wasted unless revenues increase and expenditures including subsidies are curbed. These expressions of economic conditionality are intended to be instrumental to policy outcomes.

Second, donors may believe that certain values and practices that are important to their constituents, that are intrinsic to their conception of a good society, must be respected. These may include free enterprise, basic human rights, and the rule of law. They become conditions for their participation in a development assistance relationship. In the absence of some progress along these lines, donors may not feel justified in providing further assistance.

Ethnic conditionality is warranted by both sets of criteria. Funds intended to promote economic development and improve quality of life will be dissipated unless there is internal peace and order, which may be jeopardized by ethnic conflict. Measures should therefore be taken to reduce or preempt ethnic-based grievances, by insuring the equitable division of benefits and costs among ethnic communities and by other measures intended to foster peaceful coexistence. At the same time, donors may find it impossible to work with regimes that deliberately discriminate against or impose harm on ethnic communities or that flout the rights of minorities. Under such circumstances, donors may opt for ethnic conditionality. States that persist in abusing ethnic minorities and fail to respond to the terms of ethnic conditionality would be regarded as pariahs, ineligible for development assistance.

The process would be similar to methods employed for other forms of conditionality. First, donors would engage in discussions with representatives of government, a form of constructive engagement intended to negotiate agreement on the terms of conditionality. Such agreements may represent compromises, followed by the monitoring of compliance and further dialogue. If donors can persuade themselves that there has been progress (even if less than stipulated in the terms of the original agreement), they may continue support, hoping that steady pressure will eventually persuade the government that the conditions serve its interests as well. Donors try to avoid the disruptive effects of terminating support, preferring to remain engaged and maintain pressure rather than apply sanctions. When all else fails, donors can terminate assistance until the government is willing to renew discussions. In that event, the process begins anew. Meanwhile, donors may try to continue assistance to the country through NGOs or local authorities.

Relieving the poorest countries of the heavy burden of servicing debts to bilateral and multilateral donors, debts that were imprudently contracted by previous governments and whose annual servicing consumes all or most of the nation's foreign exchange earnings, has been recognized as a useful complement to infusions of fresh resources through development assistance loans or grants. Debt relief for the 40 or so most heavily indebted poor countries would, however, be unacceptable and even futile unless accompanied by conditionality to ensure that the resultant savings would be used for developmental purposes, rather than for weapons purchases, capital flight, prestige projects, subsidies to favored constituents, or sheer corruption. President Clinton has proposed that the savings resulting from debt relief be used for education, others that they be devoted primarily to small, employment-creating public works projects or for social needs, such as public health and welfare. (Spence and Ivers 1999). The use of such savings to repair safety nets that were shredded by austerity measures imposed by structural adjustment policies could mitigate the insecurity and privation experienced by middle- and lower-income communities and thus diminish provocations for scapegoating unpopular ethnic minorities. But only if they adhere to such conditions would these governments be eligible for future assistance from development assistance agencies.

Ethnic conditionality may prove to be necessary to ensure effective or morally acceptable uses of development assistance resources in some ethnically divided countries. As the limitations of neoliberalism and developmentalism become more apparent, and as foreign assistance increasingly promotes such political values as good governance, human rights, and democratization, there will be further need to resort to this established instrument of development assistance. Ethnic impact statements and ethnic conditionality reflect the increasing salience of ethnic politics in the affairs of aid-receiving countries and the need for development assistance to take account of this reality.

Much depends on the ability of staff members of donor agencies to understand that their interventions must recognize the specific conditions, capabilities, and predispositions in every host country, including each country's ethnic politics. By now it should be clear that one approach cannot fit all, whether the issue is neoliberal economics, majoritarian elections, or large-scale infrastructure projects. Staff members must be sensitive to national specifics, and every group responsible for designing and implementing interventions must include people who have studied and are well grounded in these realities. This will better enable donor agencies to anticipate the social and political, as well as the economic, consequences of alternative methods of providing external assistance and to select intervention strategies—carrots and sticks—that avert and, where possible, actually mitigate ethnic conflict.

NOTE

An earlier version of this chapter was published in 1997 under the title "Can Foreign Aid Moderate Ethnic Conflict" by the United States Institute of Peace as no. 13 of its Peaceworks series.

REFERENCES

Anderson, Mary. 1995. *The Experience of NGOs in Conflict Intervention: Problems and Prospects.* Cambridge, MA: Local Capacities for Peace Project.
Arndt, H. W. 1978. *The Rise and Fall of Economic Growth.* Melbourne, Australia: Longman Cheshire.
Brass, Paul, ed. 1985. *Ethnic Groups and the State.* Totowa, MD: Barnes and Noble.
Carroll, T. J., and John D Montgomery, eds. 1987. *Supporting Grassroots Organizations.* Cambridge, MA: Lincoln Institute for Land Management.
Cassen, Robert, et al. 1986. "Aid and Poverty." In *Does Aid Work? Report to an Intergovernmental Task Force,* 45–58. Oxford: Oxford University Press.
Cohen, John M. 1994. *Transition toward Democracy and Governance in Post-Mengistu Ethiopia.* Discussion Paper 494. Cambridge: Harvard Institute for International Development.
Esman, Milton J. 1990. "Economic Performance and Ethnic Conflict." In *Conflict and Peacemaking in Multiethnic Societies,* ed. Joseph V. Montville, 477–90. Lexington, MA: D. C. Heath.
———. 1994. *Ethnic Politics.* Ithaca: Cornell University Press.
Faaland, Just, J. M. Parkinson, and Rais Saniman. 1990. *Growth and Ethnic Inequality: Malaysia's New Economic Policy.* New York: St Martin's.
Glazer, Nathan, and Daniel Patrick Moynihan, eds. 1975. *Ethnicity: Theory and Experience.* Cambridge: Harvard University Press.
Gurr, T. R. 1993. *Minorities at Risk: A Global View of Ethnopolitical Conflicts.* Washington, DC: U.S. Institute of Peace.
Horowitz, Donald. 1985. *Ethnic Groups in Conflict.* Berkeley: University of California Press.
———. 1990. "Making Moderation Pay: The Comparative Politics of Ethnic Conflict Management." In *Conflict and Peacemaking in Multiethnic Societies,* ed. Joseph V. Montville, 451–75. Lexington, MA: D. C. Heath.

James, Harold. 1998. "From Grandmotherliness to Governance: The Evolution of IMF Conditionality." *Finance and Development,* December, 44–47.

Kellas, James. 1991. *The Politics of Nationalism and Ethnicity.* London: MacMillan Education.

Korten, David, and Rudy Klauss. 1984. *People-Centered Development: Contributions toward Theory and Planning Frameworks.* West Hartford, CT: Kumarian.

Kottak, Conrad Phillip. 1991. "When People Don't Come First: Some Sociological Lessons from Completed Projects." In *Putting People First: Sociological Variables in Rural Development,* ed. Michael Cernea, 325–56. Oxford: Oxford University Press.

Lebanese Republic. 1995. *Solid Waste Management/Environmental Assessment Summary.* Beirut: Government of Lebanon.

Lijphart, Arend. 1977. *Democracy in Plural Societies: A Comparative Exploration.* New Haven: Yale University Press.

———. 1990. "The Power-Sharing Approach." In *Conflict and Peacemaking in Multiethnic Societies,* ed. Joseph V. Montville, 491–509. Lexington, MA: D. C. Heath.

Lipton, Michael. 1977. *Why Poor People Stay Poor: Urban Bias in World Development.* Cambridge: Harvard University Press.

Majstorovic, Steven. 1995. "Politicized Ethnicity and Economic Inequality." *Nationalism and Ethnic Politics* 1 (spring): 33–53.

McRae, Kenneth. 1990. "Theories of Power Sharing in Conflict Management." In *Conflict and Peacemaking in Multiethnic Societies,* ed. Joseph V. Montville, 93–106. Lexington, MA: D. C. Heath.

———, ed. 1974. *Consociational Democracy.* Toronto: McClelland and Stewart.

Miller, Robert, ed. 1992. *Aid as Peacemaker: Canada's Development Assistance and Third World Conflict.* Ottawa: Carleton University Press.

Montville, Joseph V., ed. 1990. *Conflict and Peacemaking in Multiethnic Societies.* Lexington, MA: D. C. Heath.

Nevette, Neil, and Charles H. Kennedy, eds. 1986. *Ethnic Preference and Public Policy in Developing States.* Boulder, CO: Lynn Reinner.

Olson, Mancur. 1963. "Rapid Growth as a Destabilizing Force." *Journal of Economic History* 23 (December).

Organization for Economic Cooperation and Development (OECD). 1999. *Development Cooperation: Efforts and Policies of the Members of the Development Assistance Committee, 1998 Report of the Chairman of the Development Assistance Committee.* Paris: OECD.

Rabushka, Alvin, and Kenneth A Shepsle. 1972. *Politics in Plural Societies: A Theory of Democratic Instability.* Columbus, OH: Merrill.

Rondinelli, Dennis. 1983. *Development Projects as Policy Experiments.* New York: Methuen.

Rostow, W. W. 1990. *Theories of Economic Growth from David Hume to the Present.* Oxford: Oxford University Press.

Rotberg, Robert I., ed. 1996. *Vigilance and Vengeance: NGOs Preventing Violent*

Conflict in Divided Societies. Washington, DC: Brookings Institution; Cambridge, MA: World Peace Foundation.

Sisk, Timothy D. 1996. *Power-Sharing and International Mediation in Ethnic Conflicts.* Washington, DC: U.S. Institute of Peace.

Sowell, Thomas. 1990. *Preferential Policies: An International Perspective.* New York: W. Morrow.

Spense, Chris, and Laura Ivers. 1999. "Summary of the Meeting on Alternative Approaches to Debt Relief." *Sustainable Development* 33 (September 27), <enb@iisd.org>.

Woodward, Susan. 1995. "Redrawing Borders in a Period of Systemic Transition." In *International Organization and Ethnic Conflict,* ed. Milton J. Esman and Shibley Telhami, 198–234. Ithaca: Cornell University Press.

Van Dyke, Vernon. 1975. "Justice as Fairness: For Groups." *American Political Science Review* 69 (June): 607–14.

Young, M. Crawford. 1976. *The Politics of Cultural Pluralism.* Madison: University of Wisconsin Press.

Contributors

Alison Brysk is associate professor of political science and chair of international studies at the University of California, Irvine. She is the author of *The Politics of Human Rights in Argentina: Protest, Change, and Democratization* (Stanford: Stanford University Press, 1994) and *From Tribal Village to Global Village: Indian Rights and International Relations in Latin America* (Stanford: Stanford University Press, 2000). Her scholarly articles and current research focus on comparative human rights, transnationalism, civil society, and symbolic politics.

John M. Cohen, trained in law and in political science, taught for several years at Cornell before joining the Harvard Institute for International Development (HIID) in 1979 as a senior faculty associate. At the HIID he specialized in public administration and grassroots rural development in sub-Saharan Africa. He contributed numerous articles to professional journals and was in frequent demand as a consultant by the major development assistance agencies. Prior to his untimely death in 1998, he and his colleague, Stephen Peterson, completed their book, *Administrative Decentralization Strategies for Developing Countries,* which was published in 1999 by the Kumarian Press.

Milton J. Esman is the John S. Knight Professor of International Studies, emeritus; professor of government, emeritus; and former director of the Center for International Studies at Cornell University. He is a longtime participant, observer, and commentator on international development and development assistance. His research and writing have focused on public administration and rural development in low-income countries, the politics of ethnic pluralism, and more recently American politics. In addition to numerous articles in professional journals, his books on ethnic pluralism include *Ethnic Politics* (1994), *International Organizations, and Ethnic Conflict* (1995, edited with Shibley Telhami) and *Ethnicity, Pluralism and the State in the Middle-East* (1988, edited with Itamar Rabinovich), all published by Cornell University Press.

Daniel R. Gibson is a social scientist in the East Asia and Pacific Region Environment and Social Development Unit of the World Bank. He presently is assigned to the World Bank country office in Beijing, China.

Ronald J. Herring is director of the Mario Einaudi Center for International Studies at Cornell University, where he is the John S. Knight Professor of International Relations and professor of government, after fifteen years at Northwestern University in the Political Science Department. He has been editor of Comparative Political Studies and worked with various academic committees of Fulbright, the Social Science Research Council, the American Council of Learned Societies, and the American Institute of Indian Studies, among others. His earliest academic interests were with agrarian relations (*Land to the Tiller: The Political Economy of Agrarian Reform in South Asia* [New Haven: Yale University Press, 1983]); his more recent interests include development policy, public authority in nature, and environmental politics. His area of geographic interest is South Asia, on which he has advised a number of international agencies.

Heather S. McHugh is a policy analyst with the Office of Transition Initiatives at the United States Agency for International Development (USAID). She has managed programs in post-genocidal Rwanda and strategic planning for humanitarian responses in other conflict-prone countries. Previously she was a foreign affairs analyst specializing in democracy, governance, and humanitarian responses for USAID's Policy Bureau. Her research has covered such subjects as ethnic conflict, civil society, postwar reconciliation, and alternative dispute resolution.

Stephen D. Shenfield is a specialist in the politics of Russia and the post-Soviet region. He obtained his Ph.D. in Soviet Studies in 1987 from the University of Birmingham (U.K.). In the 1990s he was based at Brown University's Watson Institute for International Studies. He is the author of *The Nuclear Predicament: Explorations in Soviet Ideology* (London: Routledge and Kegan Paul, 1987) and *Russian Fascism: Traditions, Tendencies, and Movements* (New York: M. E. Sharpe, forthcoming). He is currently an independent researcher.

Norman T. Uphoff is professor of government at Cornell University and director of the Cornell International Institute for Food, Agriculture, and Development. He has worked for extended periods of time in Ghana, Nepal, Sri Lanka, Indonesia, and Madagascar on different aspects of participatory and sustainable development. His Sri Lanka involvement began with a sabbatical year, 1978–79, at the Agrarian Research and Training Institute (ARTI) in Colombo, with a research fellowship from the Social Science Research Council (SSRC), after which time he was appointed to the South Asia Committee of the SSRC through 1984. Between 1980 and 1985, he worked with Cornell faculty colleagues and ARTI staff on introducing participatory irrigation management in the Gal Oya irrigation scheme in southeastern Sri Lanka. The Gal Oya case experience is reported in some detail in *Learning from Gal Oya: Possibilities for Participatory Development and Post-Newtonian Social Science,* 2d ed. (London: Intermediate Technology Publications, 1996).

Index